The Christian
in Complete Armour

THE CHRISTIAN IN COMPLETE ARMOUR

WILLIAM GURNALL

Abridged by Ruthanne Garlock, Kay King,
Karen Sloan and Candy Coan

Volume 1

THE BANNER OF TRUTH TRUST

THE BANNER OF TRUTH TRUST
3 Murrayfield Road, Edinburgh EH12 6EL
P.O. Box 621, Carlisle, Pennsylvania 17013, U.S.A.

★

First published in three volumes in 1655, 1658 and 1662
Revised and reprinted in 1864 by Blackie & Son, Glasgow, Scotland
The 1864 edition (unabridged) republished by the Banner of Truth
    Trust, Edinburgh, Scotland in 1964, 1974 and 1979
The 1864 edition (Volume 1) revised and abridged, published by
    World Challenge, Inc., David Wilkerson Crusades, Lindale,
    Texas, U.S.A. in association with the Banner of Truth Trust, 1986
© World Challenge Inc., 1986
Reprinted 1988
ISBN 085151 456 1

★

Typeset in 10½ on 12 pt Linotron Plantin
at The Spartan Press Ltd, Lymington, Hants
Printed and bound in Great Britain by
Hazell Watson & Viney Limited
Member of BPCC plc
Aylesbury Bucks

Commendations of Gurnall's book

'IF I might read only one book beside the Bible, I would choose *The Christian in Complete Armour*.'

– John Newton (1725–1807)
Converted slave trader
who wrote 'Amazing Grace'

'A beautiful feature in Gurnall's book is its richness in pithy, pointed, and epigrammatical sayings. You will often find in a line and a half some great truth, put so concisely, and yet so fully, that you really marvel how so much thought could be got into so few words.

'Solid scriptural theology, like that contained in these pages, should be valued and studied in the church. Books in which Scripture is reverently regarded as the only rule of faith and practice – books in which Christ and the Holy Ghost have their rightful office – books in which justification, and sanctification, and regeneration, and faith, and grace, and holiness are clearly, distinctly, and accurately delineated and exhibited – these are the only books which do real good. Few things need reviving more than a taste for such books as these among readers.'

– J. C. Ryle (1816–1900)
First Bishop of Liverpool

'Gurnall's work is peerless and priceless; every line is full of wisdom; every sentence is suggestive. This 'Complete Armour' is beyond all others a preacher's book: I should think that more discourses have been suggested by it than by any other uninspired volume. I have often resorted to it when my own fire has been burning low, and I have seldom failed to find a glowing coal upon Gurnall's hearth.'

– Charles Haddon Spurgeon (1834–1892)
Pastor, London Metropolitan Tabernacle

Contents

[5]

Preface

Leonard Ravenhill, a very godly friend, gave me a copy of *Christian in Complete Armour* with the solemn words, 'This book is going to revolutionize your life. It has had a profound effect on my life and I believe you are prepared to receive its message now.'

At first I put the book aside. It was too long, too wordy, and written in 17th-century English. Out of curiosity, I scanned the first twenty-five pages. That is all it took to bring me to my knees. Gurnall, the pious Puritan, had touched something deep within me. His were such probing, scorching, searing words that they shook my inner man. I devoured the entire book with great zeal.

I immediately ordered additional copies to give to minister friends. I thought that they too would become as excited about the work as I am. But I soon discovered that few ministers would or could take the time to mine the precious gold within its 1200 pages. Others complained they could not understand Gurnall's Puritan language.

Because the book and its message is so important, we prayerfully decided to find the best editorial staff we could put together to produce a shortened version in modern English. We were most excited about the results. Our editors were able to retain the meat of his message and the best of Gurnall's illustrations.

We believe that as *Christian in Complete Armour* is such an important book, it should be published in a shortened, modern version for wider acceptance.

We are delighted that the Banner of Truth Trust publishers agreed with our assessment and have decided to publish the edited manuscript in a three-volume paperback version.

Ruthann Garlock was project coordinator; she was assisted by Kay King, Karen Sloan, and Candy Coan. They put in over a full year's labor of love on the project. We are most grateful to them for their dedicated work.

I believe *Christian in Complete Armour*, either this abridgement or the full version which the Banner of Truth Trust also keeps in print, should be in the library of every man and woman of God. No Christian leader, teacher, pastor, evangelist, or Christian worker should be without it. It breathes of holiness, purity, and provokes one to prayer and fuller dedication to Jesus Christ.

Of all the Puritan writers, I believe William Gurnall speaks most directly to this generation.

I believe the Banner of Truth has been highly honored by God to be entrusted with the proclamation of God's message. Without a doubt, it is one of the most important books ever written, other than the Word of God.

I will forever bless the day it was placed in my hands.

His bondservant,
DAVID WILKERSON
Author of *The Cross and the Switchblade*

Biographical Sketch of the Author

WILLIAM Gurnall, author of *The Christian in Complete Armour*, is a man whose name seldom appears in accounts of seventeenth-century church history. Yet his enduring work on spiritual warfare has appeared in numerous editions spanning more than three hundred years, and has blessed untold thousands of Christians since its first publication.

Research reveals that he was born in November, 1616, in the coastal town of Lynn, county of Norfolk, about a hundred miles north of London. His father was first an alderman (town council member), then mayor of Lynn, a chief town of the most thoroughly Protestant district of England in the seventeenth century. The inhabitants of Norfolk and Suffolk counties were famous for their deep attachment to the doctrines of the Reformation.

An excellent scholar, Gurnall was awarded a scholarship from the city of Lynn to attend Emmanuel College, Cambridge. He began his formal training there in his 16th year, shortly after his father's death. Having been reared to honor and reverence the Puritans as the 'excellent of the earth,' and then trained at an eminently puritan college, it would have been strange indeed if Gurnall had grown up without decidedly puritan opinions. Some of his contemporaries at Emmanuel College were among the most prominent puritan writers and leaders of his time.

By way of explanation, the Puritans were a large segment of sixteenth- and seventeenth-century Protestants who sought to 'purify' the Church of England. They felt priestly vestments and elaborate ceremonies were unnecessary. Many of them held to a simple manner of worship, without the use of prayer books, and followed a simple form of church organization. Most Puritans believed all clergymen should be of equal rank, and that no bishop or high church official should exercise control over pastors of congregations.

At the age of 28, William Gurnall was appointed rector of the church at Lavenham, Suffolk, then a town of about 1,800 inhabitants, half of whom were his parishioners. A year later he married a minister's daughter, Sarah Mott, who bore him ten children. Gurnall spent the rest of his life – 35 years – in this pastorate.

During much of his lifetime he apparently suffered ill health. In the early days of his ministry at Lavenham he was once summoned to preach before the House of Commons in London. None but the most eminent and gifted ministers were asked to do this – which shows the high esteem in which Gurnall was held as a preacher. However, Gurnall begged to be excused. He stated in his letter, 'It is a burden much too weighty for my shoulders, particularly at this time, when so many infirmities oppress me that I can scarcely, without danger to my health, remain a short time in the open air. Much less therefore could I undertake so long a journey in so winterly a season.' (London was less than a hundred miles away.)

The years during which Gurnall served the parish at Lavenham were filled with momentous events in English history: a civil war, the beheading of King Charles I, the declaring of a protectorate under puritan leader Oliver Cromwell, then the death of Cromwell, and the restoration of the monarchy under King Charles II. But the most significant event for Gurnall was the passing of the Act of Uniformity.

This Act, passed in 1662, required that all ministers conform to the standards of the Church of England in matters of worship, use of the Prayer Book, and ecclesiastical authority. It was the culmination of years of conflict between the Puritans and established church leaders (though there is no indication that Gurnall himself was involved in the conflict). The result was that about two thousand Puritan ministers and teachers gave up their pastorates and other positions, were labeled Nonconformists, and subsequently suffered intolerant persecution. Gurnall, instead of siding with his puritan colleagues, chose to remain in the Church. He signed the declaration required by the Act of Uniformity, and was ordained a priest by the evangelical Bishop Reynolds of Norwich.

Herein lies the reason so little has been written about William Gurnall in the annals of church history. Though he was undoubtedly puritan in both doctrine and practice, he did not secede with the group with which he had generally agreed – a choice not likely to make him a favorite with either of the two great religious parties into which England was divided. A neutral is never popular; each party is offended at him for not casting his weight into their scale. He was just the man to be disliked and slighted by both sides.

But he was far from neutral in spiritual matters. It was during this time of civil and religious strife and controversy that Gurnall preached to his parishioners his messages on spiritual warfare. With the help of a benefactor, Gurnall published his material in three volumes between 1655 and 1662. He dedicated the first volume to the inhabitants of Lavenham. The following is an excerpt from his foreword:

The subject of the treatise is solemn: A War between the Saint and Satan. And it is such a bloody one that the cruellest war ever fought by men will be seen as but sport and child's play compared to this. It is a spiritual war that you shall read of; not a history of what was fought many ages past and is now over, but of a war now going on – the tragedy is present with us. And it is not taking place at the farthest end of the world; it concerns you and everyone who reads of it. The stage on which this war is fought is every man's own soul. There are no neutrals in this war. The whole world is engaged in the quarrel, either for God against Satan, or for Satan against God.

Gurnall died on October 12, 1679, in his 63rd year of life. The fact that a sixth edition of his work was published in the year he died is enough to show that its merits were early recognized. Other theological works of the seventeenth century were famous in their day, but are now seldom read. In regard to Gurnall, everything connected with this good man, except his book, seems to have passed away. By it alone, 'he being dead yet speaketh' (*Heb. 11:4*). The available evidence indicates that Gurnall lived and died within about 50 miles of his place of birth. He held no office other than that of rector of Lavenham, and today no trace can be found of any descendants.

William Burkitt, well-known New Testament commentator and rector of Milden, near Lavenham, delivered an address commemorating Gurnall two months after his death. He concluded his address with these words:

It will be below the merit of his person to celebrate his death by any verbal lamentations; nor can anything suit his memory but what is sacred and divine, as his writings are. May his just fame from them, and from his virtues, be precious to all succeeding ages; and when epitaphs commit-

ted to the trust of marble shall be as illegible as if they had been written in water, when all stately pyramids shall be dissolved in dust, and all the venerable monuments of antiquity shall be devoured by the corroding teeth of time, then let this short characterization describing him in his best and fullest portraiture remain of him:

He was a CHRISTIAN IN COMPLETE ARMOUR.

> *Ruthanne Garlock*
> *(with major credit to*
> *Bishop J. C. Ryle's intro-*
> *duction to the 1864 edition)*

1 : *The Saint's Call to Arms*

THE apostle Paul had a discerning heart. In writing to the early Christians at Ephesus, he knew he had to prepare them for unprecedented hardship. But first he longed to encourage and comfort them, so he reminded them of the Lord's strength:

Finally, my brethren, be strong in the Lord, and in the power of his might (Eph. 6.10).

It is as if he were thinking, 'Some of my dear friends must be quaking in their boots to see their enemies so strong and themselves so weak, so numerous while they are so few, so well equipped and expert at arms while they are just raw recruits.' He must have known a fear-wracked soul is too preoccupied with its present distress to listen to advice from anyone, even a well-meaning friend. Fear immobilizes its victim – like the distraught soldier who runs trembling to his foxhole at first rumor of an attack and refuses to come out until all threat of danger is past.

So Paul searches for an antidote to their fear and soon finds one. It is a timeless answer to the disabling condition suffered by every Christian since Adam. He tells us, 'Don't let your fears overwhelm you. March on with undaunted courage and be strong in the Lord. . . . ' And here is the great consolation: '*The outcome of the battle rests on God's performance, not on your skill or strength!*'

Surely every trembling soul will breathe a sigh of relief to hear this comforting news. Now the Christian can concentrate on the task at hand, which is to 'be strong.' It is a frequent scriptural exhortation: 'Be strong and courageous' (*2 Chron. 32:7*); 'Say to them that are of a fearful heart, Be strong' (*Isa. 35:4*). In other words, 'Marshal all the powers of your soul and muster up your whole force, for you will need all you can get!'

1. The Christian's Call to Courage

A cowardly spirit is beneath the lowest duty of a Christian. You of all men will need courage and determination if you hope to obey your heavenly Captain's orders. He commands you, 'Be thou strong and very courageous. . . . ' Why? So you can stand in battle against warlike nations? So you can make a great name for yourself? No! But ' . . . that thou mayest observe to do according to all the law, which Moses, my servant, commanded thee' (*Josh. 1:7*). That is why you need a more courageous spirit to obey God faithfully than to command an army of men; to be a Christian than a captain. The challenge exceeds the bravery of the best unless they have help from a source greater than themselves.

Secular reason sees a Christian on his knees and laughs at the feeble posture God's child assumes as his enemies descend upon him. Only divine insight can perceive what mighty preparations are actually taking place. Yet just as an unarmed soldier cannot achieve the military exploits of a well-equipped infantryman, so the carnal Christian cannot hope to do the exploits for God which the committed Christian can expect through prayer. Prayer is the main line that leads straight to the throne of God. By it the Christian approaches God with a humble boldness of faith, takes hold of Him, wrestles with Him, and will not let Him go until he has His blessing.

Meanwhile, the carnal Christian, asleep to the dangers

of his sinful state, rushes headlong into battle with a foolhardy confidence that soon turns yellow when his conscience wakes up and sounds the alarm that his sins are upon him. Then, unnerved by this surprise attack, he throws down his weapon, flees from the presence of God with guilty Adam, and dares not look Him in the face.

Every duty in the Christian's whole course of walking with God is lined with many difficulties which shoot at him through the hedges on his march toward heaven. He must fight the enemy for every inch of ground along the way. Only those noble-spirited souls who dare taken heaven by force are fit for this calling.

COWARDICE VS. COURAGE

This warfare analogy reveals why there are so many who profess Christ and so few who are in fact Christians; so many who go into the field against Satan, and so few who come out conquerors. All may have a desire to be successful soldiers, but few have the courage and determination to grapple with the difficulties that accost them on the way to victory. All Israel followed Moses joyfully out of Egypt. But when their stomachs were a little pinched with hunger, and their immediate desires deferred, they were ready at once to retreat. They preferred the bondage of Pharaoh to the promised blessings of the Lord.

Men are no different today. How many part with Christ at the crossroad of suffering! Like Orpah, they go a short distance only (*Ruth 1:14*). They profess the gospel and name themselves heirs to the blessings of the saints. But when put to the test, they quickly grow sick of the journey and refuse to endure for Christ. At the first sign of hardship, they kiss and leave the Savior, reluctant to lose heaven, but even more unwilling to buy it at so dear a price. If they must resist so many enemies on the way, they will content themselves with their own stagnant cisterns and leave the Water of Life for others who will venture farther for it. Who among us has not learned from his own experience that it requires another spirit than the world can give to follow Christ fully?

Let this exhort you then, Christian, to petition God for the holy determination and bravery you must have to follow Christ. Without it you cannot be what you profess. The fearful are those who march for hell (*Rev. 21:8*); the valiant are they who take heaven by force (*Matt. 11:12*). Cowards never won heaven. Do not claim that you are begotten of God and have His royal blood running in your veins unless you can prove your lineage by this heroic spirit: to dare to be holy in spite of men and devils.

You should find great strength and encouragement in the knowledge that your commission is divine. God Himself underwrites your battle and has appointed His own Son 'the captain of [your] salvation' (*Heb. 2:10*). He will lead you on to the field with courage, and bring you off with honor. He lived and died for you; He will live and die with you. His mercy and tenderness to His soldiers is unmatched. Historians tell us Trajan tore his own clothes to bind up his soldiers' wounds. The Bible tells us Christ poured out His very blood as balm to heal His saints' wounds; His flesh was torn to bind them up.

For bravery none compares with our Lord. He never turned His head from danger, not even when hell's hatred and heaven's justice appeared against Him. Knowing all that was about to happen, Jesus went forth and said, 'Whom seek ye?' (*John 18:4*). Satan could not overcome Him – our Savior never lost a battle, not even when He lost His life. He won the victory, carrying His spoils to heaven in the triumphant chariot of His ascension. There He makes an open show of them, to the unspeakable joy of saints and angels.

As part of Christ's army, you march in the ranks of gallant spirits. Every one of your fellow soldiers is the child of a King. Some, like you, are in the midst of the battle, besieged on every side by affliction and temptation. Others, after many assaults, repulses, and rallyings of their faith, are already standing upon the wall of heaven as conquerors. From there they look down and urge you, their comrades on earth, to march up the hill after them. This is their cry: 'Fight to the death and the City is your own, as now it is ours! For the waging of a few days' conflict, you will be rewarded with heaven's glory. One moment of this celestial joy will dry up all your tears, heal all your wounds, and erase the sharpness of the fight with the joy of your permanent victory.'

In a word – God, angels, and the saints already with the Lord are spectators, watching how you conduct yourself as a child of the Most High. This crowd of witnesses (*Heb. 12:1*) shouts joyfully from the celestial sidelines every time you defeat a temptation, scale a difficulty, or regain lost ground from your enemies. And if the fight should be too much for you, your dear Savior stands by with reserves for your relief at a moment's notice. His very heart leaps within Him to see the proof of your love and zeal for Him in all your combats. He will not forget your faithfulness. And when you come off the field, He will receive you as joyously as the Father received Him upon His return to heaven.

Would you be a valiant soldier? Then take heed to the discussion that follows.

SOURCES OF CHRISTIAN COURAGE

If you intend to bear up courageously against the opposition on your march to heaven, your principles must be well fixed. Otherwise, your heart will be unstable, and an unstable heart is as weak as a house without girders. The first crosswind will blow it down. Two things are required to fix your principles:

I. AN ESTABLISHED KNOWLEDGE OF GOD'S TRUTH

He who has only a nodding acquaintance with the king may easily be persuaded to change his allegiance, or will at least try to remain neutral in the face of treason. Some professing Christians have only a passing acquaintance with the gospel. They can hardly give an account of what they hope for, or whom they hope in. And if they have some principles they take kindly to, they are so unsettled that every wind blows them away, like loose tiles from a housetop.

When Satan buffets and temptation washes over you like a tidal wave, you must cling to God's truths. They are your shelter in every raging storm. But you must have them on hand, ready to use. Do not wait until it is sinking to patch the boat. A feeble commitment has little hope of safety when caught in a tempest. While that flounders and drowns, holy determination, grounded in the Word, will lift up its head like a rock in the midst of the highest waves.

Scripture promises, 'The people that do know their God shall be strong, and do exploits' (*Dan. 11:32*). An angel told Daniel which men would stand up and be counted for God when tempted and persecuted by Antiochus. Some would be taken in by the bribery of corrupt men; others would fall victim to intimidation and threats. But a few, who were firmly grounded in the tenets of their faith, would do great things for God. That is to say, to flatteries they would be incorruptible, and to power and force, unconquerable.

II. A HEART SET IN THE RIGHT DIRECTION

Head knowledge of the things of Christ is not enough; this following Christ is primarily a matter of the heart. If your heart is not fixed in its purpose, your principles, as good as they may be, will hang loose and be of no more use in the heat of battle than an ill-strung bow. Half-hearted resolve will not venture much nor far for Christ. Nor will the heart with false motives. A hypocrite may show some strength of spirit for the moment, but he will soon give up his profession when he is pinched on the toe where his corn is; in other words, when called to deny that which his evil heart coveted all along.

If you are a serious soldier, do not flirt with any of your desires that are beneath Christ and heaven. They will play the harlot and steal your heart. Consider Jehu. How courageous and zealous he seemed in the beginning. Why, then, did his resolve fail him before his work was half done? Because his heart was never set on God alone! The very ambition that stirred up his zeal at first, in the end quenched and killed it. He compromised with evil men to reach his goal. Then when he gained the throne, he dared not put God's plan into action for fear of provoking those same evil men and thereby losing his kingdom (*2 Kings 10:31*). In short his heart was set on the world's pleasures more than on God's favor.

2. The Christian's Call to Service

DIRECTIVES ISSUED

The soldier is summoned to a life of active duty, and so is the Christian. The very nature of the calling precludes a life of ease. If you had thought to be a summer soldier, consider your commission carefully. Your spiritual orders are rigorous. Like the apostle, I would not have you be ignorant on this point and will, therefore, list a few of your directives.

1. RENOUNCE YOUR BOSOM SINS

Those sins which have lain nearest your heart must now be trampled under your feet. And what courage and resolution this requires! You think Abraham was tested to the limit when called upon to take Isaac, 'thine only son . . . whom thou lovest' (*Gen. 22:2*), and offer him up with his own hands. Yet what was that to this: 'Soul, take the lust which is the child dearest to your heart, your Isaac, the sin from which you intend to gain the greatest pleasure. Lay hands on it and offer it up; pour out its blood before Me; run the sacrificing knife into the very heart of it – and do it joyfully!'

This is more than the human spirit can bear to hear. Our lust will not lie so patiently on the altar as Isaac, nor as the Lamb brought dumb to the slaughter (*Isa. 53:7*). Our flesh will roar and shriek, rending the heart with its hideous cries. Indeed, who can express the conflict, the wrestlings, the convulsions of spirit we endure before we can put our heart into such a command? Or who can fully recount the cleverness with which such a lust will plead for itself?

When the Spirit convicts you of sin, Satan will try to convince you, 'It is such a little one – spare it.' Or he will bribe the soul with a vow of secrecy: 'You can keep me and your good reputation, too. I will not be seen in your company to shame you among your neighbors. You may shut me up in the attic of your heart, out of sight, if only you will let me now and then have the wild embraces of your thoughts and affections in secret.'

If that will not be granted, then Satan asks for a stay of execution, well knowing that most such reprieved lusts at last obtain their full pardon. The longer we procrastinate, the harder it becomes to break through the clever coaxing of this silver-tongued defender of sin and death, and actually carry out the execution. Here history's bravest men have shown themselves putty in the enemy's hands. They return from the field with victory banners flying, and then live and die slaves to a base lust at home. They are like the great Roman who, as he rode triumphantly through the city, never took his eyes off a prostitute walking along the street: a man who conquered empires, captured by the glance of a single woman!

II. CONFORM YOUR LIFE TO CHRIST

We are commanded not to be conformed to this world – that is, not to compromise ourselves with the corrupt customs of our day. The Christian must not be such a compliant tailor as to cut the coat of his profession according to popular fashion. Instead, he must stand fixed to his principles, openly showing he is a citizen of heaven by clothing himself in the garments of truth. It takes great courage to disregard the abasement you will surely meet for your nonconformity. Sadly, there are many who cannot stand the strain. Too often we have seen a self-tailored cloak of pride tossed hurriedly over the heavenly garment of imputed righteousness by one who fears the derision of men if he dares 'confess Christ openly' (*John 7:13*). How many lose heaven because they are ashamed to go there in a 'fool's' coat!

While some will mock, others will persecute to death the Christian who will not conform in principle or practice. This was the trap laid for the three Hebrew children. They must dance to the tune of Nebuchadnez-zar's pipe, or burn (*Dan. 3:15*). Such, too, was the plot laid to ensnare Daniel, who walked so faultlessly that the only charge his enemies could bring against him was his singlemindedness in his religion (*Dan. 6:5*). Now in such a case as this, when the choice means life or death, when a

[31]

Christian must renounce his Lord or become prey to the cruel teeth of bloody men, how many retreats and self-preserving escapes will a cowardly heart invent? It is a great honor to a Christian when all his enemies can say is, 'He will not do as we do.' The Christian who faces such great opposition must be well locked into the saddle of his profession, or else he will soon be dismounted.

III. SIDESTEP STUMBLING BLOCKS

There have always been those in the church who, by serious mistakes in judgment and conduct, have laid a stumbling block in the path of professing Christians. You will need a holy resolution to bear up against such discouragements. Strive to be like Joshua. When most of the Israelites revolted and in their hearts turned back to Egypt, Joshua maintained his integrity. He declared that, though not another man would join him, yet he would serve the Lord.

IV. TRUST GOD IN EVERY CIRCUMSTANCE

There are times when a saint is called to trust in a withdrawing God. '[Let him] that walketh in darkness and hath no light . . . trust in the name of the Lord' (*Isa. 50:10*). This requires a bold step of faith – to venture into God's presence with the same temerity as Esther into Ahasuerus's. Even when no smile lights His face, when no golden scepter is extended to summon us to come near, we must press forward with this noble resolution: 'If I perish, I perish' (*Esther 4:16*).

Which leads our faith one step further: We must trust also in a 'killing God.' We must declare with Job, 'Though he slay me, yet will I trust in him' (*Job 13:15*). It takes a submissive faith for a soul to march steadily forward while God seems to fire upon that soul and shoot His frowns like poisoned arrows into it. This is hard work, and will test the Christian's mettle. Yet such a spirit we find in the poor woman of Canaan, who caught the bullets Christ shot at her, and with a humble boldness sent them back again in her prayer (*Matt. 15:22–28*).

V. STAY ON COURSE TO THE END OF YOUR LIFE

Your work and your life must go off the stage together. Persisting to the end will be the burr under your saddle – the thorn in your flesh – when the road ahead seems endless and your soul begs an early discharge. It weighs down every other difficulty of your calling. We have known many who have joined the army of Christ and liked being a soldier for a battle or two, but have soon had enough and ended up deserting. They impulsively enlist for Christian duties, are easily persuaded to take up a profession of religion, and are just as easily persuaded to lay it down. Like the new moon, they shine a little in the first part of the evening, but go down before the night is over.

This persevering is a hard word! Taking up the cross daily, praying always, watching night and day and never laying aside our armour to indulge ourselves, sends many sorrowful away from Christ. Yet this is your calling: to make the Christian faith your daily work, without any vacation from one end of the year to the other. These few examples are enough to show how much courage and determination you need. How to obtain such courage is our next order of business.

3. An Admonition to 'Be Strong in the Lord'

THE SOURCE OF THE SAINT'S STRENGTH

Having exhorted all saints to an iron resolution and flinty courage in their warfare, the apostle now leads us out of ourselves for our source of strength, and to the Lord: 'Be strong *in the Lord*.'

[33]

The strength of an earthly general lies in his troops – he flies upon their wings. If their feathers get clipped or their necks broken, he is helpless. But in the army of saints, the strength of the whole host lies in the Lord of hosts. God can overcome His enemies without help from anyone, but His saints cannot so much as defend the smallest outpost without His strong arm.

One of God's names is 'the Strength of Israel' (*1 Sam. 15:29*). He was the strength of David's heart. With Him, this shepherd boy could defy the giant who defied a whole army; without God's strength, David trembled at a word or two that dropped from the Philistine's mouth. He wrote, 'Blessed be the Lord my strength, which teacheth my hands to war, and my fingers to fight' (*Ps. 144:1*). The Lord is likewise your strength in your war against sin and Satan.

Some wonder whether a sin is ever committed without Satan having a part. But if the question were whether any holy action is ever performed without involving the special assistance of God, that is settled: 'Without me ye can do nothing' (*John 15:5*). Paul put it this way: 'Not that we are sufficient of ourselves to think any thing as of ourselves; but our sufficiency is of God' (*2 Cor. 3:5*). We saints have a reservoir of grace, yet it lies like water at the bottom of a well and will not ascend with all our pumping. First God must prime it with His awakening grace. Then it will gush forth.

Paul says, 'To will is present with me; but how to perform that which is good I find not' (*Rom. 7:18*). Both the will to do and the action which follows are of God. 'It is God which worketh in you both to will and to do of his good pleasure' (*Phil. 2:13*). God is at the bottom of the ladder, and at the top also, the Author and Finisher, assisting the soul at every rung in its ascent to any holy action. And once we have begun a work, how long will we stick to it? Only as long as we are held up by the same hand that empowered us at first. We quickly deplete the strength He gives us. So to maintain the permanence of a holy course, we must have a renewing strength from heaven every moment.

The Christian, like a chalice without a base, cannot stand on his own nor hold what he has received any longer than God holds him in His strong hands. Knowing this, Christ, when bound for heaven and ready to leave His children, asked the Father to care for them in His absence: 'Father, keep . . . those whom thou hast given me' (*John 17:11*). It is as if He had said, 'They must not be left alone. They are poor, shiftless children and cannot take care of themselves. Unless You hold on to them tightly and keep them constantly in Your sight, they will lose the grace I have given them and wander into temptation; therefore, Father, keep them.'

Even in acts of worship our strength is in the Lord. Consider prayer. Would we pray? Where will we find topics for our prayers? Alas, 'We know not what we should pray for as we ought' (*Rom. 8:26*). Let us alone, and we will soon pray ourselves into some temptation or other, and beg for the very thing God knows we should not have. To protect us, then, God puts words in our mouths (*Hos. 14:2*). But without some heart-heating affections to thaw the tap, the words will freeze on our lips. We may search in vain the corridors of our own hearts and the drafty corners of our souls. We will not find a spark upon our own hearth, unless it is some strange fire of natural desires, which will not do. No, the fire that thaws the iciness of the heart must come from heaven – a gift from God, who is 'a consuming fire' (*Heb. 12:29*).

First the Spirit stretches Himself upon the soul, as the

[35]

prophet on the child; then the soul will begin to kindle and put forth some heavenly heat in its affections. At last the Spirit melts the heart, and prayer flows from the lips of the believer as naturally as tears from the eyes. And though the saint is the speaker, the author of the prayer is God. So we see that both the strength to pray and the prayer itself are from God.

The same is true in hearing the Word. We have been instructed to hear the Word preached, but what will it profit unless God opens the ears of our understanding? For six months David listened to lectures on the law and sat unmoved. Then God, through Nathan, stirred the embers of his heart; the Word came alive and he repented. All that was said before God intervened may have been good and true, but David remained cold and unresponsive until the Spirit stirred the ashes of his understanding and kindled a holy fire. Then David's heart burned within while God spoke. The same is true in our own experience. First the Spirit of God moves upon our spirit; then we know for a surety that our strength is in the Lord. The following explanation will help you see the truth of this point.

THE SIGNIFICANCE OF GOD'S STRENGTH

I. THE NATURE OF THE SAINT'S CONSCIENCE

Man's conscience, like his physical body, is created by God. It is therefore in its very *nature* to depend on Him for being and for operation. The capacity to be and to act in and of oneself is an incommunicable property of the Deity. It can never be imparted to a creature. God alone is the source and sustainer of all life; therefore, it is His constant regenerating power that keeps the conscience alive.

Conscience may be defined as that divine influence at work in man to restrain him from sin. One evidence of its origin is that it always speaks against sin and for righteousness. Therefore, it cannot be the product of our own hearts, which in their fallen state are 'deceitful above all things, and desperately wicked' (*Jer. 17:9*). God uses the conscience to give some knowledge of His righteousness to all, so that no one can stand before Him on the Day of Judgment and plead ignorance (*Romans 1*). When you become a Christian and consecrate yourself – conscience and all – to Him, the Holy Spirit begins in earnest to perfect you in Christ.

It is said when God made the world He ended His work of creation – that is, He made no more new species of creatures. Yet to this day He has not ended His work of providence. 'My Father worketh hitherto,' Christ said (*John 5:17*). In other words, He continually preserves and empowers what He has made with strength to be and to act. A work of art, when completed, no longer needs the artist, nor a house the carpenter when the last nail is in place. But God's works on behalf of both the outer and the inner man are never off His hands.

If the Father's work is a preserving one, the Son's is a redemptive one. Both acts are perpetual. Christ did not end His work when He rose from the dead, just as the Father did not end His work when He finished creation. God *rested* at the end of creation; and Christ, when He had wrought eternal redemption and 'by himself purged our sins, sat down on the right hand of the Majesty on high' (*Heb. 1:3*). From there He continues the work of intercession for the saint, and thereby keeps him from certain ruin.

II. THE CHARACTER OF THE CONSCIENCE

The Christian's conscience is not only a creature, but it is a

[37]

weak creature, in constant combat with superior forces. It is a favorite target of Satan, perhaps because he finds it so easily distracted by the cares of this world and so easily pacified by its pleasures. Even the strongest saint will surrender if no help comes in.

Like a crown prince in the cradle, the conscience is helpless to defend itself. Satan would quickly usurp the throne if heaven did not take the saint into protection. To crush the insurrection, God conquers the believer's heart and brings His own will into it to govern the conscience. But just as in a conquered city some yield eagerly to the new government while others continuously plot its overthrow, so some parts of our old nature refuse to give up without a fight. For this reason, it takes the same power to keep a heart as to win it at first.

We Christians have an unregenerate part which is discontented at a change in management. Who among us has not felt the pull of his lower nature, extolling the virtues of self? We balk as much to come under submission to Christ's scepter as the Sodomites did to submit to Lot's judgment. We are so stubborn and self-willed that if God did not continually reinforce His newly planted colony in our hearts, the very natives (i.e., corruptions) that are left would come out of their dens and holes where they lie lurking and eat up what little good conscience we have. Our best intentions would be to these devourers as breadcrumbs to birds.

III. THE NATURE OF GOD'S PLAN

The third reason for relying on God's strength resides in the nature of His saving and keeping plan. God made it His priority to bring the saints to heaven in a way which would be a constant reminder of His love and mercy. He is a wise Father, who knows the flighty temperament of even His most obedient children. So He thinks to help them by visiting often and tucking in their empty hands this or that grace, just when it is needed most. This way of communicating gives a double accent to His love and mercy: it reminds us of the true source of all blessing, and it assures that our needs can always be met.

When you find any comfort in your soul, any added strength in duty, or any support in temptation, it distills a special sweetness into your life to consider what friend sent these blessings. They do not come from your own supply, or anyone else's. It is the heavenly Father who slips quietly in and leaves the sweet perfume of His comfort! It is His kind Spirit that holds your head and calms your heart while the trial rages within. It is His pungent fragrance that keeps you from fainting in unbelief. What soul, thus comforted, could for a moment doubt the love and concern of such a parent?

I ask you, which friend loves you more – the one who, hearing you are in need, promptly writes out a check, puts it in the mail, and considers his obligation to you paid in full? Or the one who drops everything, comes to your house, and does not leave until he is satisfied that all your needs have been cared for? But he is not through yet; he keeps coming back until the crisis is completely past. Unless you are too proud to face your benefactor, or love money above all else, you must certainly prefer the comfort of the second.

God is the latter friend. He comes to our hearts, checks the cupboards, sees how bare they are, and sends in provisions accordingly. 'Your heavenly Father knows you have need of these things . . ,' and you shall have them (*Matt. 6:32, 33*). He knows you need strength to pray, to hear, to suffer for Him; trust Him to keep your pantry well stocked.

God chooses this method to assure our strength will

never be in short supply. If the provisions were left in our own hands, we would soon be bankrupt merchants. God knows we are weak, like cracked pitchers – if filled to the brim and set aside, the contents would soon leak out. So He puts us under a flowing fountain of His strength and constantly refills us. This was the provision He made for Israel in the wilderness: He split the rock, and not only was their thirst quenched at that moment, but the water ran in a stream after them, so that you hear no more complaints for water. This rock was Christ. Every believer has Christ at his back, following him as he goes, with strength for every condition and trial.

IV. THE NATURE OF GOD

Finally, the Christian ought to rely on divine strength because this plan results in the greatest advancement of God's own glory (*Eph. 1:4, 12*). If God had given you a lifetime supply of His grace to begin with and left you to handle your own account, you would have thought Him generous indeed. But He is magnified even more by the open account He sets up in your name. Now you must acknowledge not only that your strength comes from God in the first place, but that you are continually in debt for every withdrawal of strength you make throughout your Christian course.

When a child travels with his parents, all his expenses are covered by his father – not by himself. Likewise, no saint shall say of heaven when he arrives there, 'This is heaven, which I have built by the power of my own might.' No, the heavenly Jerusalem is a city 'whose builder and maker is God' (*Heb. 11:10*). Every grace is a stone in that building, the topstone of which is laid in glory. Some day the saints shall plainly see how God was not only the founder to begin, but benefactor also to finish the same. The glory of the work will not be crumbled out piecemeal, some to God and some to the creature. All will be entirely credited to God.

A SOLEMN WARNING

Is the Christian's strength in the Lord, and not in himself? Surely then, the person outside of Christ must be a poor, impotent creature, helpless to do anything to effect his own salvation. If a living tree cannot grow without sap from the taproot, how can a rotten stump, which has no root, revive itself of its own accord? In other words, if a Christian imbued with God's grace must continually rely on His strength, then surely the one outside of God's grace, dead in trespasses and sin, can never produce such strength in himself. To be unregenerate is to be impotent. 'When we were without strength, in due time Christ died for the ungodly' (*Rom. 5:6*).

The philosophy called humanism has long been a suitor to man's pride. It boasts in his natural strength and wisdom, and woos him with promises of grand accomplishments now, and heaven later. God Himself has scattered such Babel-builders and proclaimed His pre-eminence for eternity. Confounded for ever be such sons of pride, who trust in the power of nature as though man with his own brick and mortar of natural abilities were able to make a way to heaven! You who are yet in your natural state, would you become wise to salvation? Then first become fools in your own eyes. Renounce this carnal wisdom which cannot perceive spiritual things, and beg wisdom of God, who gives without rebuke (*James 1:5*).

Here is a word for Christians. Knowing your strength lies wholly in God and not in yourself, remain humble – even when God is blessing and using you most. Remember, when you have your best suit on, who made it and who paid for it! God's favor is neither the work of your own hands nor the price of your own worth. How can you boast of what you did not buy? If you embezzle God's strength and credit it to your own account, He will soon call an audit and take back what was His all along. Even when He seems the most generous with your spiritual allowance, He still keeps the account in His own name and can at once reduce you to spiritual poverty if you misappropriate His grace.

Walk humbly, therefore, before God and manage well the strength you have, remembering that it is borrowed strength. What kind of man will waste what he begs? Or who will give to a pauper who squanders what he has already been given? How can you look God in the face and ask for more if you mis-spend what you have already so graciously received?

4. An Admonition to Appropriate
'The Power of His Might'

Paul continues his exhortation by again stressing the source of our strength: ' . . . and in the power of his might.' Two questions come at once to mind. First, what is meant by 'the power of his might'; and second, how does the believer avail himself of this power?

WHAT IS 'THE POWER OF HIS MIGHT'?

Simply put, this phrase means *his mighty power*. It is like another passage, 'to the praise of the glory of his grace' (*Eph. 1:6*), which means 'to the praise of his glorious grace.' Sometimes the Lord is described as 'strong and mighty,' sometimes as 'almighty.' What matters is that we grasp the significance of God's infinite, almighty power.

APPROPRIATING GOD'S POWER

How does the believer tap into his source of power? To be

strong in the power of the Lord's might requires two acts of faith. First, you must have a settled, firm persuasion that the Lord is almighty in power. This is a foundational truth. Second, you must not only believe that God is almighty, but also that this almighty power of God is engaged for your defense. God expects you to meet every trial, every temptation, leaning on His arm.

As a father walking over a rough path offers his hand to his child, so God reaches forth His power for His saints' faith to cling to. God did this for Abraham, Isaac, and Jacob, whose faith He tested above most of His saints before or since – for not one of the great things which were promised to them came to pass while they were on this earth. How, then, did God make Himself known to them? By displaying this attribute of His power (*Ex. 6:3*). It was all they had, to keep their footing sure. They lived comfortably and died triumphantly, bequeathing the promise to their children. They never doubted, because God Almighty had promised.

THREE REASONS FOR TRUSTING GOD'S POWER

I. HIS PAST RECORD

Throughout history God has proven the sufficiency of His power, yet it is not easy to believe that God is almighty. Moses himself was a star of the first magnitude for grace, yet see how his faith blinks and twinkles until he overcomes his doubts. He said to God, 'The people, among whom I am, are six hundred thousand footmen; and thou hast said, I will give them flesh, that they may eat a whole month. Shall the flocks and the herds be slain for them, to suffice them?' (*Num. 11:21, 22*). This holy man lost sight for a time of the almighty power of God, and began questioning how the Lord could keep His word. He might as well have said what he was obviously thinking:

[43]

'O God, have You not overestimated Your power this time? What You have promised cannot be done!' For so God interprets his reasoning: 'And the Lord said unto Moses, Is the Lord's hand waxed short?' (*v. 23*).

It was the same with Mary in the New Testament: 'Lord, if thou hadst been here, my brother had not died' (*John 11:32*). To this, her sister Martha added, 'Lord, by this time he stinketh' (*v. 39*). Both were godly women, yet they had serious doubts about the extent of Christ's power. One limited Him to *place* – 'If thou hadst been *here*. . . . ' As if Christ could not have saved Lazarus' life absent as well as present! The other limited Him as to *time* – '*Now* he stinketh. . . . ' As if Christ had brought His remedy too late, and the grave would not release its prisoner at His command. Despite their unbelief, God proved Himself faithful.

Now, Christian, before you point at the wrinkle in their faith, perhaps you should check for the holes in your own. Do not have such a high opinion of yourself as to think your own faith does not need your utmost effort continually to acknowledge the almighty power of God. When you see these heroes of the faith dash their feet against this kind of temptation, how can you be so confident?

II. YOUR PRESENT DILEMMA

Without God's strength, you cannot stand in the hour of testing. The challenge is beyond the stretch of human fortitude. Just suppose all your strength is already engaged to barricade your soul against temptation and Satan is steadily hacking away at your resolve; what will you do? You need not panic. Only send faith to cry at God's window, like the man in the parable asking his neighbor for bread at midnight, and He who keeps covenant for ever will provide. When faith fails, however, and the soul has no one to send for divine intervention, the battle is all but over, and Satan will at that very moment be crossing the threshold.

When you are in the midst of testing, do not give up in despair. Faith is a dogged grace! Unless your soul flatly denies the power of God, this courier – faith – will beat a well-worn path to the throne. Doubt cripples but does not incapacitate faith. Indeed, even as you are disputing the mercy of God and questioning in your mind whether He will come to your rescue, faith will make its way, if haltingly, into His presence. And the message it delivers will be, 'If thou wilt, thou canst make me clean.'

But if you conclude finally that God *cannot* pardon or save, *cannot* come to your rescue, this shoots faith through the heart. Then your soul will fall at Satan's feet, too disheartened to keep the door shut any longer to his temptation. Remember this: The one who abandons faith in the midst of a spiritual drought can be compared to the fool who throws away his pitcher the first day the well is dry.

III. HIS ETERNAL DESIRE

It has ever been and always will be the Father's will that we trust only Him. God demands to be called the Almighty; He insists we place our confidence in Him. That child is wise who does as his father bids. Man may be called wise, merciful, mighty; but only God is all-wise, all-merciful, almighty. When we leave out this prefix *all*, we nickname God and call Him by a creature's name, which He will not answer to. His insistence on this particular is accented in several ways:

First, in the strict command to give Him glory for His power. He has made it clear in His dealings with men that *all* power is His, and He will not share His glory with any other: 'Neither fear ye their fear, nor be afraid . . . [but] sanctify the Lord of hosts himself' (*Isa. 8:12, 13*). And not only in the midst of a marvelous display of His might. In the darkest hour, in the least likely circumstances, faith must run to the Father with praise for His greatness.

The severe discipline He administers when we fail to trust Him also shows the importance of acknowledging His omnipotence. Our faith is so important to God that He will sometimes chastise His dearest children when they stagger in this area. He expects us to trust Him even when we come off poorly by our own standards. We are not to argue or reason; we are to submit and cling to the promise of His power poured forth for us. Zacharias merely asked the angel, 'Whereby shall I know this? for I am an old man, and my wife well stricken in years' (*Luke 1:18*). And for daring to question the vastness of God's power, he was struck dumb on the spot. God longs for His children to believe His word, and not to dispute His power. The distinguishing mark of Abraham's faith was that he was ' . . . fully persuaded that what [God] had promised, he was able also to perform' (*Rom. 4:21*).

To encourage our trust, the Lord often intervenes in mighty ways on behalf of His people. Sometimes He allows an opposing force to arise, so that at precisely the right moment He can raise up a more magnificent pillar of remembrance to Himself. This pillar will stand in the very ruins of that which contested His power. Thus, when He intervenes all must say, 'Almighty power was here!'

Such was the case with Lazarus. Christ stayed away until the man was dead in order to give a greater demonstration of His power. God sometimes used the same method in the Old Testament. Remember the exodus. If God had brought Israel out of Egypt while Joseph was in favor at court, they probably would have had an easy departure. Instead, God reserved His deliverance for the reign of that proud Pharaoh who cruelly oppressed them and satisfied his lust upon them, that His children might know beyond doubt who had delivered them.

God's timely intervention is a confirmation that you can believe His almighty power is yours, engaged for your defense and help in all trials and temptations. God miraculously brought Israel out of Egypt; did He then set them down on the other side of the Red Sea to find their way to Canaan using their own skill and strength? No, 'The Lord God bare [them] as a man doth bear his son, in all the way that [they] went' (*Deut. 1:31*).

God makes the soul willing to come out of Satan's clutches, then brings him out of spiritual Egypt by His converting grace. When the saint is upon his march and the whole country rises up against him, how will he get safely past all his enemies' borders? God Himself will enfold him in the arms of His everlasting strength. We 'are kept by the power of God through faith unto salvation' (*1 Pet. 1:5*). The power of God is that shoulder on which Christ carries you, His lost sheep, home – rejoicing as He goes (*Luke 15:5*). The everlasting arms of His strength are eagles' wings, upon which you are both tenderly and securely conveyed to glory (*Ex. 19:4*).

THE FIVEFOLD BOND SECURING GOD'S POWER

I. HIS NEAR KINSHIP TO THE SAINTS

The relationship God has with His saints assures His power on their behalf. You are His own dear child, and most parents take care of their own. Even the silly hen scurries to gather her brood under her wing when trouble appears. How much more will God, who is the father of such instincts in His creatures, stir up His whole strength to defend you? A mother sitting in her house hears a sudden cry outside and, knowing the voice, says at once,

[47]

'That is my child!' She drops everything and runs to him. God responds as with a mother's heart to the cries of His children.

II. HIS DEAR LOVE FOR THE SAINTS

God's love for His saints sets His power in motion. He who has God's heart does not lack for His arm. Love rallies all other affections and sets the powers of the whole man into action. Thus in God, love sets His other attributes to work; all are ready to bring about what God says He likes. God considers all His creatures, but the believing soul is an object of His choicest love – even the love with which He loves His Son (*John 17:26*).

When a soul believes, then God's eternal purpose and counsel concerning him – whom He chose in Christ before the foundation of the world – is brought to term. Can you imagine the love God has for a child He has carried so long in the womb of His eternal purpose? If God delighted in His plan before He spoke the world into being, how much greater is His delight to witness the full fruition of His labor – a believing soul. Having performed His own will thus far, God will surely raise all the power He has in that believer's behalf, rather than be robbed of His glory within a few steps of home.

God showed us how much a soul is worth by the purchase price He paid. It cost him dearly, and that which is so hard won will not be easily given up. He spent His Son's blood to purchase you, and He will spend His own power to keep you.

As an earthly parent you rejoice to see your own good qualities reproduced in your children. God, the perfect parent, longs to see His attributes reflected in His saints. It is this image of God reflected in you that so enrages hell; it is this at which the demons hurl their mightiest weapons. When God defends you, He also defends

Himself. Now knowing that the quarrel is God's, surely He will not have you go forth to war at your own expense!

III. HIS EVERLASTING COVENANT

God's covenant engages His almighty power. He puts His own hand and seal to His promise, and like the mountains surrounding Jerusalem it stands, never to be removed. As His name is, so is His nature – a God who keeps covenant for ever. He does not parcel Himself out, a few crumbs to one, a crust to another – as one feeds the sparrows. He allows you to claim as yours whatever He has. He makes His covenant with every believer. Were some left to fight it out by the strength of their own abilities, then the strong would be more likely to stand and the weak to fall in battle. But, castled in the covenant, all are safe together – because *all* rest in the power of His might.

IV. HIS SELF-IMPOSED OBLIGATION

Since God demands our trust, He is obligated to prove Himself trustworthy. All His promises are yea and amen; He has therefore bound Himself to use His power in our defense.

Where can anyone flee in any need, or when in danger of sin, Satan, or his instruments, except to God? 'What time I am afraid,' David said, 'I will trust in thee' (*Psalm 56:3*). When you take sanctuary in God, you can rest assured He will not betray you to the enemy. Your willing dependence upon Him awakens His almighty power for your defense as surely as a newborn's cry awakens its mother, regardless of the hour. He has sworn the greatest oath that can come from His sacred lips: that all who flee to their hope in Him for refuge, shall have strong consolation (*Heb. 6:17, 18*). This should embolden your faith to expect a kind haven when you turn to God for protection. Having set up His name and promises as a strong tower,

God calls His people into His chambers, and expects them to enter and makes themselves at home.

V. HIS INTERCEDING SON

Christ's presence and activity in heaven remind God of His firm commitment to defend the saints. We have been promised that one of the Savior's ongoing activities in heaven is ever to intercede before the Father on our behalf. Intercession is purely an office of mercy to believers, that they might have given to them whatever is needed for the performance of all God has promised. Jesus Christ is our ambassador to see all carried fairly between God and us according to agreement. Although Christ sits in His exalted position beside the Father and out of the storm in regard to His own safety, yet His children are left behind in combat with Satan. They remain in His heart, and He will not forget them for a moment. Witness the speedy dispatch He made of the Holy Spirit to the apostles when He ascended. Almost as soon as He was warm in His seat next to the Father, Christ had sent the Holy Spirit to comfort not only the first Christians but all believers until His return.

OCCASIONS FOR USING GOD'S POWER

Once you realize that God omnipotent is in charge of your life, you will quit worrying about how to fight your enemies. No assault is strong enough to overpower Him, and nothing can penetrate your front lines without His permission.

The devil was shrewd enough to ask God to remove the hedge around Job before he launched his attack, but men are not generally so aware of God's power. Their own spiritual blindness deceives them into supposing their assault on a believer is against mere man. They may not be able to see an inch beyond their own noses, yet they will rush full tilt at a saint and expect to make short work of him. They do not know the supply of troops in the saint's defense is inexhaustible – because the supply line from heaven cannot be blocked by anyone other than God Himself.

The Egyptians thought they had Israel in a trap when they saw them march into a dead end by the sea. 'They are entangled in the land,' Pharaoh boasted (*Ex. 14:3*). And so they would have been, but almighty power stepped in and brought them safely through. No sooner were they past this danger, however, than they found themselves in a wilderness with not so much as a roof over their heads. Yet here they lived for forty years without trade or tillage, and without begging or robbing any of their neighbor nations.

What can almighty power not do to protect us from the wrath and power of our enemies, whether men or devils? Scripture is filled to overflowing with accounts of God's all-sufficiency. Just as His power stood between the Israelites and the Egyptians, so it marched with Joshua at Jericho and faced Goliath in the valley of Elah. This same power cast the unclean spirit from the demon-possessed Gadarene, and restored life to the widow's son.

Has His power grown weaker today, or are our enemies stronger? Certainly not, though wicked men nowadays seem bolder than the saints' enemies of old. Then, they sometimes fled at the appearance of God among His people, whereas many today would rather give the credit for their defeat to Satan himself than acknowledge God in the business. Take comfort in knowing this: God so loves His saints that He will not hesitate to give whole nations for their ransom if His providence so decrees. He ripped open the very womb of Egypt to save the life of His child Israel (*Isa. 43:3*).

The constant demonstrations of God's power in behalf of His children stand in sharp contrast to the impotent condition of those in a Christless state. The almighty power of God is a select dish. Just as He set it before Abraham and Moses, so He offers it to the saints of every age. And while they may eat their fill, the brazen sinner goes begging. He may not have so much as a drop of heavenly power for his own use. God, through His servant Isaiah, warns sinners, 'My servants shall eat, but ye shall be hungry: behold, my servants shall drink, but ye shall be thirsty' (*Isa. 65:13*).

God is almighty to pardon, but He will not use His power for a shameless sinner. He is able to save and help in time of need, but if you have not repented, how can you expect His aid? The same power God expends on the believer's salvation will be spent on your damnation, for He has bound Himself under oath to destroy every impenitent soul.

What opiate does Satan sprinkle on the pillows of the unregenerate? How can they sleep so soundly even after they have been warned of the consequences of ignoring God's gracious ultimatum? Sinner, Satan may trick you into supposing it takes wisdom or courage to refuse the terms of God's mercy, but it is really the ultimate act of foolishness. Your eternal destiny rests with God. If you will not deal with Him now, you must answer His charges later. Know this: 'It is a fearful thing to fall into the hands of the living God' (*Heb. 10:31*).

As for you, saint, strengthen yourself in the knowledge that God's strong arm reaches down to you, not in anger but in love. With the same faith that acknowledges God's existence, believe also this: His almighty power is your sure friend. You can put it to the test in the following circumstances.

1. WHEN WEIGHED DOWN BY SIN

You can be absolutely certain that no sin is powerful

enough to overwhelm God's strength. One Almighty is more than many 'mighties'! He has shown His eagerness to rescue you over and over again. Provoked to the limit by His people's sins, what does He do? He issues a sweet promise! 'I will not execute the fierceness of mine anger,' He declares. And why not? ' . . . For I am God, and not man' (*Hos. 11:9*). It is as though He said, 'I will show you the *almightiness* of My mercy!'

Who can doubt the omnipotence of God? We know He has *power* to pardon if He so chooses. But there is greater comfort than this for the believer; it rests in His *covenant* to pardon. As none can bind God but Himself, so none can break the bond He makes with Himself. These are His own words: '[I] will abundantly pardon' (*Isa. 55:7*). In other words, 'I will drown your sins in My mercy and spend all I have, rather than let it be said that My good is overcome by your evil.'

So when Satan terrifies you with his awful accusations against your soul, you can say with confidence, 'It is God and no other who justifies me. He has promised to restore my life if I submit to Him. Has He ever broken a promise? Therefore, I have committed myself to Him as unto a faithful Creator.'

II. WHEN OVERPOWERED BY TEMPTATION

If you fear you will one day fall to temptation, grab hold of God's strength now and reinforce yourself to resist. Believe you will be victorious on the day you are tested. Your Father watches closely while you are in the valley fighting; your cries of distress bring Him running. Jehoshaphat called for help when pressed by his enemies, and the Lord rescued him (*2 Chron. 20*). You can be just as sure of His help when you are pressed to the wall. Remind Him often of His promise: 'Sin shall not have dominion over you' (*Rom. 6:14*).

Though this word *almighty* is not stated in the foregoing verse, it is implied in this and every promise. Recite it to your soul: 'Sin shall not have dominion over you, saith the Almighty God!' Now if you are going to take shelter under this attribute, you must stay within its shade. What good will the shadow of a mighty rock do if we sit in the open sun? That is to say, if we wander away from God's protection by venturing into the heat of temptation, we should not be surprised when our faith grows faint and we stumble and fall into sin. We are weak in ourselves; our strength lies in the rock of God's almightiness. It should be our constant habitation.

III. WHEN OPPRESSED BY CHRISTIAN DUTY

Perhaps you find the duty of your calling too heavy for your weak faith. Look to God for strength. When you are sick of your work and ready like Jonah to run away, encourage yourself with God's words to Gideon: 'Go in this thy might . . . have not I sent thee?' (*Jud. 6:14*). Begin the work God has given you, and you will engage His strength *for* you; run from your work, and you engage God's strength *against* you. He will send some storm or other after you to bring His runaway servant home.

Are you called to suffer? Do not flinch in fear. God knows the limits of your strength. He can place the load so evenly on your shoulders that you will scarcely feel it. But still He is not satisfied. His watchful eye is always on you, and when you stagger He picks you up – burden and all – and carries you to your destination nestled in the bosom of His promise: 'God is faithful, who will not suffer you to be tempted above that ye are able; but will with the temptation also make a way to escape . . .' (*1 Cor. 10:13*). How can you fret when you are wrapped in His covenant? Your heavenly Father is so eager to care for you, that while you are timidly asking for a nibble of peace and joy, He is longing for you to open your mouth wide so He can fill it. The more often you ask, the better; and the more you ask for, the more He welcomes you.

Go quickly now. Search your heart from one end to the other, and gather up all your weaknesses. Set them before the Almighty, as the widow placed her empty vessels before the prophet. Expect a miracle of deliverance from the limitless resources of God. If you had more vessels to bring, you could have them all filled.

God has strength enough to give, but He has no strength to deny. Here the Almighty Himself (with reverence I say it) is weak. Even a child, the weakest in grace of His family, who can but whisper 'Father', is able to overcome Him. Never let the weakness of your faith keep you from the presence of God. The very sight of the pale face and thin cheeks of your faith, your love, your patience, will move His heart with compassion and carry a strong argument for His aid.

FOUR REASONS WHY GOD'S POWER IS SOME-TIMES HIDDEN

'But,' says some dejected soul, 'I have prayed over and over for strength against temptation – and to this day my hands are weak! No matter how hard I try, I cannot resist. If God's power is really engaged for me, why am I not victorious in my Christian life?'

I. YOU MAY HAVE OVERLOOKED GOD'S POWER

Check once again and you will no doubt find some hidden strength you had not noticed before. Perhaps you prayed and expected God to answer in a certain way, but while you were watching for Him from the front window, He slipped in the back door. What I mean is this: You expected sudden relief from your trial, but instead God gave you strength to pray with greater fervor. Is this nothing at all? Any physician will tell you, the stronger the cry, the stronger the child.

Not only that, but do you not find that you have more strength for self-denial than before? In other words, are you not increasingly humbled by this thorn in your flesh? If so, you have wrestled with a strong opponent – your pride – and wrestled well! What is harder or more against the grain than to force our carnal pride to its knees before God?

II. GOD MAY HAVE PURPOSELY DELAYED HIS POWER

When you have waited as long as you are willing to wait and God still has not answered, do not let your own impatience accuse Him of negligence. Instead, say to yourself, 'My Father is wiser than I. He will send what I need, when I need it. I know if He withholds His hand from me at present, it is only because He knows best.'

One reason for postponing deliverance is to give your faith an opportunity to grow stronger. When a mother is teaching her child to walk, she stands back a short distance and holds out her hands to the child, beckoning him to come. Now if she exercises her strength to go to her little one, the child is ill-served, for his unsteady legs are denied the practice they need. If she loves him, she will let him suffer a little at present to ensure his future health. Just so, because God loves His children, He sometimes lets them struggle to strengthen the legs of their unsteady faith.

Not only that, but He can also use trials as the occasion for great demonstrations of His power. Suppose a child is toddling along the river's edge, slips, and is in real danger. What does the mother do? She rushes at once to rescue him! And her arms never seemed stronger nor her embrace more comforting than in such a circumstance.

You may be a poor, trembling soul, weak in faith and ever on the brink of sinking; yet to this day your grace lives on, though full of leaks. Is there a greater demonstration of God's strength than to see such a pitiful, storm-tossed ship towed past an armada of sins and devils, into God's safe harbor at last? What a tribute to His power for so weak a vessel to foil all the battleships of Satan!

III. THE CAUSE OF HINDRANCE OF THE BLESSING MAY BE IN YOURSELF

If your heart is not set in the right direction when you appeal for deliverance, strength will not come. Ask yourself these questions when you feel shut off from God's power:

Am I really trusting God, and Him only, to meet my need? Or am I depending on my own resolve, my pastor, or some other outside source? All these things may be good, but they are only Christ's servants. Press through them to the Master Himself. Touch Him – and deliverance is yours.

Am I thankful for the strength I have? In a long-distance race, the contestants run at varying paces. Perhaps you are discouraged when you see so many strong ones pass you on the way to glory. Rather than cry after them, be thankful that you have strength to run at all! Even the lowest place in the army of saints is a great honor. Are you in the race? It is by God's grace and that alone; thank Him for the privilege. Remember this: Everyone (even the weakest saint) who finishes the race is a winner.

Has my pride stopped the flow of God's power? God will not keep supplying power if you use it for your own advancement. He knows how quickly you are carried away from Him on the wings of your pride. Because He loves you, He will recall your ration of power if it takes you out of fellowship with Him. All this He does for your own good, so that when your pride lies gasping, you will be forced back to Him.

IV. GOD MAY CALL YOU TO PERSEVERE IN THE FACE OF OVERWHELMING ODDS

Perhaps nothing that has been said answers your particular case. Your heart is clean before God; you have sincerely and prayerfully waited, yet God withholds His hand. Then you must resolve to live and die waiting, for that may be what He requires. What greater evidence of your faith and of God's grace at work in you than to persevere to the end!

Comfort yourself with the promise that when you are on your last legs, strength *will* come. The Scripture says, 'They that wait upon the Lord shall renew their strength' (*Isa. 40:31*). The prophet was not sent to the widow's house until she had baked her last loaf of bread. Job was not delivered until God's purpose had been served. Are your trials any greater than Job's? Strive to have his heart, and know your life is in the hands of a God who is full of pity and tender mercy (*James 5:11*).

2: *First Consideration: The Saint's Armour*

1. The Christian Must Be Armed

Put on the whole armour of God, that ye may be able to stand against the wiles of the devil (Eph. 6:11).

W<small>E</small> have seen that it is God's almighty power and not our own weak strength that fuels our faith and readies us for battle. Yet how do we appropriate this power in our own lives? Paul tells us: by wearing God's armour.

To put on the armour of God is to appropriate His power in a most personal way. It involves first and foremost a change of heart. The person who boasts that he has confidence in God but does not truly believe with his heart will never be safe in the war zone that separates earth and heaven. If by negligence or choice he fails to put on God's armour and rushes naked into battle, he signs his own death certificate.

The story is told of a fanatic in Munster who valiantly tried to repulse an invading army by shouting, 'In the name of the Lord of hosts, depart!' But his unregenerate soul had no such commission from the General for whom he pretended to fight, and he soon perished. His example should teach us the high price to be paid for such folly. What brave but foolish language you hear drop from the lips of the most profane and ignorant among us! They say they hope in God and trust in His mercy; they defy the devil and all his works. But all the while they are poor, naked creatures without the least piece of God's armour upon their souls. Such presumption has no place in the Lord's camp.

THE ARMED SAINT – HIS DIVINE PROVISIONS

Paul's admonition to put on armour falls into two general parts. First, a direction telling us *what* to do: 'Put on the whole armour of God. . . . ' And second, *why* we should do it: '. . . that ye may be able to stand against the wiles of the devil.'

So to begin, every recruit in Christ's army should be properly fitted with armour. The first question that comes to mind is, What is this armour?

I. CHRIST AS ARMOUR

We are told, 'Put ye on the Lord Jesus Christ' (*Rom. 13:14*), where Christ is presented as armour. The apostle does not exhort the saints simply to put on temperance in place of drunkenness, or for adultery to put on chastity. Instead, he tells them to 'put on the Lord Jesus Christ,' implying that until Christ is put on, the creature is unarmed. It is not the man decked out in morality or philosophical virtues who will repel a full charge of temptation sent from Satan's cannon; it is the man suited up in armour – that is, in Christ.

II. THE GRACES OF CHRIST AS ARMOUR

I speak now of the 'girdle of truth, the breastplate of righteousness,' and so forth. We are instructed to 'put on the new man' (*Eph. 4:24*), who is made up of all the graces. The point is this: To be without Christ and His graces is to be without armour.

THE UNARMED SINNER – HIS DIM PROSPECTS

A person in a Christless, graceless state is naked and unarmed – totally unequipped to fight sin and Satan. In the beginning, God sent Adam out in complete armour.

But by sleight of hand, the devil stripped him. As soon as the first sin was completed, '[Adam and Eve] were naked' (*Gen. 3:7*). Sin robbed them of their armour and left them poor, weak creatures. It cost Satan some fancy footwork to make the first breach, but once man opened the gates to let him in, the devil named himself king and brought to court a whole cortege of deadly sins, without ever drawing a sword.

Here is what I mean: Instead of confessing their sin, Adam and Eve tried to hide from God and became evasive in their dealings with Him. They blamed one another, shifting the responsibility for their disobedience rather than appealing for mercy. How quickly their hearts were hardened by deceit! Man's basic nature has not changed since that day. This is exactly the condition of every son and daughter of Adam; naked Satan finds us, and slaves he makes us until God, having bought us with the blood of His dear Son, comes to reclaim each penitent soul for service in His own kingdom.

To better understand the seriousness of being caught without God's armour, study these four consequences of being naked and unarmed.

I. ALIENATION FROM GOD

'Ye were without Christ, being aliens from the commonwealth of Israel and strangers from the covenants of promise' (*Eph. 2:12*). If you are not a kingdom child, you have no more to do with any covenant promise than a citizen of Rome has to do with the charter of London. You are alone in the world, without God. If you get into trouble, you must plead your own case. But if you are a citizen of heaven, God has power to grant you special immunity in any situation. And while the devil's spite is directed toward you, he dare not come upon God's ground to touch you without permission.

What a desperate condition, for a soul to be left to his own defense against legions of lusts and devils! He will be torn like a silly hare among a pack of hounds – no God to call them off, but Satan to urge them on. Let God leave a people, no matter how militant, and before long they lose their courage and cannot fight. A company of children could rise up and chase them out of their own front yard. When the Israelites panicked at news of invincible giants and walled cities, Caleb and Joshua pacified them with this assurance: 'They are bread for us; their defence is departed from them' (*Num. 14:9*). How much more must that soul who has no defense from the Almighty be as bread to Satan?

II. IGNORANCE

Only an ignorant soul is foolish enough to ride out of his castle unarmed during a siege. He obviously has not studied the enemy, or he would know what peril lies beyond his gates. To make matters even worse, if he fights without putting on Christ, he must fight in the dark. The apostle writes, 'Ye were sometimes darkness, but now are ye light in the Lord' (*Eph. 5:8*). As a child of light, you who are Christians may be in the dark from time to time concerning some truth or promise. But you always have a spiritual eye which the Christless person lacks. The unregenerate man is always too ignorant to resist Satan, whereas the Christian's knowledge of the truth pursues and brings back the soul even when taken prisoner by a temptation.

Do not let anyone deceive you. Spiritual darkness can never be expelled except by union with Christ. As the physical eye once put out cannot be restored by human means, so neither can the spiritual eye – lost by Adam's sin – be restored by the efforts of men or angels. This is one of the diseases Christ came to cure (*Luke 4:18*).

III. IMPOTENCY

'When we were yet without strength, in due time Christ died for the ungodly' (*Rom. 5:6*). What can an unarmed soul do to shake off the yoke of Satan? No more than an unarmed people can do to shake off the yoke of a conquering army! Satan has such power over the soul that he is called the strong man who keeps the soul as his palace (*Luke 11:21*). If he has no disturbance from heaven, he need fear no mutiny within. He keeps everything under his control. What the Spirit of God does in a saint, Satan in a diabolical sense does in a sinner. The Spirit fills the heart with love, joy, holy desires; Satan fills the sinner's heart with pride, lust, lying. And like the drunkard filled with wine, the sinner filled with Satan is not his own man, but an impotent slave.

IV. FRIENDSHIP WITH SIN AND SATAN

A soul that refuses to put on Christ declares himself a rebel and makes himself the enemy of God. I think we can safely say that whoever is God's enemy must be Satan's friend – and how will you make someone fight against his own friend? Is Satan divided? Will the devil within fight against the devil without?

Sometimes Satan and a carnal heart appear to scuffle, but it is a farce – like the parrying of two fencers on stage. You would think at first they were in earnest, but when you see how wary they are and where they strike one another, you soon know they do not mean to kill. Any doubt is removed when you see them after the match, making merry together with the proceeds from their performance! Likewise, when you see an unrepentant heart make a groan or two against sin, follow him off the stage of good works where he has gained the reputation of a saint by playing the hypocrite. There you will doubtless see him and Satan together in a corner as friendly as ever.

[63]

You have seen some of the side effects of being without God's armour: ignorance, impotence, alienation from God, and friendship with sin and Satan. If putting on Christ is the sure cure for such morbid afflictions, why do we see so many refuse the sweet medicine of His grace?

1. THE NATURAL INCLINATION OF MAN'S SOUL

When you look around and see the devil's vast empire and what a little spot of ground contains Christ's subjects – what heaps of precious souls lie prostrate under Satan's feet and what a tiny regiment of saints march under Christ's banner of grace – perhaps you ask yourself, 'Is hell stronger than heaven? Are the arms of Satan more victorious than the cross of Christ?' But if you consider what I am about to tell you, you will wonder that Christ has *any* to follow Him rather than that He has so few.

Every son of man is born in sin (*Ps. 51:5*). So when the prince of this world first approaches a young soul with this or that wicked proposal, he finds the soul unarmed and in its natural state already familiar with his policies. Yielding to Satan's control will therefore not cause much of a stir in the naturally sinful heart. But when Christ campaigns for a soul, He proposes sweeping changes. And the selfish soul, which generally likes things as they are, answers Him with the same scorn as the rebellious citizens in the parable: 'We will not have this man to reign over us!' (*Luke 19:14*). The vote is unanimous: All the lusts cast their ballots against Christ, and rise up like the Philistines against Samson, whom they called the destroyer of their country (*Judges 16:23, 24*). If God's grace did not step in and override the veto, the whole world would be held in Satan's sway.

Satan's conquests are limited to ignorant, graceless souls who have neither strength nor sense to oppose him.

They are born imprisoned in sin; all he has to do is keep them there. But when he assaults a saint, whose freedom was won at the Cross, once for all, then he is laying siege to a city with gates and bars. Sooner or later, he must retreat in shame, unable to pluck the weakest saint out of the Savior's hand. Doubt your own strength, but never doubt Christ's. In your gravest conflicts with Satan, trust Him to bring you out of the devil's dominion with a high hand, in spite of all the force and fury of hell.

II. THE SUPERNATURAL MALICE OF SATAN

Do not doubt for a moment that Satan will hurl all his fury at those who love God's Word. His acquaintance with the Good News of Christ goes back a long way, to the dawn of the ages, in fact. He has seen its power demonstrated over and over again, and he knows it houses an arsenal of arms and aids for battered souls.

The very first assault the gospel made against the kingdom of darkness shook its foundation and put the legions of hell on the run. They are fleeing still. When the seventy missionaries commissioned by Christ returned with their reports that even demons were subdued by the power of the gospel, Christ replied, 'I beheld Satan as lightning fall from heaven!' (*Luke 10:17, 18*). In essence He tells them, 'What you say is not news to Me; I watched when Satan was cast out of heaven. How well I know the power of the gospel!'

Do you wonder that Satan works so hard to dispossess the gospel which dispossesses him? By the light of the gospel many who were once his friends find the way to truth and life. By the same light, saints move with blessed assurance toward their eternal home. Nothing torments the devil more than to see his old companions neglect their former sinful pleasures and spend time studying the Scriptures instead. He knows that a saint without a knowledge of the gospel is as vulnerable as an army without ammunition. Therefore, he labors either by persecution to drive God's Word away, or by political policy to persuade a people to send it away from their coast.

For it is God's Word which teaches us how to put on Christ and His graces so that we are fitly armed. Never flatter yourself into thinking you can do without this priceless book. We have all known those who content themselves with a profession of Christ and a smattering of gifts and works, and do not wish to know if there is more to the Christian life. They are the ones whose graces freeze when winter winds buffet their souls. But the saint whose faith has been insulated from error by the truth of the gospel will be able to withstand all Satan's icy blasts.

THE ARMOUR – ITS CREATOR

You have by this time been sufficiently warned of the consequences of being unarmed. Let us take a closer look now at our proper battle array. Not just any armour will do; better none at all than armour which has not been proven. Only the armour of God meets the proof test. Two particulars show this to be true.

I. GOD IS THE SOLE DESIGNER OF HIS SAINTS' ARMOUR

A true soldier goes to the front with no arms except what his general commands. It is not left to everyone's fancy to bring whatever weapons he pleases; this would only breed chaos. The Christian soldier is similarly bound to God's orders. Though the army is on earth, the council of war sits in heaven and issues directives: 'Here are your orders . . . these are your weapons.' And those who do more or use other than God commands, though with some seeming success against sin, shall surely be called to account for their boldness.

The discipline of war among men is strict in this case. Some have been court-martialed and executed even though they have beaten the enemy, because they forgot their rank or acted without orders. The discipline of God is also very precise on this point. He will say to all who invent ways of their own to worship Him or who fabricate their own forms of penance, 'Who has required this at your hands?' This is truly to be 'righteous over-much,' as Solomon says (*Eccl. 7:16*), when we presume to correct God's law and add supplements of our own to His rules. God told Israel that the false prophets were wasting their time because they did not come on His errand (*Jer. 23:32*). You, too, are wasting your time if you are doing anything that is not by God's design.

God's thoughts are not like man's, nor His ways like ours. If Moses in his own wisdom had directed Israel's flight from Egypt, we would have expected him to plunder the Egyptians of their horses and arms. But God would have His people come out naked and on foot, and Moses kept close to His orders. It was God's war they waged, and therefore only reasonable they should be under His command. They encamped and marched by His order; they fought at His command. And the tactics and weapons they used were all prescribed by God. What are we to learn from their example? In our march to heaven, fighting with the cursed spirits and lusts that stand in our way, we too must go by God's rules, which are spelled out for us in His Word.

Christian, take special care not to trust in the armour of God, but in the *God* of the armour. All your weapons are only 'mighty through God' (*2 Cor. 10:4*). The ark was the means of Israel's safety, but when the people began to glory in it instead of in God Himself, it hastened their overthrow. Just so, duties and ordinances, gifts and graces, are havens for the soul's defense; but they must be kept in their proper place. Satan trembles as much as the Philistines at the ark, to see a soul diligent in the use of his 'graces', i.e., patience, temperance, virtue, etc. But when the creature trusts more in them than in the Lord, he is on shaky ground.

II. GOD MAKES HIS SAINTS' ARMOUR AND TRAINS THEM IN ITS PROPER USE

As we have already seen, it is not armour as armour but as armour of God that makes the soul impregnable. Is prayer armour? Are faith, hope, and righteousness? Only if they are of God's design and by His appointment. That which is born of God overcomes the world, a faith born of God, a hope born of God. But the spurious, adulterous brood of self-seeking duties and graces with which some Christians gird themselves, having sprouted from mortal seed, cannot be divine.

Look closely at the label to see whether the armour you wear is the workmanship of God or not. There are many imitations on the market nowadays. It is Satan's game, if he cannot keep the sinner satisfied in his naked, lustful state, to coax him into some flimsy thing or other that by itself will neither do him good nor Satan harm. Perhaps it is church attendance, or good works, or some self-imposed penance by which he intends to impress both God and man. Do such impersonators believe in God? Oh, they hope they are not infidels. But what their armour is, or how they came by it, and whether it will hold up in an evil day, they never stop to question. Thus thousands perish who supposed they were armed against Satan, death, and judgment – when all along they were miserable and naked. These people are worse off than those who have not a rag of pretense to hide their shame from the world's gaze.

To most of us, a careful copy of a masterpiece looks quite as good as the original. But when the master himself appears, he can tell in an instant which is real and which the imposter. It is the same with that self-righteous hypocrite who is a pretender to faith and hope in God. Here is a man in glittering array with his weapon in his hand. With the sharp sword of his tongue he keeps both the preacher and the Word of God at arm's length: 'Who can say I am not a saint? Name one commandment I do not keep, one duty I neglect!' he demands indignantly. Many are impressed by his seeming piety. It takes the Spirit's discerning eye to expose him, and even then it is harder to convict him because Satan has so cleverly tampered with him already. He must first be disarmed and unclothed of his own filthy self-righteousness, because God's armour can never be made to fit over the suit he has fashioned for himself. On the other hand, the soul that stands naked and humble before God is fully aware of the magnitude of his need and is eager for help. Which would you say is easier: to set a freshly broken bone, or to attempt the repair of one that has already been falsely mended?

Oh, pious hypocrite, either deny the name of Christ, whose insignia you only pretend to march after, or throw away the phony armour of self-righteousness and come to Him in true repentance. Do not dare to call anything the armour of God which does not glorify Him and defend you against the power of Satan!

THE ARMOUR – ITS VARIOUS PARTS

Notice the total adequacy of the saint's equipment: 'the *whole* armour of God' (*Eph. 6:11*). When properly worn, the Christian's armour is complete, and that in a threefold respect.

I. ALL THE PARTS TOGETHER COVER THE WHOLE SAINT, SOUL AND BODY

Thus the powers of the one and the senses of the other are divinely protected. No part is left exposed. Otherwise, Satan's dart may fly in at a little hole, like the deadly one that penetrated the joints of Ahab's armour (*1 Kings 22:34*). If all the man is armed except for the eye, Satan can shoot his fireballs of lust in at that opening and set the whole house aflame. Eve only looked on the tree, and a poisonous dart struck her to the heart. Suppose the eye is shut, but the ear is open to corrupt conversation. Then the devil will wriggle in at that hole. Or if all the outward senses are well guarded, but the heart not kept with all diligence, a man's own thoughts will soon betray him into Satan's hands.

Our enemies are on every side, so our armour must be 'on the right hand and on the left' (*2 Cor. 6:7*). The apostle called sin an enemy that surrounds us (*Heb. 12:1*). Satan divides his temptations into several squadrons. One he employs to assault here, another to storm there. We read of fleshly wickedness and spiritual wickedness. While you are repelling the enemy's temptation to fleshly wickedness, he may be entering your city at the other gate of spiritual wickedness. 'But,' you say, 'all my actions are above reproach.' Well, then, what armour do you have to defend your head, your judgment? If he surprises you in this area and plants a seed of heresy, it may soon take root and choke your faith.

Thus we see what need we have of universal armour covering every part.

II. EACH PIECE HAS A SPECIAL FUNCTION

God designs each part of the armour for a particular purpose; therefore, the saint must be properly attired. In other words, it will not do to cover the heart with the helmet, or to hold the buckler where the breastplate ought to be. Indeed, there is a series of graces, each with a special function to bring life and health to the soul – much like the network of veins and arteries which carries blood through the body. Prick one vein, and the blood of the whole man may spill from that outlet; neglect one duty, and the strength of all the graces may be lost.

The apostle Peter urged Christians to increase the whole body of grace. Is this not true health – when the whole body thrives? *Faith* is the grace which leads the procession. If you have faith, then add *virtue*: 'Add to your faith virtue,' says Peter (*2 Pet. 1:5*). These graces are of mutual benefit to one another. Good works and gracious actions get their life from faith; faith, in turn, fattens and becomes strong on works – so says Martin Luther.

Your works may bear luscious-looking fruit, but you are not safe from the devil's blight unless you add to your virtue *knowledge*. Knowledge is to faith as sunshine is to the farmer. Without it, faith cannot see to do her work. Nor can the work, once finished, be adequately inspected in the dim light of half-truths. If you do not ground yourself in the truth of the gospel, Satan will play upon your ignorance to thwart your spiritual growth. He has a clever proposition for every occasion. In one instance he may try to persuade you that you are not humble enough, and cause the weeds of self-condemnation to choke out the assurance of your salvation. Another time, he will flatter you into a false sense of pride in your humility, and the pestilence of self-righteousness will wipe out the Spirit's crop of fruit in your life. Satan is not particular what lie he tells you; one will work as powerfully as another if he can get you to believe it.

But knowledge is not the end of the work of grace. To it we must add *temperance*. Without it, both faith and reason may soon relinquish their rightful place to temporal pleasures. Temperance is an excellent steward. It regularly inspects the soul and sets the saint's affections in order so that he does not ignore holy duties to pursue his own entertainment. If you allow your love of creature comforts – or even your pleasure in family and loved ones – to outrun your love for the Lord, you cannot be a victorious soldier for Christ. Therefore, pray for temperance, which keeps the spiritual gauge of your heart well within the safety range, and sounds a warning when your heart grows too warm in its temporal affections or too cold toward Christ.

Imagine yourself now well equipped and marching toward heaven while basking in prosperity. Should you not also prepare for foul weather – i.e., a period of adversity? Satan will line the hedges with a thousand temptations when you come into the narrow lanes of adversity, where you cannot run as in the day of your prosperity. You may manage to escape an alluring world, only to be flattened when trouble strikes, unless you know how to persevere. Therefore, the apostle commands, 'to temperance [add] *patience*' (*2 Pet. 1:6*).

Do you have patience? An excellent grace indeed, but not enough. You must be pious as well. So Peter continues, 'to patience [add] *godliness* (*v. 6*). Godliness encompasses the whole worship of God, inward and outward. Your morals may be impeccable, but if you do not worship God, then you are an atheist. If you worship Him and that devoutly, but not according to Scripture, you are an idolator. If according to the rule, but not according to the spirit of the gospel, then you are a hypocrite. The only worship that leads to the inner chamber of true godliness is that which is done 'in spirit and in truth' (*John 4:24*).

By now we have examined quite a fine collection of

graces, and perhaps you would like to try them out. But wait – all your armour is not yet on. You have spiritual kinfolk, heirs of the same promise with you; therefore, you must add to godliness, *brotherly kindness* (*v.* 7)..It is one of our Lord's great commandments. Our love for one another is the insignia of our allegiance to Him. If Satan can set us at odds with a brother, he gives a deep wound to our godliness and to the whole cause of Christ. He knows we will hardly join hands in a duty if we cannot join hearts in love.

Not only do you have a God-given responsibility toward the family of believers, but your heavenly Father asks also that you walk blamelessly toward those outside His family. So you must add to brotherly kindness, *charity* (*v.* 7). This grace empowers you to do good to the worst of men. The more they curse you, the harder you must pray for them. 'Father, forgive them,' Jesus prayed as His executioners raked in His side for His heart's blood.

Where is Christ's compassion in the church today? It is evident the lack of this last piece of armour gives Satan great advantage in our time. We have become penny-pinchers with God's mercy for fear our charity will be too broad – whereas in the biblical sense, if it is not as wide as the world, it is too narrow for the command which bids us 'do good to all.'

I want to speak for a moment now to pastors: Where is our charity if every sermon is directed only to the saints and makes no effort to rescue poor, captive souls out of the devil's clutches? He may haul them to hell by the wagonload, while we are busy comforting the saints and preaching their privileges. May God give us a compassion for lost souls that will move us to reprove and exhort them in love, and snatch them from Satan's deadly grasp! It is true that ministers are stewards to provide manna for the saints, but does this mean the rest of our hearers should have no portion at all?

III. EACH PIECE IS COMPLETE AND PERFECT

Not only is the armour perfect as a whole, but God provides for each piece to be complete and perfect as well. Here the saint is called to keep his armour ready for use and shining. He must not only seek after all the graces, but also grow and mature in every particular grace – even to perfection itself. As you are to add to your faith virtue, so you must add faith to faith. Your graces are precious, like silver: the more you use them, the brighter they shine.

'Be ye . . . perfect, even as your Father which is in heaven is perfect' (*Matt. 5:48*). And purify yourselves, as God is pure. There we have an exact copy set – not that we could equal the purity and perfection which is in God, but to make us strive toward that goal. For instance, if your patience groans at the weight of a little burden, you can be sure a greater one will knock you on your back. Begin, then, at once to exercise and build up your patience so you will be spiritually strong when the load increases.

OUR GRACES – WHY WE MUST PERFECT THEM

Here are a few reasons why you should be maturing in the graces that are yours in Christ:

I. BECAUSE OUR GRACES CAN SUSTAIN INJURY

In an army called to active duty, weapons are frequently battered and broken. One man has his helmet dented, another his sword bent, a third his pistol broken. So replacements are often necessary. In one temptation you may have your helmet of hope beaten off your head, in another your patience crushed or your charity trampled upon. You need an armourer's shop near at hand to make up your losses as quickly as possible, for Satan is most likely to attack when you are least prepared to repel his charge.

'Simon, Simon, Satan hath desired to . . . sift you,' Jesus said to Peter (*Luke 22:31*). The devil knew the disciples were weak at this time. Christ, their captain, was about to be taken from the head of their regiment. They were discontented among themselves, arguing about who would have the best seat in heaven. And their supply of stronger faith, which the Spirit was to bring, had not yet come. Therefore, Christ sent them to Jerusalem to wait together until He could dispatch His Spirit to them (*Acts 1:4*). This example shows us, in the weakness of our graces, whom to ask for a fresh supply.

    II. BECAUSE SATAN IS STILL PERFECTING HIS WRATH
        AND SKILL

He is called 'the old serpent,' and for good reason: subtle by nature, yet ever more cunning; wrathful by nature, yet ever more enraged. Like a bull, the longer he is baited, the madder he grows. And considering what little time he has left, we who are to fight with him must enter the arena well equipped.

    III. BECAUSE WE FULFILL GOD'S PURPOSE WHEN WE
        GROW IN GRACE

The end of all God's working is to perfect His saints in their virtues and comforts. He is the wise caretaker of our souls. When He uses afflictions to lop and prune our spirits, it is only to purge so we can bring forth more and better fruit (*John 15:2*). The same tribulation which yields bitter results in the arid soul of the wicked is used to produce the sweet fruit of the Spirit in the fertile soul of the saint.

Why is God so intent on perfecting His saints? To prepare a spotless bride for His Son, and complete His grand design! He has furnished His church with all the instruments and gifts necessary 'for the perfecting of the

saints, . . . for the edifying of the body of Christ' (*Eph.*
4:12). If we fail to advance in spite of His provisions, we
make void the counsel of God. Therefore, the apostle
scolds the Christian Jews for their poor performance in the
school of Christ: 'When for the time ye ought to be
teachers, ye have need that one teach you again which be
the first principles of the oracles of God' (*Heb. 5:12*).

THE ARMOUR – ITS PROPER USE

I. THE ARMOUR MUST BE PUT ON

God both designs and makes His saint's armour; it is
therefore perfect in every detail. The obligation which
rests with the saint is to '*put on* the whole armour of God.'

Briefly, what is implied in the command to 'put on'? We
know it is more than a putting on by conversation. There
is little value in saying 'I have faith,' or 'I have hope,' or 'I
have charity' if you are not at that moment believing or
trusting or loving. It is one thing to have armour in the
house, and another thing to have it buckled on – to have
grace in principle, and grace in action.

II. THE ARMOUR MUST BE KEPT ON

The Christian's armour is made to be worn – no taking it
off until you have finished your course. Your armour and
your garment of flesh come off together. Then there will
be no more need of shield or helmet, no more late night
watches. Those military duties and field graces – as I may
call faith, hope, and the rest – shall be honorably
discharged. In heaven you shall appear, not in armour,
but in robes of glory.

Nevertheless, for the present you must wear your
assigned suit night and day. You must walk, work, and
sleep in it or you are not a true soldier of Christ. Paul set
himself a goal: 'Herein do I exercise myself, to have always
a conscience void of offence toward God, and toward men'

(*Acts 24:16*). Here we see this holy man at his arms, training like a true soldier, his own heart the target range on which he practises all the graces in preparation for battle. We have ample reasons to conduct ourselves in like manner.

For one thing, Christ commands it. He tells us to have our armour on, our grace in action: 'Let your loins be girded about, and your lights burning' (*Luke 12:35*). He speaks as a general to his soldiers: 'Oil your armour; light your torch; be ready to march. Prepare to fight at the first alarm of temptation!' Again He speaks, this time as a master to his servants: 'If the lord of the manor is called away and the hour of his return uncertain, will a faithful servant bolt the door, douse the fire, and retire? No, he will stand watch through the night, ready to greet the master whenever he comes.' Meaning, it is not fit for the Master to stand at our heart's door knocking, and find our graces sleeping.

Every duty of the Christian demands this constant effort. Pray he must, but how? 'Without ceasing.' Rejoice, but when? 'Evermore.' Give thanks – for what? 'In everything' (*1 Thess. 5:16–18*). We must hold our shield of faith and helmet of hope to the very end (*Eph. 6:16, 17*). Where the soldier is placed, there he stands and must neither stir nor sleep till he is discharged. When Christ comes, only that soul whom He finds so doing shall have His blessing.

Why is Christ so insistent that His soldiers remain on alert? Because *Satan's actions demand it*. Satan's advantage is great when he catches our graces napping. When the devil found Christ so ready to repel his temptation, he soon had enough. It is said, 'He departed . . . for a season' (*Luke 4:13*). But in his shameful retreat it seems he comforted himself with hopes of surprising Christ unawares at another time more advantageous to his design. And we do find him coming again at the most likely time to have had his way – but only if his enemy had been man and not God (*Matt. 27:42*).

Now if this bold tempter watched Christ so closely, does it not seem likely he will scout you, too, hoping sooner or later to find your graces slumbering? What he misses now by your watchfulness he may gain later by your negligence. In fact, he hopes you will push yourself to exhaustion with continual duty. What fiendish pleasure he would derive from turning the tables on your sincere efforts for Christ. 'Surely,' says Satan when he sees a fervent Christian, 'this will not last long.' When he finds him most sensitive to the Spirit and scrupulous in conduct, he says, 'This is but for a while; he cannot keep it up for long. Soon he will unbend his bow and unbuckle his armour, and then I will have at him.' But this can never happen as long as we are continually applying to God for our strength.

Satan is not the only pitfall; *the nature of our graces makes diligence essential*. If not watched closely, they will play the truant. And a soul long absent from the school of obedience will not be eager to return and take up his old assignments. The reason is twofold. First, having neglected his duties, he is ashamed to face the Master. Second, he knows how much he has forgotten through neglect, and what late hours he must keep to recoup the loss. He goes to duty like the scholar who has not looked at his books for some time: his lesson is almost out of his head. Whereas another, who is always mulling it over, has it at his fingertips and is eager to begin his next assignment.

I cannot say enough about the need to keep your wicks trimmed and your lamps burning. One of Satan's favorite maneuvers is the surprise attack. Imagine the confusion in a town if an alarm suddenly sounded in the dead of night, signaling the enemy was already at the gates – but all the soldiers were home in bed. What turmoil would ensue! One hunts his pants, another his sword, a third does not know what to do for ammunition. Thus in utter chaos they run up and down, spreading panic – which could never happen if the enemy had found them upon their guard. A similar uproar will occur if you do not keep your spiritual armour on. You will be feverishly searching for this grace and that when you should have already reported to Christ for active duty.

Not only are active graces necessary for your own protection, but also for the help and comfort of other Christians. Paul had this in mind when he disciplined himself to keep a good conscience so as not to be a scandal to other believers. He knew that the cowardice of one may make others run; that the ignorance of another may do mischief to many. How often has the waywardness of a saint seduced a fellow Christian to leave the narrow path for the broad road that leads to destruction? This is among the gravest of errors for we are commanded to do just the opposite! God told the Reubenites and Gadites to go before their brethren armed for battle, until the land was conquered. Thus you are to assist your fellow brethren who may not have the same measure of grace or comfort as you. Help such weak ones; be their shieldbearer. This you will not be able to do unless your own grace is exercised, your armour buckled on.

Perhaps you are a parent with a family under your wing. They fare much as you do. If your heart is feasting on Christ, you will never find yourself in short supply when caring for their spiritual needs. On the other hand, if your own heart is malnourished, they will go hungry for spiritual food. In the same way that a mother eats more while she is nursing her infant, you should, for the sake of those under your roof, be more careful to nourish your own graces and cherish them.

THE ARMOUR – ITS PROPER PLACE

Not only should the armour be put on and kept on, but it should also be visible to everyone you meet. Men boast of their faith, their repentance, their love for God – precious graces, indeed. Why, then, do so few let us see these walking abroad in their daily conduct? Surely if such guests were truly residing in a soul, they would at least look out the window or take a short stroll occasionally and be seen in this duty and that holy action.

Grace – here I mean those divine attributes infused into your human spirit by the Holy Spirit – is a living creature. It is not a souvenir of your salvation, which you may tuck away in some obscure closet of your soul. No, grace will show itself. It will walk with you wherever you go. It will buy with you and sell for you, and have a hand in all your enterprises. It will encourage you when you are sincere and faithful for God, and it will complain and chide when you are otherwise.

FINAL EXHORTATION

Enough has been said to show the tendency of our graces to be overcome by a sleeping disorder in this life. Christ, though He roused His disciples twice on the evening of His arrest, yet found them napping a third time. If you do not exercise your godly character you, too, will be caught sleeping. Your time is short and your way long; put on the graces of Christ at once lest you be overtaken the night before you reach sight of your Father's house.

There is a dual advantage in possessing these graces – first to yourself, and then to others. While you are here on this earth, others will fare better when your graces are healthy. Your enthusiasm in your heavenly course will aid those who travel with you. When they see what good medicine God's grace is to your soul, they will soon be begging for their own portion. What is more, the booming voice of your graces will drown out the sins of others. Let me give you a practical illustration. The diseased swearer does not know such a powerful cure is present when the Christian is mealy-mouthed and does not reflect the character of God. But if a godly man has his antidote ready and the courage to administer it in a wise and loving reproof, he can make sin flee the place and run with shame into its hole.

God deserves the best service you can give Him in your generation, so start letting His divine attributes manifest themselves in your life now. He does not give you a limited supply of His grace, to be meted out a little at a time. Do not do like so many and tuck it away in a savings account, which you intend to use someday but not now. Surely God is not so miserly with His Spirit that you must budget your graces! On the contrary, the eye of Providence is never shut; He who keeps you does not slumber. The psalmist assures us, 'The eyes of the Lord are upon the righteous' (*Ps. 34:15*). He has fixed His gaze for ever and with infinite delight pleases Himself in the object of His affection. When was His ear ever deaf to your cries or His hand short from supplying your needs? Does not your welfare occupy the thoughts of God, and are there any other than thoughts of peace which He entertains? A few drops of this oil will keep the wheels of your faith in motion.

2. Why the Christian Must Be Armed
THE DANGER IF UNARMED
To better understand the nature of our enemy let us note

the term Paul uses here: *wiles*, or methods. The word in the Greek connotes 'that art and order one observes in handling an argument.' Now because it implies extraordinary skill and a sharp wit to compose that kind of discourse, *wiles* is used to express the subtlety of Satan in planning his strategy against the Christian. The expert soldier is keenly aware of this order, as well as the scholar. He understands there is method in forming an army, as well as in framing an argument.

Because the devil is a very subtle enemy, the saint must always be on his guard. Satan is called the old serpent. The serpent is subtle above other creatures; and an old serpent, above other serpents. If Satan was too crafty for man in his perfection, how much more dangerous to us now in our maimed condition – for we have never recovered from that first crack Adam's fall gave to our understanding. And as we have lost knowledge, so Satan has gained more and more experience. Granted, he lost his heavenly wisdom as soon as he became a devil, but ever since, he has increased his craft. And while he does not have wisdom enough to do himself good, yet he has knowledge enough to do others harm. God showed us where Satan's strength lies when He promised to bruise the *head* of the serpent; with his head crushed, he will soon die.

We shall now consider this matter of Satan's subtlety by examining his two main strategies: tempting and accusing.

SATAN AS TEMPTER TO SIN

Let us first look at the devil as a tempter to sin. None is more skillful than this master manipulator, who uses every avenue to get to his victim.

I. SATAN CHOOSES *WHEN* TO TEMPT

'To everything there is a season,' Solomon said (*Eccl. 3:1*). This same wise man tells us why man so frequently misfires and is thwarted in his enterprises: 'Because he knows not his time' (*Eccl. 9:12*). Distracted by the cares or pleasures of the world, too many report for duty after the troops have left. Satan watches and knows a deserted soldier may be eager for some other entertainment. In the same way that Christ directs a righteous man to speak words of comfort and counsel in season, so Satan shows his shrewdness in choosing the appropriate moment to speak words of seduction and temptation. And a word in season from Satan is a temptation ripe for plucking.

The devil especially likes to tempt when the Christian is newly converted. No sooner is the child of grace born than this vicious dragon belches forth white-hot temptations upon him. The first cry of the new creature in Christ startles all the legions of hell. They are as troubled by it as Herod and Jerusalem were when they sat in council to take away the life of the newborn King. Satan did not hesitate to tempt the apostles while they were yet infants in Christ. He knew grace within was weak and the nourishment promised at the Spirit's coming had not yet arrived. Is an enemy ever more likely to take a town than when only the children are home? Indeed, the disadvantages are so many that we would despair for every babe in Christ if we did not know he is wrapped in covenant grace and held tightly in the strong arms of God's promise.

Another time Satan attacks is when the Christian is enduring some great affliction. Satan first got permission from God to weaken Job in his temporal estate, then he tempted him to impatience. He let Christ fast forty days before he came, and then fell to his enticing work – just as an army blocks off a town and waits to negotiate until it is pinched for provisions and likely to agree to almost anything. If you wish to stand firm in the midst of suffering, forewarn yourself of this fact: Temptation is never stronger than when relief seems to dress itself in the very sin that Satan is suggesting. For example, suppose your family falls on hard times and you see no way out of your predicament. This is the very moment Satan will come to whisper in your ear, 'What are you going to do? Surely God would not have your children starve! Your neighbor's garden is just beyond the hedge. He has enough and to spare. The night is dark. Who will see if you step across and take only what you need?'

Satan will also come on the scene when you are on some notable errand for God's glory. He will raise himself up like a snake in your path, hissing his venomous lies. This old serpent never was a friend to kingdom work. What a handsome excuse he served the Jews: 'The time is not come!' God's time *was* come, but not the devil's; and therefore he perverted the sense of Providence, as if it were not yet time for the Messiah.

Two periods stand out in Christ's life: His entrance into public ministry at His Baptism, and the culmination of it at His Passion. At both He had a fierce encounter with the devil. This should give you an idea of how the master tempter works. The more public your place, and the more eminent your service for God, the greater the probability that Satan is at that very moment hatching some deadly scheme against you. If even the cadet corps need to be armed against Satan's bullets of temptation, how much more the commanders and officers, who stand in the front line of battle!

Satan will not always wait until you are on an important mission to tempt you, however; he will seize every opportunity along the way to practise his enticing skills.

His job is made a little easier if he can find some object to enforce his temptation. Thus he took Eve when she was looking with longing at the tree. Since her own eye first enticed her, it was all the easier for Satan to take the object of her affection, polish it to a high gloss, and with it quicken the lust which lay dormant in her heart. If we lean out the window to hear temptation's serenade, Satan is satisfied that his suit may in time be granted. If we do not wish to yield to sin, we must take care not to walk by or sit at the door of the occasion. Do not look on temptation with a wandering eye if you do not wish to be taken by it, nor allow your mind to dwell on that which you do not want lodged in your heart.

Another time the tempter comes is just after a great manifestation of God's love. Such is the weak constitution of our character that it cannot bear well either prolonged smiles or frowns from God. If God smiles and opens Himself to us a little, then we are prone to become proud and lifted up. If He frowns, then we sink in our faith. Thus the one, like fair weather and warm sun, brings up the weeds of corruption; and the other, like sharp frost, nips and even kills the flowers of grace. Danger lurks in either climate; therefore, Satan takes advantage to entice a saint to one sin or the other, which he knows will cause the flower of his heavenly joy to fade.

Finally, at the hour of death, when the saint's physical strength lies prostrate, this bully falls upon him. It is his last opportunity for a skirmish, so he gives a final, mighty effort. At the very moment the Christian is stepping into eternity, the tempter treads upon his heel. If he cannot trip up the saint so as to prevent his arrival in heaven, he will at least see to it that he goes with more pain.

II. SATAN CHOOSES *HOW* TO TEMPT

Not only does he choose when he will tempt, Satan also

chooses the best methods for displaying his temptations.

One strategy is to hang out false colors. He comes up to the Christian disguised as a friend, so that the gates are opened to him before his true identity is discovered. Paul says we should not be shocked to find false teachers masquerading as apostles of Christ, ' . . . for Satan himself is transformed into an angel of light' (2 Cor. 11:13, 14). Of all his plots, this is perhaps the most dangerous to the saints: when he appears in the mantle of a prophet and silverplates his corroded tongue with fair-sounding language. In this manner he corrupts some in their judgment by interpreting gospel truth in such a way that God appears to condone questionable behavior. These Christians get caught up in the world's morality under the guise of Christian liberty.

Not everyone will swallow such heresy, so Satan tempts them with other wares, though still in the disguise of a saint himself. He desecrates Scripture by magnifying faith to the exclusion of every other grace. Or he labors to undermine repentance and overpraise good works. He pulls back in seeming horror at the corruption of church administrations, and thus draws unstable souls from the body of believers. Under the pretense of zeal, he kindles wrath in the Christian's heart and makes his spirit boil over into desires for revenge in situations where God would have him forgive. Luke records such an occasion, where the disciples wanted 'fire to come down from heaven.' They thought their zeal was kindled by a holy fire until Christ told them, 'Ye know not what manner of spirit ye are of' (Luke 9:54, 55). How we need to study the Scriptures, our hearts, and Satan's wiles, that we may not bid this enemy welcome and all the while think it is Christ who is our guest!

Another of the enemy's methods is to spy on the saint's

affairs. Satan is the greatest intelligence agent in the world. He makes it his business to inquire into your inclinations, thoughts, affections, and plans. Then he sets to work accordingly – finding which way the stream goes, opening the passage of temptation, and cutting the channel to the fall of your affections. You can scarcely stir out of the closet of your heart without Satan knowing your destination. Some corrupt passion or other will betray your soul and be the informer to Satan, saying to him, 'If you want to surprise such a one, you will find him in the wood of worldly employment, up to his ears in the desires and cares of this life.'

Is ambition the lust the heart favors? Such pleasing projects he will put that soul upon! How easily, having first blown him up with vain hopes, he draws him into horrid sins. This is how he hurried Haman, who was willing to do anything to become the prince's favorite, into that bloody plot against the Jews, fatal at last to himself (*Esther 7:9, 10*).

In his approaches to a sensitive soul, Satan uses an especially subtle strategy. When he comes to tempt, he is modest and asks for just a little. He knows he may get through several askings what he would be denied if he asked all at once. This is how he wriggled into Eve's bosom. He did not dare her to eat the fruit at first. He knew she would probably be frightened away by such a bold challenge. Instead, he asked a provocative question which would set the stage for his debut as man's archenemy: 'Hath God said?' In other words, 'Are you sure you are not mistaken? You know how generous God is! He lets you eat everything else in the Garden; why would He deny you the best of all?' Thus he digs about and loosens the root of her faith, and then the tree falls more easily with the next gust of temptation.

[87]

Conversing with Satan is a dangerous policy indeed. Many have yielded to go a mile with him who never intended to go two. But when once on the way, they have been lured farther and farther, until at last they are so lost and confused they do not know how to leave his company. Yield at first, and you relinquish your strength to resist him in the rest. In this manner Satan leads his victims down winding stairs into the abyss of sin, one step at a time. They are in danger of becoming for ever lost unless they heed God's call and turn at once from their sins.

Perhaps you are one of the strong ones, able to reject every offer of a certain temptation. Do not relax your guard; Satan is not finished with you so easily as you may think. He will call in his reserves. As a wise captain always has fresh troops to move in a pinch, so Satan is seldom at a loss for recruits. When one temptation is beaten back, he quickly sends another to fill the gap and reinforce the line.

In this way he tempted Christ to doubt God's providence by bidding Him turn stones into bread. He implied that it was high time for Jesus to fend for Himself. After all, He had been neglected by His Father for forty days, and no relief was in sight. To this challenge Christ calmly replied, 'It is written, Man shall not live by bread alone, but by every word that proceedeth out of the mouth of God' (*Matt. 4:4*). Yet our Lord had no sooner quenched this dart, than Satan had another on the string – tempting Him to presumption. The devil took Him to the highest point of the temple and said, 'Cast thyself down; for it is written, He shall give his angels charge concerning thee . . . ' (*v. 6*). Here was a clever argument indeed: 'If you have such confidence in God and His Word as you pretend, show it by throwing yourself down, for you have a word between you and the ground – *if* you dare trust God.' Christ had His answer ready, and was prepared to receive Satan's charge on the right hand and on the left, being so completely armed that no temptation could penetrate His armour.

Satan uses this same method with us. When we have resisted one way, he attacks in another. In fact, he plants his succeeding temptation upon our very resistance of the one before. You must have a watchful eye and skill at all your graces to stand your guard.

Still another strategy Satan uses is his shrewd retreat. We read not only of Satan's being cast out, but of the unclean spirit going out voluntarily, with a purpose to come again and bring worse company with him (*Matt. 12:43–45*). Satan is not always beaten back by the dint and power of conquering grace; sometimes he retreats willingly, then lays his own siege. He waits until the Christian is out of his trench, intending to snap him up on the plains if he cannot take him in his fortification. When Satan seems to have conceded defeat, do not assume the battle is won. His flight should strengthen your faith, but not weaken your guard.

III. SATAN CHOOSES *WHAT* OR *WHOM* TO USE AS INSTRUMENTS OF TEMPTATION

We have seen that he decides when and how he will tempt; now we shall see that he decides what or whom he will use to do his work.

As the master workman, Satan cuts out the temptation and gives it shape, but sometimes he has his journeymen finish it. Knowing his work may be carried on better by others, he carefully considers who can do the work to the greatest advantage of his evil cause. Just as every politician is not fit for an embassage, so not just anyone qualifies for the devil's special service. He screens his prospects with care. In this he is unlike God, who is not at all limited by His choice of instruments, because He *needs* no one and is able to do as well with one as with another. But Satan's power is finite, so he must patch up the defect of the lion's skin with the fox's.

The ambassadors Satan prefers are chiefly of four sorts: persons of prominence and power; persons of superior intellect and diplomacy; persons of holiness, or at least reputed to be; and persons able to influence those in power.

First: Satan singles out persons of prominence and power. They may be either in the state or in the church. If he can, he will secure both the throne and the pulpit, as the two generals that command the whole army. A head of state may influence thousands; therefore, Paul said to Elymas, when he tried to dissuade the deputy from the faith, 'O full of all subtilty and mischief, thou child of the devil' (*Acts 13:10*). As if he had said, 'You have learned this from your father the devil – to haunt the courts of princes and wield your influence over rulers.'

Satan doubles his leverage in gaining such leaders to his side. First of all, they have the power to draw others to their way. Corrupt the captain, and he will bring his troops with him. Let Jeroboam set up idolatry, and all Israel is soon in a snare. Second, should the sin stay at court and the infection go no further, yet a whole kingdom may pay dearly for the sin of its leader. David succumbed to Satan's temptation to number the people, but the entire nation suffered the plague of punishment with him (*1 Chron. 21*).

Besides trying to infiltrate the ranks of government, Satan also aims at those in office in the church. What better way to infect the whole town than to poison the cistern where they draw their water? He takes special delight in corrupting the heart of a minister. If he can wiggle into a pastor's heart, then he is free to roam among

God's flock undetected – a devil in shepherd's clothing. Who will persuade Ahab to go to Ramoth-Gilead and fall? Satan can tell: 'I will be a lying spirit in the mouth of all [God's] prophets' (*1 Kings 22:22*). How shall sinners be hardened in their sins? Let the preacher place cushions under their consciences and sing a lullaby of 'Peace, peace,' and it is done. How may the worship of God be discredited? Let the world observe the scandalous conduct of a minister, and many, both good and bad, will reject the truth of the gospel on the strength of the lie his life tells.

Second: Satan also employs persons of superior intellect and diplomacy. What a grand accomplishment for him to preach his accursed ideologies from the podiums of the great minds of history! So well does he succeed, that very few of this rank are found among Christ's disciples: 'Not many wise . . . are called' (*1 Cor. 1:26*). Perhaps it is because the blessing of perception so easily becomes the curse of deception. Indeed, God will not have His kingdom, either in the heart or in the world, maintained by carnal principles. No! It is a gospel command that we walk in godly simplicity. Jacob got the blessing by a trick, but he could have had it cheaper with plain dealing.

Satan inquires for the sharpest minds – a Balaam, an Ahithophel, or a Sanballat – to peddle his curse and get mankind to buy. He is always searching for a better salesman, 'that if it were possible [he might] deceive the very elect' (*Matt. 24:24*). From his own experience, Paul knew Satan's power over the mind and feared for the Corinthians, whom he had espoused to Christ. He did not want to see their 'minds corrupted from the simplicity that is in Christ' (*2 Cor. 11:3*). If God has blessed you with an excellent mind, be thankful – but be also mindful of Paul's warning!

The great idol which the more intelligent part of the world worships and makes the icon of their faith is human reason, from which many heresies spring. Prideful by nature, man would like nothing more than to be his own god (though for clambering so high he got his fall). Find a doctrine that nourishes a good opinion of man in his own eyes, and he will show himself a glutton at its table.

Men like also to feast on fleshly liberty, another of their natural appetites, and Satan knows just how to nurture this desire. Man is a son of Belial, without yoke; and if he must wear one, the one which has the softest lining and pinches the flesh least will please him best. Therefore, when sincere teachers of the Word press sincere obedience to it, Satan's overseers come and say, 'What hard taskmasters you have! They harness you to continual duty. Come, we will show you an easier way to heaven.' He who sells cheapest will have the most customers. But in the end, truth with self-denial is a better bargain than error with all its flesh-pleasing.

Third: Does Satan prefer the company of persons of power and intellect? He also delights to entertain those who have a reputation for holiness. What works as well as a live bird to draw others into the net? Such is the craft of Satan – and the frailty of the best among us – that the holiest men have been his bait to snare others. That great patriarch Abraham tempted Sarah to lie: 'Tell them you are my sister!' (*Gen. 12:13*). The old prophet of Bethel led the man of God out of his way, the holiness of the prophet's life and the reverence of his age lending authority to his counsel (*1 Kings 13:18*).

Oh, how this should make you watchful if you are one whose long travel and great progress in the ways of God have gained you a name of eminence in the church! What you say and do, because you are a leader, causes others to look less to themselves and more to you to set the pace and make the rules.

Fourth: Satan chooses persons able to influence those in power. If he can win family or friends to his side, he has easy access to the real object of his desire. Some think this is why he spared Job's wife – so he could send by her own hands his cup of poison: 'Curse God and die!' We know David would not have received from Nabal what he took from Abigail. Satan thought to send the apple to Adam by Eve's hand; he sent defeat to Samson by Delilah. And he used Peter, a disciple, to tempt Christ. Some martyrs have confessed that their hardest work was to overcome the prayers and tears of their friends and relatives. Paul himself expressed these same feelings when he said, 'What mean ye to weep and to break mine heart? For I am ready, not to be bound only but also to die at Jerusalem for the name of the Lord Jesus' (*Acts 21:13*).

WARNING

Study Satan's tricks, and acquaint yourself with his tactics. Paul takes for granted that every Christian understands them in some measure: 'We are not ignorant of his devices,' he says (*2 Cor. 2:11*). Can this be said of you? Do you know how subtle and clever your enemy is? What pleasant company he can pretend to be?

'Sit down at my gaming table,' says Satan. 'Here are some tempting prizes: your earthly estate, your life, your liberty.' Now you must agree, these things are good and lawful. But here is Satan's gimmick: he expands the rule of his game so that if you play for him, you will certainly violate the irrevocable and unchangeable laws of God. If you cannot have good things by plain dealing but must resort to sleight of hand, you know the prize is counterfeit and will turn to dung in your hands. How utterly foolish to fast shuffle with God by compromising His truth. You may think you have won a hand or two, but when the game is over, you will find yourself bankrupt.

If Satan can entice you to sin for what he assures you is a worthy prize, you are in serious trouble, but the worst is yet to come. Once he has you sitting at his table, he will begin in earnest to teach you the tricks of his trade. This diabolical dealer will show you how to slip your sins under the table, telling you no one – not even God – will see. He has been teaching this trick since Adam, who thought he could hide behind a fig leaf. What did Joseph's brothers do when they had left him for dead but hide their deed under the coat they had bloodied? And how did Potiphar's wife respond when Joseph turned away from her adulterous gaze? She hid her sin (again in his coat) and accused him of her own wickedness.

Beware of playing such games of chance with God. No coat is large enough to hide your sin; no hand is quick enough to slip it under the table and miss the all-seeing eye of God. If He does not call you to account for it in this life, you can be sure you will answer for it in the next.

The gravest discipline God can dispense this side of eternity is to leave a sinner to his own pursuits when he is hell bound in the company of Satan. One of the dangers of playing the devil's games is that you come to like them. They are as addictive as wine, and create an insatiable thirst. Practise the devil's tricks long enough, and your blackened soul will begin to devise mischief of its own to help satisfy your ravishing appetite for sin. No sins speak of a higher attainment in wickedness than those which are the result of deliberate, premeditated plotting. Set your heart toward wickedness, and Satan will lend you his own chariot and drive you himself to perform the deed.

PRECAUTIONS

These are sobering thoughts and would strike fear to the very marrow of our spirits if we did not have a powerful prescription for spiritual health written in God's own hand. Read carefully, then follow it to the letter.

I. ASK GOD FOR COUNSEL

Heaven overlooks hell, and God at any time can tell you what plots are hatching there against you. He who makes the watch knows every pin in it. God made this crooked serpent (though not the crookedness in him), so He knows everything about him. Satan is also God's prisoner; and the Lord, who is his keeper, has him always in His sight.

Everything transacted in heaven or hell passes through Christ's hands. The Son knows all the Father knows, and He is ready to reveal to His saints all they need to know in this life (*John 15:15*). We live in days of high political intrigue. Only the few who stand on the upper end of the world understand the mysteries of state; the rest of us know little more than what we read in the newspaper. It is the same with regard to the plots which Satan is furtively weaving against the souls of men. Only a few have an inkling as to the purpose of Satan's designs against them. These are the saints, to whom God's Spirit reveals not only what He has prepared for them in heaven but also the warp and woof of Satan's deadly schemes here on earth.

II. KNOW YOUR HEART

Be intimately acquainted with yourself, and you will better know Satan's design against you. He takes his method of tempting from the inclination he finds there. As a general walks about the city and views it well, then directs his assault where he has the greatest advantage, so Satan surrounds and considers the Christian in every part before he tempts.

[95]

III. READ GOD'S WORD ATTENTIVELY

It gives a history of the most remarkable battles between the great soldiers of Christ and their adversary Satan. You can read how Satan has foiled them, and how they recovered lost ground. There is not a lust of which you are in danger, but you have it disclosed; there is not a temptation which the Word of God does not arm you against. It is reported that a certain man planned to poison Martin Luther, but Luther was forewarned by a faithful friend who sent him a picture of the would-be murderer. The Bible shows you, Christian, the faces of those lusts which Satan hires to destroy your precious soul. 'By them is thy servant warned' (*Psalm 19:11*).

SATAN AS ACCUSER OF SIN

By this time you should be well acquainted with Satan's temptations. No doubt he has often peddled them at your door, for he delights to gain a saint as his steady customer. You may be a hard sell, and I pray God you are; but do not think for a moment that Satan will be easily turned away. If you do not like his box of temptations, then he will reach into his sack of accusations and display them so cleverly you will think he brings them at God's request!

As the Holy Spirit is first a sanctifier and then a comforter, so Satan is first a tempter, then a troubler. Joseph's mistress first tried to entice him to gratify her lust; then, that string breaking, she took another tack to charge him. And we have already seen that for evidence she used his own coat to cover her malice. Just so, it is not hard for Satan to find some hole in the saint's coat, even when he walks most circumspectly.

When Satan wishes to tempt to sin, he knocks at the door of the will. When he wishes to accuse of sin, he pays a call on the conscience. But he does not have absolute knowledge or power over these, for they are locked to all but God. Satan knows he cannot pick a lock to which God holds the key, so he thinks up cunning ways to trick the saint into opening the door for him.

Satan, as the serpent, has a unique way. Other animals use direct motion but the serpent goes askew, writhing its body. When you see a snake creeping along, you can hardly tell which way it is heading. Satan moves in a similar fashion, turning this way and that to conceal his true intentions. Here are some of the methods he uses to accuse your soul and cloud your relationship with the Father.

I. SATAN ACCUSES THE SAINTS OF HIS OWN WICKED THOUGHTS

He lays his own evil imaginings like foundling children at their door. How clever he is at this deception! When thoughts or inclinations contrary to the will and ways of God creep in, many dear Christians mistake these miserable orphans for their own children, and take upon themselves the full responsibility for these carnal passions. So deftly does the devil slip his own thoughts into the saint's bosom that by the time they begin to whimper, he is already out of sight. And the Christian, seeing no one but himself at home, supposes these misbegotten notions are his own. So he bears the shame himself, and Satan has accomplished his purpose.

What recourse does the child of God have? Stay in close fellowship with the Father. Then you will be able to repulse the devil's accusations by the sword of the Spirit. But be prepared for another assault. Like Nebuchadnezzar, Satan will probably throw a fit of jealous rage and stoke the fires of his wrath seven times hotter until the flames of his blasphemous emotions engulf you. By this he hopes to frighten you and so muddle your spiritual senses that you may yet be persuaded to draw a wrong conclusion

– that you are no longer a child of God, for instance. The truth is, if you sin at all in this situation, it is because you doubt God's keeping power instead of doubting these mongrel emotions. My counsel in this case is to do with such feelings as you would with outlaw gangs who travel around the country harassing good citizens. While you may not be able to keep them from passing through your town, you can certainly see to it they do not settle there.

II. SATAN EXAGGERATES THE SAINTS' SINS

His aim is to discredit not the sins but the saints. Here his chief tactic is to deliver his accusations as if they are an act of the Holy Spirit. He knows a charge from God's cannon wounds deeply; therefore, when he accuses a conscientious Christian, he forges God's name on the missile before he fires it. Suppose a child were conscious of gravely displeasing his father, and some spiteful person, to harass him, wrote and sent him a counterfeit letter full of harsh and threatening accusations, copying the father's name at the bottom. The poor child, already painfully aware of his sins and not knowing the scheme, would be overcome with grief. Here is real heartache stemming from a false premise – just the kind of thing Satan relishes.

Satan is a clever investigator. He closely observes the relationship between you and God. Sooner or later he will catch you tardy in some duty or faulty in a service. He knows you are conscious of your shortcomings and that the Spirit of God will also show distaste for them. So he draws up a lengthy indictment, raking up all the aggravations he can think of, then serves his warrant on you as though sent from God. This is how Job's friends reacted to his trouble. They gathered up all the evidence of his infirmities to use against him, implying they had been sent by God to declare him a hypocrite and denounce him for it.

While Satan is a master inquisitor, we know that not all our rebukes come from him. God's Word clearly states that 'whom the Lord loveth he chasteneth' (*Heb. 12:6*). How, then, can we discern the spiteful accusations of Satan from the loving reprimands of God and His Spirit?

Try this test: If such rebukes contradict any prior work of the Spirit in your soul, they are Satan's and not the Spirit's. Satan's purpose in emphasizing your sin is to try to unsaint you and persuade you that you are only a hypocrite. 'Oh,' hisses Satan, 'now you have shown your true colors! See that horrid stain on your jacket – what other saint every committed such a sin! Your whole life is a sham! God wants nothing to do with such a desperately wicked person as you.'

And with a single blow Satan dashes all in pieces. The whole mansion of grace which God has been building many years in your soul and all the special comforts the Holy Spirit has brought are blown down by one gust from his malicious mouth. He leaves your life a shambles, and tells you it is your own fault.

Do not despair. Pacify your fears with this precious truth: Once the Spirit of God has begun a sanctifying work, causing you to hope in His mercy, He never will nor can bring contrary news to your soul. His language is not 'yea and nay', but 'yea and amen' for ever. If you play the prodigal, God will frown and chide you roundly for your sin, as He did David through Nathan: 'Thou art the man!' (*2 Sam. 12:7*). Yet not a word is heard from Nathan telling David to unsaint himself and call in question the work of God in his soul. That prophet had no such commission from the Lord. He was sent to make David mourn for his sin – not from his sin to question his state of grace, which God had so often put beyond doubt.

Besides planting seeds of doubt about the sanctifying

work of the Spirit, Satan often sends rebukes of the conscience that deny the riches of God's grace. When you find your sins represented to you as exceeding either the mercy of God's nature or the grace of His covenant, this comes from that jealous suitor, the devil. The Holy Spirit, as Christ's intermediary, woos sinners to embrace the grace of the gospel. Would He say anything that would spoil the courtship or lower Christ's esteem in the eyes of His beloved? Surely you must know where such lies originate! When you hear someone compliment another person as wise or good, then at last come in with a *but* that dashes all, you know he is no friend but some sly enemy who, by seeming to commend the person, really desires to discredit him. And so, when you find God represented to you as merciful and gracious, *but* not to such a great sinner as you; strong and mighty, *but* not able to save someone like you, you can say, 'Be gone, Satan, your speech betrays you. This is not a message sent to me by the Lover of my soul!'

III. SATAN APPOINTS HIMSELF BOTH JUDGE AND JURY TO TRY THE SAINTS

The devil is at church as often as you are. And he stands outside your closet door and listens to what you say to God in secret, all the while studying how he may accuse you. The rebellious spirit who dared to criticize God's rule of heaven will not hesitate to pass judgment on the way you rule your soul. He is like those who listen to sermons only to find fault so they can call the minister an offender for some misplaced word or other. Satan delights in taking your duties to pieces and so disfiguring them that they appear superficial, though they are truly zealous; pharisaical, though they are really sincere. He will not rest until he can hand in a verdict of 'Guilty!' against your soul.

When you have done your best, then this persuasive

critic goes to work, 'There,' he will say, 'you played the hypocrite – appearing noble, but really serving self. Here you wandered; there, you were lazy; farther along, puffed up with pride. What reward can you hope for at God's hands, now that you have spoiled His work?' Such constant nitpicking makes many poor souls lead a weary life. Are you one of these – spiritually exhausted? Does he snipe at everything you do until you know not whether to pray or not, to listen or not? And, when you have prayed and listened, whether it is to any purpose or not? Thus your soul hangs in doubt, and your days pass in sorrow, while your enemy stands in a corner and laughs at the trick he has played upon you. It is his master plan that if he cannot rob you of your righteousness, he will deprive you of your joy.

IV. SATAN TRIES TO ROB THE SAINTS OF THEIR COVE-
     NANT PROMISE

He comes to fetch you away from the green pastures of covenant comfort and drag you into the depths of despair. He does this under the false pretense that you are not humble enough over sin. The apostle knew what sophisticated mind-games the devil plays. He called them his 'devices' (*2 Cor. 2:11*), meaning his clever arguments. Here Satan relies heavily on his smooth tongue. Everything he says is flagrant lies and double-talk, but where is the Christian who has not been taken in, at least momentarily, by his bluff?

Satan reasons like this: 'There ought to be a proportion between sin and sorrow. But there is no proper proportion between *your* sin and *your* sorrow; therefore, you are not humbled enough.' What a plausible argument at first glance! For Satan can show you ample Scripture to prove his point. Manasseh was a great sinner, and an ordinary sorrow would not do for him. He 'humbled himself greatly before . . . God' (*2 Chron. 33:12*). 'Now,' says Satan, 'weigh your sin in the balance with your sorrow; are you as great a mourner as you have been a sinner? For many years you have waged war against the Almighty, making havoc of His laws, loading His patience to the breaking point, wounding Christ with the dagger of your sins while you grieved His Spirit and rejected His grace. And now do you think a little remorse, like a rolling cloud letting fall a few drops of rain, will satisfy? No, you must steep in sorrow as you have soaked in sin.'

To show you the flaw in his thesis, we must distinguish between two kinds of proportion in sorrow.

First, an exact proportion of sorrow to the inherent nature and demerit of sin. This is not feasible; the injury done in the least sin is infinite, because done to an infinite God.

Second, a relative proportion of sorrow to the law and rule of the gospel. And what is the law of the gospel concerning this? That genuine heart-sorrow is gospel-sorrow: 'They were pricked in their heart' (*Acts 2:37*). This gospel sorrow is indeed repentance unto life, given by the Spirit of the gospel for your relief. Oh, tempted soul, when Satan says you are not humbled enough and tells you to keep wallowing in your own sorrow, see how you may be saved. Christ is the footbridge by which you may safely cross the raging river of your sins. You are a dead man if you think to answer your sin with your own sorrow; you will soon be above your depth, and drown yourself in your own tears, but never be rescued from the least sin you have committed. The strength of your sorrow is not what carries you to heaven – but true heart repentance.

Now a prick to the heart is more than a wound to the conscience. The heart is the seat of life. Sin, wounded there, lies dying. If your heart is false, I cannot help you nor can the gospel itself. But if you are sincere, you have boldness with God (*1 John 3:21*) and His promise of forgiveness (*1 John 1:9*).

THE SAINT'S PROPER REACTION TO SATAN'S ACCUSATIONS

If you have been giving serious thought to the foregoing discussion, you may be asking yourself, 'What can I do of a practical nature to withstand Satan when he comes to criticize my duties for Christ?'

I. LET HIS ACCUSATIONS MAKE YOU MORE CAREFUL

This is God's purpose in allowing Satan to spy on you. Is a child ever more circumspect that when the teacher has scheduled a conference with his parents? Likewise, if you know Satan is watching and is sure to tell tales about you to God, you ought to be more careful to keep your slate clean. This should challenge you to study your heart well and read God's Word faithfully. Then when Satan attacks, you will have a rebuttal ready to counter every accusation.

II. LET THEM MAKE YOU MORE HUMBLE

To be honest with ourselves, we must admit that many of his charges are all too true. If Satan, whose eyes of understanding are so darkened, can charge us with this much, what could the light of God uncover! What a wonderful opportunity again to acknowledge your own sinfulness, and the overriding mercy of God! By this attitude, we take the very bricks Satan is throwing at us, and use them to build a monument to the glory of our gracious Lord.

III. LET THEM SHOW YOU THE FALLACY OF HIS LOGIC

Then you can answer his criticisms wisely. The fallacy is double. First, he will point out that you are not perfect but are expected to be; then he will tell you that since you are not perfect, God will have nothing to do with your pitiful efforts.

To persuade you that your service and yourself are hypocritical, proud, selfish, etc. is generally not too difficult, because something of these sins is found in everyone – even Christians! You must learn to distinguish between pride *in* a work and a proud work, between hypocrisy *in* a person, and a hypocrite. The best of saints have the stirring of such corruptions in them. Comfort yourself with this: If you find a voice within your heart pleading for God and entering its protest against evil, you and your efforts are acceptable in His sight.

God sees your failures as symptoms of your sickly state here below and pities you as He would a lame child. How we despise a person who mocks another because he stutters or limps! Such are the flaws in your new nature. Note Christ's words in His prayer against Satan: 'The Lord rebuke thee . . . is not this a brand plucked out of the fire?' (*Zech. 3:2*). It is as though He said, 'Lord, will you allow this envious spirit to blame your poor child Joshua for those infirmities of his old nature which still cling to his perfect state? He is just newly plucked out of the fire. No wonder there are some sparks unquenched, some corruptions unmortified, some disorders unreformed.' And what Christ did for Joshua, He does incessantly for all His saints, apologizing to the Father for their infirmities and pleading leniency on their behalf.

The second distortion in Satan's argument is in reasoning that because the residue of our old nature still clings to our present efforts, God does not accept them. 'Will God,' he asks, 'take such broken coins from your hand? Is He not a holy God?' Now here is where you must learn discernment. There are two kinds of acceptance I want to discuss: the acceptance of something in payment of a debt, and the acceptance of something offered as a token of love and gratitude. He who will not take broken money or half of what is owed to satisfy a debt, will, if his friend sends him only a bent sixpence as a token of love, accept it joyfully. It is true the debt you owe God must be paid in good and lawful money. But, for your comfort, Christ is your paymaster. Send Satan to Him; have him bring his charge before Christ, who is ready at God's right hand to open the books and show the debit column blotted out with His own blood, and the debt stamped 'Paid in Full.'

From the day of your salvation, your performance and obedience are entered in a separate ledger as tokens of your love and thankfulness to God. And such is the gracious disposition of your heavenly Father that He accepts your mite. Love refuses nothing that love sends. Not the weight nor the worth of the gift, but 'the desire of a man is his kindness' (*Prov. 19:22*).

GOD'S PERFECT RESPONSE TO SATAN'S AC-CUSATIONS

What immeasurable comfort to know we are not left on our own to ward off Satan's blows to our conscience. Is he clever? Your God is more so, who can safely lead you through the devil's labyrinth of lies right back to Himself!

1. GOD USES SATAN'S OWN SCHEMES TO MAKE HIS SAINTS WISE

With them he unmasks the devil and exposes the children of Beelzebub, those offspring of the enemy who show the same craft as their infernal father in vexing the spirits of the saints. These are some of the 'children of Satan' whom Satan sends out to molest a saint's peace.

Those who dig up the saint's old sins, which God has

forgiven and forgotten, merely to grieve his spirit and muddy his name; these show their devilish malice indeed, who take such pains to travel many years back to find a handful of dirt to throw on the saint's face. Thus Shimei taunted David, 'Come out, thou bloody man' (*2 Sam. 16:7*). When you meet such reproaches, answer them as the French theologian Beza did those who, for lack of better ammunition, charged him for some impious poems he penned in his youth. 'These men,' he said, 'begrudge me the pardoning mercy of God.'

There are also those who lie in wait for the saint to stumble, then point at every faltering step to make him seem graceless, and themselves graceful by comparison. Such pawns of the devil bring a curse upon themselves, although they think little of it. Consider Amalek, the remembrance of whose name God threatened to blot from under heaven (*Deut. 25:19*). Do you recall what he did to deserve God's wrath? He had his soldiers slay those at the rear of Moses' company who were feeble and could not keep up with the rest! We can hardly imagine a greater cruelty, yet in God's sight it is even worse to smite with the edge of a mocking tongue the feeble in grace.

Some wicked men sin with the evil purpose of troubling the saints' spirits. Perhaps you have watched a blasphemer in action. When he discovers there are those present who love the Lord and cannot bear to hear His name taken in vain, he deliberately uses foul language that grates on the chaste ears and troubles the sensitive spirits of his listeners. This rascal strikes father and child at one blow. He thinks dishonoring God is not enough, but insists that the saints stand by to see and hear the wrong done to their heavenly Father.

Perhaps worst of all are those who blame a child of God for the consequences of their own sins. This is why Ahab called the prophet the troubler of Israel when it was really himself and his father's house who were to blame. What a grief to Moses' spirit for the Israelites to lay at his door the blood of those who died in the wilderness. God Himself can testify Moses was their constant bail when at any time His hand was raised to destroy them.

The finest of God's servants in this crooked generation of ours lie under the same curse. 'We may thank them,' say the profane, 'for all the miseries of our nation; we were doing fine until they tried to reform us.' Do not blame the good medicine that was administered, but the corrupt body of the nation that could not keep it down!

II. GOD USES SATAN'S TRICKS TO MAKE HIS SAINTS THANKFUL

You know what boulders the devil rolls into your path. If today the road is clear, what relief and joy your soul must feel! None surpasses Satan at stirring up trouble, yet you have peace in your conscience. To whom are you obliged for your serenity of spirit? To none but your God, who holds Satan in custody and will not let him enter the garden of your soul. Satan is plotting to undermine your comfort every day. This thief sees your pleasant fruits as they hang, and his mouth waters at them; but the wall is too high for him to climb. God keeps him out of your paradise. It is not the grace of God in you, but the favor of God as a shield about you that defends you from the wicked one. What more do you need to hear to make your heart swell in gratitude?

III. GOD USES THE DEVIL'S WILES TO MAKE HIS SAINTS WARY

You are not dealing with a fool, but with one who has wit enough to spill your comfort and spoil your joy if not closely watched. Your peace is the dainty tidbit he gapes for. To keep the flies out of your cupboard in summer is no harder than to bar Satan from your conscience. He has robbed the saints of many a sweet meal and sent them supperless to bed; be always on your guard, for he roams your way also.

THE SAINT'S FORTIFICATION

'Well,' you say, 'I need no more arguments to prove the troublesome nature of my adversary. Tell me now what I can do to fortify myself against his attacks.'

I. BEWARE OF SATAN AS A SEDUCER

If you want to be protected from your enemy as a troubler, you must take heed of him as a seducer. You can be sure he takes heed of you! The handle of the hatchet with which he chops at the root of the Christian's comfort is commonly made of the Christian's own wood. Satan is only a creature and cannot work without tools. He can indeed make much from a little, but he cannot make anything out of nothing. We see this in his assault on Christ, where he troubled himself to no purpose because he came and found nothing in Him (*John 14:30*).

But when he comes to us he finds fossils of our old natures, which tell him much about the disposition of our hearts. These are the artifacts our carnal hearts once held so dear: our strength, our lusts, our pride. He holds them out to us, thinking to draw us away from our new-found grace in Christ. Beware of his enticements. Do not drink from his cup; there is poison in it. Do not even look on it as it sparkles in the temptation. What you drink down with sweetness, you will be sure to bring up again as gall and wormwood.

Above all sins, guard against bold or arrogant ones. You are not beyond the danger of such. If caught in the web of presumptuous sin, call quickly to God for help. If you hesitate, you only give Satan time to entangle you more tightly. But if you cry out to God in true repentance, He will come at once to rescue you. The sooner you yield to the Spirit, the less damage is done to your soul.

II. CLING TO GOD'S PROMISE OF JUSTIFICATION

Another way to fortify yourself against Satan is to study that grand gospel truth of a soul's justification before God. Acquaint yourself with this truth in all its aspects: the free mercy of God's grace; the accomplishment of Christ's sacrifice; the effectiveness of faith in appropriating these blessings (*Rom. 3:24, 25*). An effectual door once opened to let the soul in to this truth will spoil the devil's market.

When Satan comes to take away your peace, if you do not understand the full significance of your justification in Christ you will be easily overcome. A saint without assurance of salvation is as unprotected as the rabbit that darts into a thicket to escape a fox, but is easily followed by the print of her own feet and the scent she leaves behind. In Christ you have a hiding place where the enemy dare not come: 'the clefts of the rock, in the secret places of the stairs' (*Song of Sol. 2:14*). While the devil may be in hot pursuit of your soul, the very scent of Christ's blood, by which you are justified, is noxious to him and will stop him in his tracks. Run straight into this tower of the gospel covenant, and roll this truth on the head of Satan, as the woman cast the stone on the head of Abimelech: 'To him . . . that . . . believeth on him that justifieth the ungodly, his faith is counted for righteousness' (*Rom. 4:5*).

III. AVOID ENTRAPMENT

Be sure also, Christian, to keep to the plains. That is, do not let Satan lure you into doctrinal traps where you can neither fight well nor flee. One of his tactics is to lead you through a maze of impertinent questions intended to retard your progress toward heaven. Sometimes he asks a soul which it embraces – free will or predestination. And whichever answer it gives, he confounds it with his crafty reply. Another time, he will demand to know the exact day and hour of your salvation, and if you cannot answer, he will challenge your right to claim kinship to Christ.

When Satan badgers you with trivial inquiries, do not try to reason with him. Answer him with your present position in Christ and His sure work of grace in your soul. Never forget that the simple truth of the gospel reduces all the intricacies of Satan to a worthless heap of lies.

Now suppose you escape the trap of pointless questions; what will you do when Satan leads your faith down a trail of obscure scriptures? I am talking about those difficult passages which rush past the understanding as a mountain stream past the eye, until dizzy and disoriented, the saint drops in despair for his own condition. The wine of the gospel is heady stuff! Too much study in difficult places can confuse your soul and weaken your faith. Once again, keep to the plains. Combat Satan's attack with simple scriptures – those most likely to nourish your faith and cheer your spirit. When you meet such straightforward scriptures as speak to your own case, use them to ford the flood of temptation, and do not venture beyond your depth.

Satan will try to draw you off your steadfast course to heaven in still another way – by the presence of circumstances you cannot understand. With them Satan argues against God's love, and for your soul. First (by God's permission) he pillaged Job's earthly possessions, and then fell to work on his spiritual estate. He used every circumstance and everybody at his disposal. He had Job's wife blame God; he had Job's friends condemn the man himself. Satan convinced them all – except Job – that an afflicted condition and a state of grace could not live together in the same house.

Here is a timely warning when you find your soul adrift in a heavy fog of tribulation: Neither accuse God foolishly of your enemy's mischief, nor charge yourself with belonging to the enemy. God can chart a straight course in the worst storm. He can be righteous when He uses wicked instruments, and gracious when He dispenses harsh providences. Do not over-react to changes in your temporal estate. Christ told us to expect some rough sailing before we reach heaven's shore.

Your perspective should be very different from that of the unregenerate. Like naive children, they think everyone loves them who gives them plums. They do not realize that prosperity can be a curse to bind them in a deeper sleep of false security. Remember how Jael served Sisera (*Judges 5:25, 26*). She gave him milk though he asked for water, that she might more surely nail him to the ground – milk having the property, it is said, to incline to sleep. But the Christian in an afflicted state has a key to decipher God's providence. The Spirit, through the Word, teaches you to read the shorthand of His dispensations: Every son whom He loves, He corrects. Behind the travail of every affliction is a blessing waiting to be born.

IV. MAINTAIN ASSURANCE OF SALVATION

Still another way to fortify yourself against Satan is to preserve the hope of your salvation, which is promised through Christ's atoning sacrifice. Record God's special visits to you in the memory book of your heart. Paste in keepsakes of the occasions when He declared a holiday and came to you in festive robes of mercy, holding forth the scepter of His grace more familiarly than usual. Keep old receipts written in His own hand for the pardon of your sins.

"But,' the doubting soul may ask, 'what if I cannot

grasp this assurance, or vouch for those evidences which I once thought to be true?' Then try the following prescriptions as a tonic for your ailing faith.

First of all, renew your repentance, as if you had never repented. Put forth fresh acts of faith, as if you had never believed, and you will beat Satan at his own game. Let him tell you that your former actions were hypocritical, or that they are old and worthless. What can he say against your present affirmation of faith? In this way, the very accusations he uses to drive you away from God, instead draw you closer to Him.

If he still haunts you with fears of your spiritual condition, then apply to the throne of grace and ask for a new copy of the old evidence, which you have misplaced. The original is in the pardon office in heaven, of which Christ is the Master. And if you are a saint, your name is on record in that court. Appeal to God, and hear the news from heaven, rather than listen to the tales your enemy brings from hell. If you would argue less with Satan and pray more to God about your fears, they would soon be resolved. Can you expect truth from a liar, or comfort from an adversary? Turn your back on him and go to God. Try not to worry. Sooner or later you will receive your certificate of assurance.

If your soul is so buffeted that you cannot seem to hear God's reassuring answer above Satan's howling, sail away from the enemy and head straight for God's harbor. Make an honorable retreat into those assurances and strengths which Christ provides for His endangered soldiers. There are two places of advantage into which deserting souls may retire: the name of God, and the absolute promises of the gospel. I think of these as the fair havens, which are chiefly of use when the storm is so great that the ship cannot live at sea. As there was nothing inherent in the creature to move the great God to make such promises, so there can be nothing in the creature to hinder the Almighty from keeping them, where and when He pleases. This act of faith in retreating to the promises, accompanied with a longing desire after that grace you are seeking, while it may not fully satisfy all your doubts, will nevertheless keep you from sinking.

Finally, if Satan continues to hound you, call in help and do not listen to the devil's counsel to the contrary. The very strength of some temptations lies in trying to keep them hidden. Telling a trusted, godly friend of your struggles often brings relief. Satan knows this too well, so in order more freely to rifle the soul of its peace and comfort, he frightens it into silence. 'Oh, my,' Satan says, 'if your friends knew such a thing of you, they would cast you off. You had better hope they never find out!' He has kept many a poor soul in misery by swearing it to secrecy. You lose two blessings by keeping the devil's secret – the counsel of your fellow brethren, and their prayers. And what a serious loss this is!

THE ASSURANCE OF VICTORY IF ARMED

We have seen the perilous straits of the unarmed soul; turn your thoughts now to the glorious prospects of a soul fitly armed. Who would decline the honor of serving in the army of the King of kings – especially when victory has already been declared! This is the assurance Paul gives every saint who puts on the whole armour of God: 'That ye may be able to stand against the wiles of the devil.' With this statement he places the enemy's potential back in proper perspective. He never intended to scare the saints into cowardly flight or woeful despair of victory when he acknowledged the enemy's might. Rather, he hoped to rouse them to vigorous resistance by promising them strength to stand in battle, and a sure victory afterwards. These two ideas are implied in the phrase 'to stand against the wiles of Satan.' Sometimes *to stand* implies a fighting posture (*Eph. 6:14*), sometimes a conquering posture – 'I know that my Redeemer liveth, and that he shall *stand* at the latter day upon the earth' (*Job 19:25*). The earth which today is the field for all the bloody battles between the saints and Satan, will one day be Christ's footstool, when not an enemy shall dare to show his head.

SATAN'S DAMNATION

Satan, with all his wit and wiles, will never defeat a soul armed with true grace, nor will the contest ever end in a stalemate. Look into the Word. You will not find a faithful servant sifted and winnowed by this enemy, who did not come off with an honorable victory. Witness David, Job, Peter, and Paul, who were the hardest put to it of any upon record. And lest some should attribute their victory to their own inherent strength, the glory of the victories is attributable to God alone, in whom the weak are as strong as the strongest. There are two reasons why the Christian who seems to be so overmatched is yet so unconquerable (*2 Cor. 12:9; James 5:11*).

I. THE CURSE THAT LIES UPON SATAN

God's curse blasts wherever it comes. The Canaanites, along with their neighboring nations, were easy prey for Israel, though they were famous for war. Why? Because they were cursed nations. The Egyptians were a shrewd people. 'Let us deal wisely,' they said. Yet God's curse lay like a thorn at Egypt's heart, and was finally her ruin. In fact, when the Israelites, themselves children of the covenant, sinned and became the object of God's curse, they were trampled like dirt under the Assyrians' feet.

An irrevocable curse clings to Satan from *Genesis 3:14*,

15: 'And the Lord God said unto the serpent, Because thou hast done this, thou art cursed. . . . ' And as the curse works eternally against Satan, so it operates eternally in favor of the saints.

For one thing, it prostrates Satan under their feet: 'Upon thy belly shalt thou go' (*v. 14*). This prostrate condition of Satan assures believers that the devil can never lift his head – his wily schemes – higher than the saints' heels. He may make you limp, but he cannot take your life. And the bruise which he gives will be rewarded with the breaking of his own head – the utter ruin of him and his cause.

Besides restricting his posture, God also limits his food. Satan cannot devour whomever he chooses. The dust is his food, which seems to confine his power to the wicked, who are 'of the earth earthy', mere dust. But the graces of those who are of a heavenly extraction are reserved for Christ's food, and their souls surely are not a morsel for the devil's tooth.

II. THE LIMITS GOD PLACES UPON SATAN

The devil may not tempt anyone unless God allows it. When Christ went into the wilderness, He was led, not by an evil spirit, but by the Holy Spirit (*Matt. 4:1*). All that transpired was by God's permission. And the same Holy Spirit that led Christ into the field brought Him off with victory. As soon as He had repulsed Satan, we see Him marching into Galilee in the power of the Holy Ghost (*Luke 4:14*).

When Satan tempts a saint, he is only serving as God's messenger. Paul called his thorn in the flesh 'the messenger of Satan' (*2 Cor. 12:7*). Another translation reads ' . . . the *messenger Satan*,' implying that the messenger was sent by God to Paul. Indeed, the errand he came on was too good to be Satan's own, for Paul himself says it was to keep him humble. This tempter to sin never meant to do Paul such a service, but God let him go to Paul to accomplish His own divine will. The devil and his instruments are both God's instruments. We will be well advised to let God alone to wield the one and handle the other.

Let Lucifer choose his way; God is a match for him at every weapon. If he assaults the saint by persecution, God will oppose him. If he works by a subtlety, God is ready there also. The devil and his whole council are mere fools to God. The more wit and craft in sin, the worse, because it is employed against an all-wise God who cannot be outwitted. In Paul's words, 'The foolishness of God is wiser than men' (*1 Cor. 1:25*). God is wiser in His creatures' weak sermons than Satan is in his deep plots; wiser in His ignorant children than Satan in his Ahithophels and Sanballats. '[God] disappointeth the devices of the crafty' (*Job 5:12*). By displaying His wisdom in pursuing the saints' enemies, God adds a sweet relish to their ultimate deliverance. After He had hunted Pharaoh out of all his lairs and burrows, He broke the very brains of that wicked ruler's plots and served them up to His people, garnished with His wisdom and power.

SATAN'S INTENTIONS AND GOD'S INTERVENTION

Satan has never been nor will he ever be a worthy opponent of God Almighty. Our Lord so far surpasses the devil in wisdom that He can take the very temptations the enemy uses to batter the saints, and use them instead to build a tabernacle of grace and comfort for His children! This is the noblest kind of conquest – to wrestle the devil's tools from his own hands and use them to rebuild what he has been so busily tearing down. Thus God lays, as it were, His own plans under Satan's wings and makes him hatch them. (Remember how He used the evil plot of

Joseph's brothers to accomplish His own grand design.)

All the while Satan is planning evil, you can be sure God is providing for your good. If you will but ask Him, He will turn the temptations of Satan *to* sin, to the purging of your heart *from* sin. Here is how He does it.

I. SATAN'S INTENTION: TO DEFILE THE SAINT'S CON-
   SCIENCE

Satan designs every temptation to bring as much discomfort as possible to the saint, hoping to rob him of his peace and create self-doubts about his sincerity.

But God does not sit idly by. We have a sure promise that 'the eyes of the Lord are upon the righteous' (*Ps. 34:15*). First of all, He uses the temptations of Satan to one sin as a preventive against another. God omnipotent sits in the devil's council and overrules proceedings there to the saint's advantage. He allows the devil to annoy the Christian with certain troublesome temptations which He knows will drive the soul to watchfulness. So Paul's thorn in the flesh prevents his pride. God sent Satan to assault Paul on his strong side so that in the meantime He might fortify the apostle where he was weak.

Second, God uses the temptation to sin as a purgative against future sin. Peter never had such a conquest over his self-confidence, never such an establishment of his faith, as after his denial in the high priest's hall. This man, who recanted when questioned by a serving maid, became a bold confessor of Christ before councils and rulers. If you should trip over a temptation and fall headlong into sin, do like Peter. Use the experience to discover your prevailing infirmity and take measures to overcome it.

Third, God uses temptation to promote the whole work of grace in the heart. A good husband, seeing the roof leak in one corner, will send for a repairman to check the whole house. And a good wife, finding a stain on her husband's shirt, will wash the whole garment. This kind of concern for one's spiritual condition distinguishes a sincere heart from a hypocrite, whose repentance is only partial. Judas confessed his treason, but not a word of his thievery and hypocrisy. If he had been truly repentant, his sorrow for one sin would have broken his heart for the others also. David, when overcome by one sin, renewed his repentance for all (*Ps. 51*).

II. SATAN'S INTENTION: TO DEFILE OTHER SAINTS

Satan plants temptation in one saint, hoping it will blossom into sin and its seeds will be carried to other hearts by the winds of conformity or disillusionment so that they are either encouraged to sin by example, or discouraged in their own walk by the scandal.

God once again fools Satan, by making such sins a seasonable warning to others to look to their standing. When you see a meek Moses provoked to anger, you keep more careful watch for such chokeweeds in your own unruly heart!

God also comforts His afflicted saints by showing them what a rocky road some of His dearest children traveled on their way to heaven. Is your conscience distressed by your sin? Is your soul grief-stricken because Satan has convinced you there is no hope of pardon? The lives of some of the greatest saints are an indisputable rebuttal to Satan's accusations against you. David's sins were great, yet he found mercy. Peter denied his faith, yet he is now in heaven. Does God love you any less than them? Has He not promised to pardon *all* who are of a contrite heart (*Ps. 34:18*)?

Another way God uses Satan's attacks is as a training ground for his saints. The saint who has been severely tested is best equipped to help other suffering saints. The best drill sergeant is not the general behind the desk but the man who has served in the front line of battle. So here you put your faith to work in earnest; all your graces are called into action. If you fall to temptation and come under Satan's rule for a time, you learn what an evil taskmaster he is. He wields an iron rod in one hand and a cruel lash in the other, with which he intends to drive all his subjects to hell. But the sincere child of God, when he sins and feels the sting of Satan's whip, knows how to escape. He runs to the Word and to God Himself. And laying open his wounded heart before Christ, he yields to the kind ministrations of the Spirit.

This kind of experience with sin and Satan will prompt you to warn fellow saints about the devil's dealings and will also teach you how to comfort those who lie wounded and bleeding from Satan's scourging. None will handle poor souls as gently as those who remember the pain of their own experience. These lessons of life, not tutors or books or even head-knowledge of Scripture, equip you to speak a word in season to a weary soul. Christ Himself was trained in the same school. His sufferings (which were all along mingled with temptations) were the lecture from which He emerged with wisdom and compassion, to restore and comfort distressed souls. For the devil's part, he should have let Christ alone, and His saints also. For the enemy's evil design is turned inside out by God, who uses the transitory suffering of one as a permanent source of comfort for many.

III. SATAN'S INTENTION: TO DEFILE THE SAINT'S
RELATIONSHIP WITH GOD

Satan aims to make a breach between God and the saint. He hates both, and therefore labors to divide these dear friends. 'If I can get such a one to sin,' he thinks, 'God will be angry and will whip him soundly.' By this means, the devil assumes the saint will question God's love for him and consequently will cool in his devotion to God.

How does God respond to such deceitful maneuvers? He makes Satan's temptations the courier of His love to the saints. The devil thought he had the game in his own hands when he got Adam to eat the forbidden fruit. He supposed he now had man in the same predicament as himself. But did he catch God by surprise? Of course not! God knew the outcome before the match was ever begun and used Satan's temptation to usher in that great gospel plot of saving man by Christ. At God's command, Christ undertook the charge of wresting His fallen creatures from Satan's clutches and reinstating them to their original glory, with access to more than they ever had at first.

And what did Satan get for all the energy he spent on Job, but to let that holy man know at last how dearly God loved him? When he foiled Peter so shamefully, do we not find Christ claiming Peter with as much love as ever? Peter was the only disciple to whom Christ sent the joyful news of His resurrection by name – as if He had said, 'Be sure to comfort Peter with this news. I want him to know I am still his friend, despite his cowardice.' God never condones wickedness in His saints, but He does pity their weakness. He never sees a saint in mourning without planning to clothe him in the sunlight of His love and mercy.

God can, in fact, use His saints' failures to strengthen their faith, which, like a tree, stands stronger for the shaking. Times of testing expose the heart's true condition. False faith, once foiled, seldom comes on again; but true faith rises and fights more valiantly, as we see in Peter. Temptation is to faith as fire is to gold (*1 Pet. 1:7*). The fire not only reveals which is true gold, but makes the true gold more pure. It comes out less in bulk, being separated from the dross that was mixed with it, but is greater in quality and value.

Faith before temptation has much extraneous stuff that clings to it and passes for faith; but when temptation comes, the dross is discovered and consumed by the fiery trial. The quality of faith that emerges is like Gideon's handful of men – stronger when all these worthless accessories to faith are sent away than when they were present. And here is all the devil gets: Instead of destroying the saint's faith, he is the means of refining it, thereby making it stronger and more precious.

The love of tempted saints is enkindled to Christ by the fires of temptation. Did you edge too close to the flames and singe your soul? Where will you go for cleansing, if not to Christ? And will His kindly aid not rekindle your love for Him above all others? Christ's love is fuel to ours; the more He puts forth His love, the more heat our love gets. And next to Christ's dying love, none is greater than His rescuing love in temptation. The greatest opportunity a mother has to show her child how much she loves him is when he is in distress – sick, poor, or imprisoned. Christ is both mother and nurse to our love. When His children lie in Satan's prison, bleeding from the wounds of their consciences, He hurries to reveal His tender heart in pitying, His faithfulness in praying, His mindfulness in sending help to them, and His dear love in visiting them by His comforting Spirit. No child is more dutiful in all the family than the one who has repented of his rebellion. Jesus Christ, whom Satan thought to shut out of the soul's favor, comes in the end to sit higher and surer than ever in the saint's affections.

Do you see now why God allows His children to meet with temptation? He is in control! He holds the reins on Satan and will not let him trample you. If you never experienced the mighty power of Satan arrayed against you, you could not know the almighty power of God displayed for you.

On this same stage God spreads out the panoply of His wisdom, and lets you watch while He reduces all the wit and wiles of Satan to utter foolishness. God will be admired by His saints in glory not only for His love and faithfulness in their salvation, but also for His wisdom in the way to it. Wisdom is the attribute man admires above all others, and the one Satan chose as his first bait, when he made Eve believe she should be like God in knowledge and wisdom. Therefore God, to give Satan the more shameful fall, lets him use all his cunning in tempting and troubling the saints. But in the end the way to His throne, where His wisdom as well as His mercy shall sit in state, will be paved with the skulls, as I may so speak, of devils.

Rest easy, worried Christian. The duel is not between the church and Satan, but between Christ and Satan. These are the champions of the two sides. Gather round and watch the all-wise God joust with His crafty opponent. You shall behold the Almighty smite off this Goliath's head with his own sword, and take this wicked knight in the trap of his own schemes. That faith which ascribes greatness and wisdom to God will shrink up Satan's challenge into a thing of nothing. Unbelief fears Satan as a lion; faith treads upon him as a worm.

Observe God at work, and be assured that what He is about will be an excellent piece. Man's wisdom may be leveled with folly, but God's design is never interrupted. None can drive Him from His work. A builder cannot work when night draws the curtain, and he is driven off his scaffold by a rainstorm. But all the plots of hell and commotions on earth have not so much as shaken God's hand to spoil one letter or line He has been drawing. The mystery of His providence may hang a curtain before His work so that we cannot see what He is doing, but even when darkness surrounds Him, righteousness is the seat of His throne for ever. Where is our faith, saints? Let God be wise, and all men and devils be fools. Even if a Babel seems more likely to go up than a Babylon to be pulled down, yet believe God is making His secret approaches and will besiege Satan's stronghold.

What does it matter though the church be like Jonah in the whale's belly, swallowed up out of view by the fury of men? Do you not remember that the whale had no power to digest the prophet? Do not be too quick to bury the church before she is dead. Be patient while Christ tries His skill before you give it over. By your prayers, bring Christ to its grave to speak a resurrection word. The saints of old exhibited admirable faith in circumstances which were just as dire. Jeremiah purchased a field from his uncle and paid for it in full, even though the Chaldean army was quartered about Jerusalem, ready to take the city and to carry him into captivity with the rest of the Jews (*Jer. 32*). All this was by God's decree, so Jeremiah could show the people how completely he believed in the fulfillment of the promise for their return from captivity, in spite of the sad state of affairs. Indeed, we dishonor the Word of God if, when the church's power is at its lowest ebb, we do not take the single bond of His promise as a guarantee of its deliverance.

3: *Second Consideration: The Nature of the War and the Character of the Enemy*

1. The Nature of the War

For we wrestle not against flesh and blood, but against principalities, against powers, against the rulers of the darkness of this world, against spiritual wickedness in high places (Eph. 6:12).

We have studied at some length the Christian's need to be armed and the nature of that armour. Let us turn our thoughts for a while to the nature of the war that is raging. Here Paul lays all on the table. He does not underrate the fierceness of the struggle nor the strength of our foe. In this he is unlike Satan, who dares not let sinners know the true character of God, but must draw them on to the field with false reports and keep them there with lies and subterfuge. Paul, on the other hand, is not afraid to show the saints their enemy in all his power, the weakness of God being stronger than all the powers of hell.

Look now at the nature of the war in three particulars: the sharpness of combat, the universality of combat, and the duration of combat.

WHY SAINTS MUST WRESTLE

I. THE SHARPNESS OF COMBAT

Your state in this life is set out by the word *wrestling*. Though sometimes it is used to define a form of recreational sport, here it describes the sharpness of your encounter with the enemy. Paul uses it to convey the notion of a bloody and lasting war between the Christian and his implacable opponent. Two things make wrestling a sharper combat than others.

First, it is a single combat. Strictly speaking, wrestling is not a team sport, but primarily a 'one-on-one' contest where one opponent singles out another and enters the arena with him, as with David and Goliath. Each wrestler exerts his whole force and strength against the other. Such combat is much fiercer than fighting in an army where, though the battle is sharp and long, the soldier is not always fighting. He can stop occasionally to get his breath. In fact, he may escape without a scratch, because in war the enemy's aim is not at one man in particular but at the whole regiment. In wrestling, however, each contestant is the sole object of his challenger's fury, and must be shaken and tried until one or the other is proclaimed victorious.

Whether you like it or not, you must go into the ring with Satan. He has not only a general malice against the army of saints, but a particular spite against every single child of God. As our Lord delights to have private communion with His saint, so the devil delights to challenge the Christian when he gets him alone. The whole issue of your spiritual destiny is personal and particular. You give Satan a dangerous advantage if you see his wrath and fury bent in general against the saints, and not against you specifically: Satan hates *me*; Satan accuses *me*; Satan tempts *me*. Conversely, you lose much comfort when you fail to see the promises and providences of God as available for your own specific needs: God loves *me*; God pardons *me*; God takes care of *me*. The water supply for the town will do you no personal good unless you have a pipe that carries it to your own house. Let it serve as both a caution and a comfort to know your spiritual combat is singular.

Second, wrestling is a close combat. Armies fight at some distance; wrestlers grapple hand-to-hand. You may be able to dodge an arrow shot from a distance, but when the enemy actually has hold of you, you must either resist manfully or fall shamefully at his feet. When Satan comes after you, he moves in close, takes hold of your very flesh and corrupt nature, and by this shakes you.

II. THE UNIVERSALITY OF COMBAT

'We wrestle' encompasses everyone. You may have noticed that the apostle changes the pronoun 'ye' in the former verse, into 'we' in this, that he may include himself. He wants you to know the quarrel is with every saint. Satan neither fears to assault the minister nor disdains to wrestle with the lowliest saint in the congregation. Great and small, minister and people, all must wrestle – not one part of Christ's army in the heat of battle and the other at ease in their quarters.

III. THE DURATION OF COMBAT

The length of a man's combat with Satan measures the same as the length of his life. He is, as Jeremiah said of himself, born 'a man of strife' (*Jer. 15:10*). And once he becomes a saint, the struggle increases. From your spiritual birth to your natural death, from the hour you first set your face toward heaven until you set your foot inside the gate, you will have wars with Satan, sin, and self. Israel's march out of Egypt is, in a figurative way, our open declaration of war against the forces of darkness. And when did they have peace? Not until they reached Canaan.

No condition the Christian finds himself in here below is quiet. Is it prosperity, or is it adversity? Here is work for both hands – to keep pride and complacency down in the one, faith and patience up in the other. The Christian has nowhere he can call privileged ground. Lot wrestled with the wicked inhabitants of Sodom, his righteous soul vexed with their filthy behavior. Then what happened at Zoar? His own daughters brought a spark of Sodom's fire into his bed, and he was inflamed with incestuous lust (*Gen. 19:30–38*)!

Some have thought if they were only in such a family, under such a ministry, removed from a certain temptation, then they would not be such weak Christians. I confess a change of air is a great help to an invalid, but do you think you can thus escape Satan's presence? No! Even if you were to take the wings of the morning, he would pursue you. A change in circumstances may make him change his method of tempting, but nothing temporal can make him lay down his designs. As long as his comrade, your old nature, is alive within, he will be knocking at the door without. This diabolical opponent will challenge you at every opportunity. He delights to sneak up on you from behind, while you are kneeling, trowel in hand, planting seeds for the kingdom. He knows a scuffle with him will at least detain you, if he cannot stop you altogether.

You wrestle at a disadvantage, for you must wrestle with a body of flesh. The flesh is to you as the horse is to the rider – you cannot go on your journey without it. If the flesh is kept high and lusty and given free rein, then it is spoiled and unruly. But if the bit is too tight and the spirit pinched, then it is weak and soon tires, able to gain little ground.

You also wrestle with a body of sin as well as of flesh, and both mutter and murmur when the soul undertakes any enterprise for the Master. Sometimes they keep the Christian from duty, so that he cannot do what he would like. As Paul said, 'I would have come several times, but

Satan hindered me.' 'I would have prayed,' the Christian may say, 'and meditated on the word I heard, but this enemy (that is, Satan working through the flesh) kept me from it.'

You can see that the Christian is assailed on every side by his enemies. How can it be otherwise, when the rumblings of war are deep in the natures of both man and Satan? A pack of wolves may snarl and pick at one another, but they are soon quiet again because the quarrel is not in their nature – they are of the same disposition. But the wolf and the lamb can never be made friends. Their differences are irreconcilable. The spiritual application is this: Satan and your old nature may lie down together, but sin and grace never will. Sin will lust against grace, and grace draw a sword upon sin whenever they meet.

HOW NOT TO WRESTLE
When we wrestle against Satan, we wrestle for God; it follows then that our refusal to wrestle against Satan is a passive resistance against God. There are other times when we actively wrestle against God. Isaiah warns, 'Woe unto him that striveth with his Maker' (*Isa. 45:9*). I do not need to tell you the outcome! What kind of contest is it when thorns fight fire, or stubble battles flames? But our deceitful hearts will sometimes trick us into such an uneven match. Be ever watchful, then, that you do not wrestle against God in one of the following ways.

I. DO NOT WRESTLE AGAINST GOD'S SPIRIT
Genesis 6:3 speaks of the Spirit as 'striving' with man. This does not mean God is trying to overcome or destroy man. He could do that at a word, without any stir or scuffle. No, His striving is a loving contest with us. Seeing

us run at such a gallop headlong to our ruin, He sends His Spirit to pull us back before we destroy ourselves. This is the same kind of strife you would witness if someone were attempting to take his own life and another intervened and struggled to take the weapon from him.

The lusts of men are those bloody instruments of death with which sinners are harming themselves. The Holy Spirit strives to get them out of our hands and replace them with Christ's grace and eternal life. When you repulse such loving strife, you are justly counted a fighter against Him. 'Ye stiff-necked, and uncircumcised in heart and ears, ye do always resist the Holy Ghost,' said Stephen (*Acts 7:51*).

II. DO NOT WRESTLE AGAINST GOD'S PROVIDENCE

Questioning God's acts, whether of mercy or justice, is called contending or reproving Him (*Job 40:2*). He is a bold man for sure who dares to name himself the plaintiff and God the defender. No! God is the Judge, and He will find you in contempt of court for bringing such false accusations against Him. Contend with the Almighty? Reprove God? You had better cry with Job: 'I am vile; what shall I answer thee? I will lay mine hand upon my mouth' (*Job 40:4*). Hear his plea: 'Only pardon what is past, and you shall hear such language no more!'

Christians, take heed of this wrestling above all other. Contention is always unfortunate – whether with neighbors or friends, wife or husband – but worst of all with God. If God cannot please you and your heart rises against Him, what hopes are there of your pleasing Him? Love cannot think any evil of God, nor endure to hear any evil spoken of Him. It must take God's part, as Jonathan took David's when Saul disparaged him. Love will allow you to groan when afflicted, but not to grumble. When you complain, you reveal a mutinous spirit against God, and

[129]

stab love to the heart.

Complaining about the providence of God is bad enough. But what about the times we willfully oppose Him? God in His mercy uses every means to draw us to Himself, but by steadfastly resisting, we wrestle against Him with both hands. Is it His mercy he offers, and we ignore Him? Or is it affliction, and we turn away? The one should draw, the other drive us to Him. If we continue in our stubbornness, the worst thing He can do is remove Himself from us. Suppose you prove incorrigible and He says at last, 'I will afflict you no more.' What He means is, 'I will be in your debt until another world, when I shall pay you in full for your sin.'

III. DO NOT WRESTLE BY YOUR OWN RULES

We wrestle against God when we disregard His rules and substitute our own. Maybe you do not wrestle against God's providence, and you do wrestle against sin. This seems commendable, but God requires more: You must wrestle by His rules and His alone. Timothy tells us, 'If a man also strive for masteries, yet is he not crowned, except he strive lawfully' (2 Tim. 2:5). Check your own conduct against the errors of some who have waged their own battle, and not Christ's:

Some, while they wrestle against one sin, embrace another. Our lusts are diverse and will fight for rank among themselves. When malice wants revenge, craft says, 'Hide your wrath – but do not forgive.' When passion sends out for whores, hypocrisy cancels the request but for fear of the world, not God. The man who allows one sin to command another, and thus to rule his soul, cannot be God's champion.

Some wrestle because they are pressed into service. Their slavish fears frighten them and keep them from their lusts for the moment. But the real combat for such a wrestler is between his conscience and his will, rather than between his soul and his lusts. In such a case, the will at last prevails, for a lust held in check but not discarded grows as wild as a trapped stallion. Finally conscience can no longer hold the reins nor sit in the saddle, but is thrown down. Then the lust ranges where it can have its fullest meal and will continue to gorge itself until conscience revives and runs to God for help.

Others wrestle with sin but do not hate it. They wrestle in jest, not in earnest. Until the love of a sin is quenched in the heart, the fire will never die out. How is this accomplished? Jerome says one love extinguishes another – that is, the love of Christ must quench the love of sin. Then and not until then will the soul's decree stand against sin.

HOW TO WRESTLE
Now that you know some of the wrong ways to wrestle, you will be well advised to take these tips on the right way to manage your combat.

I. ENLIST GOD AS YOUR SECOND
My meaning is, engage God by prayer to stand behind you. God has an offensive and defensive agreement with you, but He waits to be called in. If you go into battle without Him, you have more valor than Moses, who would not stir without God even though He sent an angel as His lieutenant (*Ex. 33*). Or you must think yourself wiser than Jacob, who, to overcome Esau, turned from him and fell upon God. He knew if he could wrestle with God, he could trust God to deal with his brother. Enlist the Lord, and the back door is shut. No enemy can come behind you; instead, your enemy will fall at your feet. 'Oh, Lord, I pray thee, turn the counsel of Ahithophel into foolishness,' David prayed (*2 Sam. 15:31*). Heaven

[131]

said 'Amen' to his prayer, and David's foe hanged himself.

II. STAY IN TRAINING

Your bout with sin and Satan is not a weekend sport; it is the final conflict. So you dare not give your enemy a handhold. Wrestlers strive to fasten upon some part of the body which will let them more easily throw their adversary. To prevent this, ancient wrestlers used to anoint their bodies before a match. You should do likewise. Strive to put off the old man – that corruption David called his own iniquity (*Ps. 18:23*). Observe what it is and mortify it daily; it is a favorite handhold of Satan's. He will beat a shameful retreat when he finds no iniquity in you to catch hold of – and he dare not touch that in you which is holy.

Is your flesh mortified? Now anoint your soul with the frequent meditation of Christ's love. It will help you disdain the offer of sin and, like oil, will make your spirit supple and your will agile to evade the enemy. Satan will find little welcome where Christ's love dwells. Love will kindle love, and flame as a wall of fire to keep him away.

III. USE YOUR ADVANTAGE WISELY

If you are a smart wrestler, you will fall with all your weight upon your enemy when you have him on the ground. Though in most sports the referee would call 'Foul!' if you were to strike when your opponent is down, this is not the case with wrestling. The object is to put your opponent on his back and keep him there. Do not so compliment sin as to let it breathe or rise. Do not repeat Ahab's sin and let the enemy loose when God has decreed his destruction.

Learn a little wisdom from Satan's brood. Though they had Christ on His back, they still took precautions. They never thought they had Him sure enough – not even when dead. So they sealed and watched His grave. You should do the same to hinder the resurrection of your sin: seal it down with stronger purposes and solemn covenants, and watch it by a wakeful, circumspect walk.

A WORD OF ENCOURAGEMENT TO WRESTLERS
Perhaps you are discouraged, not only by the strength of the enemy, but by your own apparent weakness and the constant contention with sin and self. Be encouraged! There is strong consolation for the Christian who struggles with the truth of God's grace and his own inner conflicts with sin. Gideon cried out in despair, 'If the Lord be with us, why is all this befallen us?' (*Judges 6:13*). We understand his perplexity because we identify with his sufferings. Our hearts, too, cry out, 'Why do I find such struggling in me, provoking me to sin, pulling me back from that which is good?'

God has a ready answer if we will stop whining long enough to hear it. 'Because,' He says, 'you are a wrestler, not a conqueror.' It is as simple as that. Too often we mistake the state of a Christian in this life. He is not immediately called to triumph over his enemies, but is carried into battle to fight them. The state of grace is the commencement of your war against sin, not the culmination of it. God Himself will enter the battle in disguise and appear to be your enemy, rather than leave you no enemy to wrestle with. When Jacob was alone, He sent a man to wrestle with him until dawn.

Take comfort in the fact that you *are* a wrestler. This struggling within you, if upon the right ground and to the right end, only proves there are two nations within you, two contrary natures, the one from earth earthly, and the other from heaven heavenly. And for your further comfort, know that although your corrupt nature is the elder, yet it shall serve the younger (*Gen. 25:23*).

Wrap your weary soul in this promise: There is a place of rest reserved for the people of God. You do not beat the air, but wrestle to win heaven and a permanent crown. Here on earth we overcome to fight again. One temptation may be conquered, but the war remains. When death comes, however, God strikes the final blow. We know peace is sweet after war, pleasure after pain. But what tongue can express the joy that will flood the creature at the first sight of God and his eternal home? If we knew more of that future blissful state, we would worry less about our present conflict.

2. The Character of the Enemy

The apostle Paul goes into some detail describing the assailants that appear in arms against the Christian. When he says they are 'not flesh and blood,' we are not to interpret this as an absolute negation. Rather, he means *not only* or *not chiefly* flesh and blood. First, consider what *is* meant by 'flesh and blood.'

THE SAINT'S MINOR ASSAILANTS: 'FLESH AND BLOOD'

1. OUR INNER CORRUPTIONS ARE 'FLESH AND BLOOD' because they are propagated to us by natural generation. Thus Adam is said to beget a son in his own likeness, sinful like himself, as well as mortal. The holiest saint on earth passes on this corrupt and sinful nature to his child – as the circumcised Jew begets an uncircumcised child, and a bare grain of wheat, when sown, comes up again with a husk.

We may also call our inner corruptions 'flesh' because of the operations of our unregenerate nature, which is fleshly and carnal. The thoughts of the corrupt mind are incapable of perceiving the things of God. All its desires, delights, cares, and fears are wrapped up in this present world, and are therefore fleshly. Just as the sun hides the heavens above it while revealing the things beneath, so carnal reason leaves the creature in the dark concerning spiritual truths, while enlightening his carnal knowledge most excellently. Every creature has its proper diet: the lion does not eat grass, nor the horse, flesh. Just so, what is food to the carnal heart, is poison to the gracious; and what is tasty to the gracious, is odious to the carnal.

Now according to this interpretation of flesh and blood, the apostle is not saying that the war is over between your old and new natures. You know from experience this is not the case. The Spirit lusts against the flesh and the flesh against the Spirit throughout the whole course of a Christian's life. Were there no devils, you would still have your hands full resisting the corruptions of your own heart. What Paul wants you to see is that your old nature is only a private in the war against your new nature. Satan comes to the battle as an ally of the flesh and launches a massive attack. He is the general who marshals your sinful inclinations, exercises them mercilessly, and sends them out as a united front against the power of God in your life. Compare it to the following situation. Suppose that while a king is fighting to subdue his own mutinous subjects, some superior foreign troops should join with them and take command. Then the king no longer fights primarily against his subjects, but against a foreign power. You see the spiritual analogy: Even as the Christian is fighting against his own inner corruptions, Satan joins his power to the residue of the old nature and assumes command. It could be said that our sin is the engine, and Satan, the engineer.

This knowledge should make every one of us diligent to

keep our lusts unarmed – for they will be all too eager to declare their allegiance to Satan when he comes to tempt. Our own naked grace is no match in such a circumstance – as the odds are two to one against us. But if we cling to God for strength and wisdom, then we will be able to deal mightily with this serpent and his lusty brood.

II. HUMAN BEINGS ARE 'FLESH AND BLOOD'

'We wrestle not with flesh and blood' – that is, not with other *men*. 'Handle me, and see,' Jesus said, 'for a spirit hath not flesh . . . ' (*Luke 24:39*). Now according to this interpretation, observe first of all how scornfully the Holy Spirit speaks of man, and second, where He lays the stress of the saint's battle: not in resisting flesh and blood, but in combating principalities and powers in the unseen world of spirits.

First of all, note that the Spirit reduces man to flesh and blood. Man has a heaven-born soul, which makes him kin to angels – and what is more, kin to God. But this is passed by in silence, as if God would not own that which is tainted with sin and no longer the creature as He first made it. The soul, though of divine extraction, is so immersed in sensuality that it deserves no other name than flesh to express its weakness and frailty. It is the word the Holy Ghost uses to express the impotence of a creature. For example, 'They are men, and their horses are *flesh*' – that is, weak (*Isa. 31:3*). On the contrary, when God wishes to emphasize the power and strength of a thing, He contrasts it to flesh: 'Our weapons are not carnal, but mighty' (*2 Cor. 10:4*).

How this should humble you! The flesh, which you so often glory in, is but one step from filth and corruption. Your redeemed soul is the salt that preserves you, or else you would stink above ground. Are you proud of your beauty? It is the vanity of vanities! How soon will time's plough make furrows in your face, or illness so change your complexion that your doting lovers will abhor to look at you!

Is it strength you boast of? Alas, it is an arm of flesh that withers while you stretch it forth. Soon your blood, which is now warm, will freeze in your veins. Your marrow will dry in your bones, your sinews shrink, and your legs bow under the weight of your puny body.

Perhaps wisdom is your heart's pet. The same grave that covers your body will bury all the wisdom of your flesh. Your goodly schemes will come to nothing. Only those thoughts which are the holy respirations of your soul will have meaning beyond the grave.

Perhaps it is not beauty, or strength, or intellect that you expect to sustain you; maybe it is your birth and breeding. Whoever you are, you are baseborn until born again. The same blood runs in your veins with the beggar in the street (*Acts 17:26*). We enter and leave the world alike; as one is not made of finer earth, so he does not disintegrate into purer dust.

If such is the composition of all flesh, why place your faith in any man? Do not trust in princes; they cannot keep their crowns on their own heads, nor their heads on their own shoulders. Neither trust in wise men, whose designs so often recoil upon themselves. Man's carnal wisdom may predict whatever it likes, but God turns the wheel and brings forth His own providence regardless. Nor trust too much in spiritual leaders. They, too, are flesh, and their judgment is not infallible. The holy man's mistake may lead you astray, and though he repents, you may go on and perish. Trust not in any man – not even yourself. 'He is a fool,' the wise man said, 'who trusts his heart.'

Just as you should not trust in the flesh, neither should

you be afraid of the flesh. You have seen what a rusty bucket it is, how subject to decay. This was David's resolve: 'I will not fear what flesh can do unto me' (*Psalm 56:4*). If you are a Christian, what is there to fear? You have no life to lose if you have already given yourself to Christ. And while God has not promised immunity from suffering, He has undertaken to bear your losses and pay you a hundredfold, though your reward may not come until another world.

One more comforting thought. Is man mere flesh? Our heavenly Father knows it and makes allowances for our weakness: 'He knoweth our frame, he remembereth that we are dust' (*Psalm 103:14*). When you begin to faint under the weight of duty or temptation, God rushes to you as a mother to her distraught child, revives you with His own sweet breath, and will not let your spirit die.

Now, Christian, you know you are not to fear flesh and blood; yet neither can you ignore it. As long as the seeds of corruption reside in man's carnal nature, Satan will interweave his crafty plots with man's – so that we wrestle not with man alone, but with man led on by Satan. The Christian must wrestle with two sorts of men: good and bad. Satan strikes in with both.

First, the Christian wrestles with good men. Many sharp conflicts have taken place between saint and saint, scuffling in the dark through misunderstanding of the truth and each other. Abraham fell out with Lot. Aaron and Miriam quarreled with Moses, until God interposed and ended the dispute by disgracing Miriam (*Num. 12:10*). In the very presence of Christ Himself, the apostles argued heatedly about who should be greatest among them.

In all these civil wars among saints, Satan is the great, unseen instigator. Like Ahab, he fights in disguise, playing first on one side and then on the other, aggravating every petty injury, always provoking to wrath and revenge. For this reason, the apostle warns, 'Neither give place to the devil' (*Eph. 4:27*). In other words, 'Do not fall out among yourselves unless you long for the devil's company. He is a soldier of fortune and therefore runs to any place where there is hope of war.' He is attracted to the heat from our anger like a moth to a flame. He cannot work well without fire, so he is himself a kindle-coal. He lays himself upon any embers of contention he finds among the saints and fans them until they glow white-hot. These he uses at his forge to heat our spirits into wrath. Then we are malleable, easily hammered as he pleases.

Contention throws the soul into chaos, and the law of grace cannot act freely when the spirit is in commotion. Even meek Moses spoke foolishly when he became provoked. If nothing else, this thought should sound a retreat to our petty differences: that a Joab had a hand in creating them. He sets an evil spirit between brethren. What folly it is for us to bite and devour one another to make sport for the devil. We are prone to mistake our heat for zeal, whereas usually the strife between saints is a fire-ship sent by Satan to scatter our unity and order. United we are an armada invincible, and Satan knows he has no other way but strife to sink us.

To this end, he is not satisfied with stirring up strife among good men; he also prods evil men to challenge the saint. Christ says because you are not of this world, the world hates you (*John 15:19*). The saint's nature and life are anathema to the world. Fire and water, heaven and hell, could as soon be reconciled. Hence come wars. The fire of persecution never goes out in the hearts of the wicked, who still say in secret as they once shouted in the

Colosseum, 'Christians to the lions!'

Now in all the saints' wars with the wicked, Satan is commander-in-chief on the wicked side. It is their captain's work the wicked do, his lusts they fulfill. The Sabeans were the ones who plundered Job, but they went on Satan's errand. The heretic spreads corrupt doctrine and perverts the faith of many, but he is only a minister of Satan (*2 Cor. 11:15*), who gives him his call, his wiles, and his wages. Persecutors, whether by their tongues or their hands, are but the devil's instruments (*Rev. 2:9, 10*).

When you see people striving furiously against the truths or servants of Christ, pity them as the most miserable people on earth. Do not fear their power, nor admire their talents. They are emissaries of Satan. The martyrs of old called them his drudges and slaughter-slaves. Augustine said in a letter to Lycinius (a brilliant but wicked man who once had been his student), 'Oh, how I weep to see such a sparkling wit as yours prostituted to the devil's service! If you had found a golden chalice, you would have given it to the church; but God has given you a golden head, talent, and wit, and with them you are drinking yourself to the devil!'

When you see men of power and intellect using their talents against God, weep for their souls. Better they had lived and died slaves and fools, than to do the devil's business with their God-given abilities.

When reproached and persecuted by wicked men, look beyond them. Spend your wrath on Satan, who is your chief enemy. Men are only his puppets. They may be won to Christ's side and so become your friends at last. Anselm explains it in the following manner. 'When the enemy comes riding up in battle, the valiant soldier is not angry with the horse, but with the horseman. He works to kill the rider so that he may possess the horse for his own use.

Thus must we do with the wicked. We are not to bend our wrath against them, but against Satan who rides them and spurs them on. Let us pray fervently, as Christ did on the cross, that the devil will be dismounted and these miserable souls delivered from him'. Greater honor is earned by taking one soul alive out of the devil's clutches, than by leaving many slain upon the field.

Augustine showed this same compassion toward the wicked. Erasmus records that he begged the emperor's officers to give him custody of the heretics who had been sentenced to death for persecuting believers. What was his motive in this? To minister to their souls like a kind physician, that if possible he might work a cure and make them sound in the faith.

THE SAINT'S CHIEF ASSAILANTS: EVIL SPIRITS

If the saints' battle only pitted flesh against flesh, some might be able to win it by their own efforts. But Paul dashes any silly notion of an independent victory when he describes the character of our greatest enemies. They are not 'flesh and blood,' but a host of evil spirits directed by the devil himself, and sent out to war against the saints.

Having been for ever denied pre-eminence above the stars, Satan has determined to have it beneath them. Since the day he was thrown out of heaven, he and his followers have worked tirelessly to establish their dominion on earth. The Epistle to the Ephesians reveals the scope of their influence: first, their system of government; second, the magnitude of their power; third, their territory; fourth, their inherent nature; and fifth, the subject of their dispute with God.

1. THEIR SYSTEM OF GOVERNMENT

The word *principalities* is used to designate the territory which that usurper Satan has claimed belongs to him. To

[141]

deny the devil's exalted position in the present wicked world is to contradict God Himself. Christ referred to him as 'the prince of this world' (*John 14:30*). And as princes have a people and a province which they rule, so Satan has his.

An earthly dictator is fortunate if he has a handful of subjects he can trust. The rest he must control by force, or he may shortly lose his throne as well as his head. But Satan has no reason to fear an assassin's bullet. He can trust all his subjects and never has to worry about rebellion – except when the Holy Spirit intervenes. As a matter of fact, the wicked go beyond mere obedience to the devil; they willingly bend their knees and bow their heads to *worship* him (*Rev. 13:4*). It is, nonetheless, no more than he demands.

Satan is a diabolical dictator, whose laws are evil to the core. His will is called a '*law* of sin' because it is given with such authority (*Rom. 8:2*). He hands down orders to the eager sinner, who quickly runs to obey. Little does he know the law is written in his own blood and nothing but damnation is promised for fulfilling the devil's lust!

Satan knows he must have the co-operation of all his subjects in order for his kingdom to thrive, but he is especially pleased to use the most wicked. As princes appoint ministers of state to enforce their whims and wishes, so Satan sends out special emissaries to carry out his plans. He too has his chosen disciples like Elymas, whom Paul called 'full of subtilty . . . and child of the devil' (*Acts 13:10*). It is to this inner circle of dark hearts that he imparts the mysteries of iniquity and the depths of degradation.

But even with these chosen few he does not share everything. He always holds his own purse and the sinner's too, so that he is the investor and the sinner only the broker to trade for him. In the end, all the ill-gotten gains drop into the devil's pocket. Everything the sinner has – time, strength, intellect, and all – is spent to keep the devil on his throne.

(a) *Satan's claim to his throne*

'How,' you may ask, 'did such a low creature come to hold such a mighty principality?' Not lawfully, you can be sure, though he is clever enough to show a claim which appears legitimate.

For one thing, he claims the earth by conquest. It is to some degree true that he won his crown by power and politics, and that he keeps it the same way. Yet 'conquest' is a cracked title.

A thief has no legal right to the wallet he takes from his victim simply because he puts it in his pocket and claims it is his own. Nor is the wrong thus committed ever made right by the passing of time. Years may go by before he is discovered; he will be as guilty on the day of his arrest as on the day he perpetrated the crime. Now a thief on the throne is no different from one in the alley. Satan has indeed kept his stolen title a long time, but he is no less a criminal than on the day he first took Adam's heart from God.

Christ's conquest of your soul is just, because the ground of His war is righteous. He comes to recover what was His all along. Satan, on the other hand, is a false contender and his conquest is a hoax because he cannot ever say of the least creature, 'It is my own.'

Satan also claims his principality by election. Count the ballots and you will see he holds his present position in the world by the unanimous vote of man's corrupt nature. Never mind that he rode into office on a lie; Adam fell for it, and so have all the sons of Adam since. Christ put it very succinctly: 'Ye are of your father the devil, and the lusts of your father ye will do' (*John 8:44*).

Still, Satan's claim to a democratic victory is flawed, for man was created as God's subject, and has neither the power nor the authority to oust the eternal King in favor of another. We may choose to ignore God's sovereignty, but we cannot strip it from Him. Though sin disabled us to keep God's law, it does not excuse us from our need to keep it, or from the terms of God's government.

Finally, Satan presents a counterfeit deed of gift from God to claim the earth as his. This imposter is so brazen that he actually presented his worthless claim to Christ Himself, pretending to possess absolute power as the prince of this world. He showed our Lord all the earthly kingdoms and said, 'All this power will I give thee, and the glory of them: for that is delivered unto me; and to whomsoever I will I give it' (*Luke 4:6*).

There was a truth here – yet more than the truth. In a sense God did deliver this world to Satan, but not to do whatever he pleases. The devil is prince of the world, not by the preference of God, but by His permission. And God can revoke His permission at any time.

(b) *God's present concession to Satan's claim*

From our limited human perspective, we must wonder why God allows His apostate creature to hold such a principality in the world. Why does He let this rebel parade with such pomp and arrogance before men and angels? There are several reasons we might consider.

First, to punish sin. Letting Satan crack his whip over man is one way God punishes rebellion: 'Because thou servedst not the Lord thy God with joyfulness, and with gladness of heart . . . therefore shalt thou serve thine enemies . . . in hunger' (*Deut. 28:47, 48*). Satan is an overseer given in God's wrath. The devil is God's slave, and man the devil's. Sin has chained the creature to Satan, and now he drives him mercilessly.

A second reason God has allowed Satan to flaunt his power is to show that the Lord's power is greater. No one will doubt God's almighty power when they see Him flick this mighty dragon off the earth and into hell as though he were a gnat. Just as man alone is no match for the devil, so Satan with all his troops is no match for God. What a glorious name God will have for Himself when He has finished this war!

The workmanship of heaven and earth gave God the name of Creator. Providence gave Him the name of Preserver. But His triumph over Satan gives Him a name above every other – that of Savior. As Savior He both preserves rescued man from destruction and creates a new creature in him – a child of grace. Then the Savior nestles this babe in His bosom and carries him safely past all the commotions of Satan, until at last he reaches heaven.

There is no greater evidence of God's mercy than His plan of redemption. All His other majestic works will flow as rivers into this one mighty sea, on whose shores the saints will stand with great rejoicing. Know this for certain: If we had not been Satan's prisoner first, we would not fully understand or appreciate our deliverance at last.

Finally, God permits Satan's temporary reign in order to increase the saint's eternal joy. Does this sound like a paradox? Think about your own life, and you will find that often the occasions for the greatest joy arise from the ashes of suffering. Scripture gives three illustrations of great joy: the joy of a new mother, the joy of a prosperous farmer, and the joy of a successful soldier. The exultation of all three is harvested from hard soil. It costs the travailing woman great pain, the farmer many months of backbreaking labor, and the soldier grave peril, before they come to their reward. But at last they are paid in full. And it is a peculiar attribute of sorrow that its past remembrance so often adds a sweetness to our present joy.

Here is the spiritual corollary: if Christ had come and entered into affinity with our natures peaceably, then returned to heaven with His spotless bride, we doubtless would have shared the joy of marriage with Him. Yet the way He chose to carry His saints to heaven will embellish our joy and adoration – for we will have the memory of the sharp pains caused by sin and Satan to compare to the immeasurable joy of being His bride. The nuptial song is joined to the victory march of a conqueror who has rescued His beloved from the hands of her captor as he was leading her to the chambers of hell.

(c) *How to test your true allegiance*

Look around you and you will see Satan's empire flourishing on the right hand and on the left. His rule spans continents and oceans; his subjects are as numerous as the sands of the sea. Oh, how we need to be sure we are not counted among them, for even in Christ's own territory, the visible church, Satan has planted his subjects. To discover your heart's true allegiance, study the following guidelines.

First, find out whose subject you are. You recall that Christ had His saints in Nero's court; well, the devil has his servants in the outer court of Christianity. If you claim to belong to Christ, you must prove it by something stronger than an outward conformity to His ordinances.

When a king's subjects go as merchants to live in a foreign country, he expects them to learn the language and observe the national customs insofar as possible. This does not undermine their allegiance to him; on the contrary, it makes them the more valuable as his subjects. Similarly, Satan does not care if you stand in the courtyard of the visible church and learn the language of the saints gathered there. He can yield to this and be no loser. In fact, he can often be served all the better by a hypocrite who offers a show of piety to the church, but saves back his heart for the devil.

Christ and Satan create a spiritual dichotomy which you cannot ignore. It divides the whole world. You belong to one camp, and only to one. Christ will allow no equal, and neither will Satan; therefore, you cannot side with both. The test of your allegiance is really quite simple. You are the subject of the one you crown in your heart – not the one you flatter with your tongue.

To know if Christ is really your Prince, answer these questions:

(i) *How did your prince come to the throne?* You are Satan's subject by birth, just like the rest of the human race. It stands to reason that Satan would not voluntarily resign his place in your heart. And you know you cannot resist his power by your own efforts. Only Christ by His Holy Spirit can bring a change of government to your heart. Have you ever heard a voice from heaven calling out to you as it did to Paul, prostrating you at God's feet and turning you about-face toward heaven? Has Christ come to you like the angel to Peter in prison, wrenching the chains of darkness from your mind and conscience, making you obedient? If so, you may claim to have your freedom.

But if in all this I seem to speak a strange language, and you know no such work to have been done upon your spirit, then I fear you are still in the old prison. Do you suppose for a moment that an invading nation could overthrow a government and the citizens not know? Can one king be dethroned and another crowned in your soul, and you hear no scuffle at all? When Christ is crowned, the joyous celebration at His coronation will resound throughout your whole being. When He comes to you and wrests your spirit from Satan, you will know it. You must say, like the man sent by Jesus to wash in the pool of Siloam, 'Whereas I was blind, now I see' (*John 9:25*). Are you able to say it is thus with you?

(ii) *Whose law do you obey?* The laws of the prince of darkness and the Prince of peace are as contrary as their natures – one a law of sin (*Rom. 8:2*), and the other a law of holiness (*Rom. 7:12*). Unless sin has already blinded you so that you can no longer discern between the holy and the profane, you should have no problem resolving this issue.

When Satan comes to tempt you, observe your behavior. How do you respond to his enticements? Do you stand fast on the ordinances of God and refuse to be swayed? Or does your soul embrace the temptation as a bosom friend, glad for an excuse to entertain it? If so, you are under the power of Satan! In the words of Paul, 'Know ye not, that to whom ye yield yourselves servants to obey, his servants ye are?' (*Rom. 6:16*).

(iii) *Where do you go for protection?* Who has your confidence? A good prince is eager to protect his subjects. He expects them to trust him with their safety. Obedient subjects therefore commit state matters to the wisdom of their prince and his council. When wronged, they appeal for justice; when guilty, they submit to the penalty of the law and bear their proper punishment.

Do you trust the wisdom of God to deal justly with you? An impenitent man is afraid to trust himself to God's care. He knows what a thorough housecleaning his soul needs, but he likes the filth and wants to keep it. So he locks the doors and windows to all that is pure and righteous, and spreads a lusty feast for his own sinful nature to devour in private. Now the same fear that drives the wicked man away from God, encourages the gracious one to throw open his heart to the Spirit's knock. He welcomes the prospect of a cleansed soul and understands that the purging God sends is to get rid of carnal refuse and make room for added blessings.

(iv) *With whom do you sympathize?* He is your prince whose victories and losses you take to heart. What do you say when God's Spirit stands in the threshold of your will and blocks the sin Satan is soliciting? If on Christ's side, you will love Him all the more for keeping you from sin. But if otherwise, you will harbor a grudge against God because He kept you from your heart's real desire. When Satan returns, as he surely will, he will find you still pining for the lust that was turned away from your door. And he always gratifies the soul that longs for sin.

When you see God blessing the efforts of His children, how do you respond? Hearing that the gospel thrives, does your spirit swell in songs of praise? If you are still a child of the devil, any triumph over sin is a defeat for your camp. The sound of the saints' rejoicing will clang in your ears like a miscast bell. You will go muttering to your house, like Haman, inwardly furious that some favorite sin of yours has been snatched away and given to Christ for destruction. But if God is truly your Father, your heart will leap to hear the bells of victory whenever sin is defeated by your fellow soldiers.

(v) *Have you joined the troops that fight to subdue the insurrections of evil men spurred on by Satan?* Just standing on the sidelines and cheering other saints to victory is not enough. You too must run the race that is set before you. If you are a saint, you belong to God and you run, not for yourself, but for Him. His desires must come before your own. If subjects could choose where they would like to live, most would ask to stay in the palace with the prince.

But usually this is not in the best interests of their lord. So those who love him most not only gladly deny themselves the delicacies of court, but volunteer for service along the border where the enemy is strongest. And they thank their prince for the honor of serving him!

Paul, upon these terms, was willing to have his day of coronation in glory postponed and his day of tribulation on earth extended, so that he could keep on sowing seeds for the kingdom. Serving God is what makes life worthwhile. It gives us a great opportunity to prove our gratitude to Him for redeeming us from Satan's power and translating us into the kingdom of His dear Son. Begin at once, Christian, to redeem your time. What you mean to do for God, do quickly.

Check your heart. If you find that a transfer of title has indeed been made out to Christ, praise God that you are a citizen of heaven and not of hell. Mark the day of your spiritual birth on the calendar of your heart and call for a celebration! It is your marriage day: 'I have espoused you to one husband . . . Christ,' Paul told the Corinthians (*2 Cor. 11:2*). This same Christ has given you the promise of eternal life. Do you know that from the hour you come under His dominion, all the sweet fruit of the tree of life is yours? It is a perfect gift given in perfect love to the bride which He is even now perfecting.

Dear saint, remind yourself often of the change that God has made in you. Satan will tempt you to doubt the wisdom of choosing Christ as your sovereign, so nail God's promises on the upper doorpost of your heart. They will keep your soul in quarantine; Satan will run from them as from the plague. And don't let time erode the memory of the smoky hole where Satan kept you in the bondage of sin, or he may entice you back with his old lies and broken promises. Compare this horror to the taste of heaven you have already received and know that your greatest joy on earth is but a whiff of all that heaven holds.

Clinging to such a wonderful prospect should give you the courage you need to serve Christ faithfully while Satan's principality prospers all around you. You cannot excuse yourself from service. Even though you may not be called to preach and baptize, you can still be used to help those who are. Your prayers whet the minister's sword; they break down barriers so Christ's kingdom can be enlarged.

You serve a prince who knows your heart. Nothing pleases Him more than for you to love Him completely. How He longs to know that if you were free to choose your own king and to make your own laws, you would choose none other than Himself, nor any laws except those He has already decreed.

II. THEIR POWERS

In the second branch of Paul's description of the archenemy, he talks about the strength, or powers, by which the devil supports his claim to sovereignty. If he were a powerless potentate, we could simply disregard his self-exaltation. But he, along with the horde of demons who are his accomplices, does have a degree of power to back his claim. It may be helpful to explore the devils' power by considering the following: their names, their nature, their number, their order and unity, and the mighty works that are credited to them.

First, then, how do their names reflect their power? The devils have names of great power ascribed to them in Scripture. Satan is singled out as the most powerful of all. He is called the 'strong man' (*Luke 11:21*) – so strong that he keeps his house in peace, defying all the sons of Adam. We know from our own experience that flesh and blood is no match for him. Christ must come from heaven to

[151]

destroy him and his works, or we would all die in our sins.

He is also called the 'roaring lion' (*1 Pet. 5:8*), the beast that rules the whole jungle. When a lion roars, the sound of his voice so petrifies his prey that he can walk calmly among them and devour them without resistance. Such a lion is Satan, who moves with ease among sinners, preying on them at will (*2 Tim. 2:26*). He takes them alive as easily as the fowler entices a bird into the net with a scrap of bread. If the truth were known, the devil finds most sinners so naive and spiritless that he needs only to appear with a proposition, and they yield without the slightest twist of the arm. Only the children of the most high God dare to oppose him and, if need be, resist to blood.

Another name for Satan is 'the great red dragon,' who with his tail (i.e., wicked men) sweeps down the third part of the stars of heaven (*Rev. 12:3, 4*). He is also called 'the prince of the power of the air' (*Eph. 2:2*), because as a prince he can muster his subjects and call them to report for duty at any time.

But his most powerful title of all is 'the god of this world' (*2 Cor. 4:4*). It is given to him because sinners grant him a godlike worship, mistakenly holding him in reverence as the saints do God Himself.

The nature of demons also makes them mighty. Remember, these fallen creatures were once angels and have not yet been stripped of all their power. Scripture verifies the potency of angels: 'Bless the Lord, ye his angels, that excel in strength,' wrote David (*Ps. 103:20*). It is also recorded that the Israelites ate angels' food – that is, the food of the mighty (*Ps. 78:25*). This power of angelic nature appears first of all in its superiority over the rest of God's creatures. Angels are placed at the pinnacle of creation. Man is beneath them, according to *Hebrews 2:7*. Now in the works of creation, the superior has power over the inferior: the beasts over the grass and herbs, man over the beasts, and angels over man.

Next, angels are superior because of the spirituality of their nature. The weakness of man resides in his flesh. His soul is made for great enterprises, but it is weighed down by a lump of flesh and must row with a strength suitable to its weak partner. Devils, being angels by virtue of creation, have no such encumbrance, no fumes from a fleshly intellect to cloud their understanding, no clog at their heel to retard their motion. They are as swift as a flame of fire carried on the wind. Being spiritual, they cannot be resisted with human force. Neither fire nor sword can hurt them. No one is strong enough to bind them except God, the Father of spirits.

By his fall the devil lost much of his power in relation to the holy and happy estate in which he was created, but not his natural abilities. He is an angel still, and still has an angel's power.

In addition to their names and nature, the vast number of devils adds to their power. What is lighter than a grain of sand? Yet number makes it weighty. What creature is smaller than lice? Yet what grief a plague of them brought the Egyptians! Think how formidable devils must be, who are by nature so powerful and by number such a multitude. Satan has enough devils to harass the whole earth; not a place under heaven where he has not stationed his troops; not a person on earth without some of these cursed spirits tracking him wherever he goes.

For special service Satan can send a legion to keep garrison in a single person (*Mark 5:9*). And if he can spare so many to attack one, how many must there be on the muster roll of Satan's whole army? Do not be surprised to find your march to heaven difficult, since you must pass through the very quarters of this demonic multitude.

[153]

When God cast these rebels out of heaven, they became aliens on earth. Ever since, they have been wandering fitfully, seeking to do mischief to the children of men – especially those traveling on heaven's road.

Besides their vast number, the unity and order among devils makes their number even more formidable. We cannot say there is love among them. Such a heavenly fire cannot burn in a devil's bosom. Yet there is unity and order in their common goal to overcome both God and man. Knit together not by ligaments of love but of hatred and policy, they know their prospects are utterly hopeless if they do not all agree in their evil design.

How faithful they are to this wicked brotherhood! Our Lord testified to this when He said, 'If Satan cast out Satan, he is divided against himself' (*Matt. 12:26*). Did you ever hear of a mutiny in the devil's army? Or that any of these apostate angels freely yielded one soul to Christ?

They are many, and yet there is but one spirit of wickedness in them all. 'My name is Legion; for we are many,' the devil said to Christ (*Mark 5:9*). Note he did not say, '*Our* name. . . . ' These cursed spirits work together in their schemes and will enlist human co-operation whenever they can. Not content with bare obedience, they work on the darkest souls to extract an oath of faithfulness, as in the case of witches.

Yet another declaration of the power of devils is their mighty works. What dreadful effects this prince of the power of the air can produce in nature! He is no creator, so he cannot make the least breath of air, drop of water, or spark of fire. But let him loose in God's storehouse, and he will use the Creator's tools so deftly that no man can stand before them. He can hurl the sea into such a commotion that the depths boil like a pot, and fan the air into storms and tempests that threaten to bring the very heavens crashing down to earth. He can light the fuse of the celestial cannon, causing such dreadful thunder and lightning as shall not only frighten but do grave damage as well. If you doubt it, read how he killed Job's children by sending a gale-force wind that buried them in the ruins of their house (*Job 1:19*).

Nor is his power limited to the natural elements. It also gives him control over beasts. Recall the herd of swine he drove into the sea. He apparently has some power (with God's permission) over the bodies of men as well, for we read that Job's boils were not merely a natural physical affliction, but the print of Satan's fangs on his flesh.

Now all such attacks Satan counts small game. His great spite is at the souls of men. He uses a physical disturbance only to upset the equilibrium of the soul. He knows how quickly its rest and peace are disturbed by the groans and complaints of the body under whose roof it dwells. Truly, if Satan had no other way to work his will on us except by taking advantage of our frail constitutions, he would still have a great advantage. I grieve to see the soul fallen so far beneath its divine origin! The body, which was intended to be its servant, has instead become its master, and rules with a merciless hand.

Regardless, Satan is not limited to harassing our bodies to get to our souls. He has a nearer way of access. When man first fell, he splintered his soul's barricade against sin and left the way wide open for the spirit Satan to enter, bag and baggage, and make himself at home. He would not leave a soul on earth uninhabited if God did not call a halt to the procession. Christ's saving and keeping power is the only thing that protects anyone from this intruder

Satan is crafty and admires the wisdom of God, so he works in the wicked in much the same way God works in His saints. God works effectually in the saints (*Gal. 2:8; 1*

Thess. 2:13); Satan works effectually in the children of disobedience (*Eph.* 2:2). But the fruits of their labor bear no resemblance at all. The Spirit brings knowledge and righteousness to the saints' hearts (*Eph.* 5:9), while Satan brings envy and all unrighteousness to the wicked. The Holy Spirit fills with comfort; Satan fills with terror – as with Judas, who first became traitor to his Master and later hangman to himself.

If you are a saint, you do not need to fear that Satan will infiltrate your soul. God will not permit it. But the devil can and does attack along the borders of your faith. Though you are not the proper subject of his power, you are and always will be the chief object of his wrath. He wrestles with you at every opportunity, and you will only overcome him as long as God supplies His strength in your behalf. If He steps aside, you will immediately find out how helpless you are against your strong opponent. He has sent the finest among your ranks home, trembling and crying to God, with their hearts' blood streaming from their wounded consciences.

All this study of Satan's power may cause you some discouragement, but that is not my intention at all. These are valuable lessons, which will help you on your march toward heaven and fit you for the kingdom.

By studying Satan, we see that power is no basis for pride. Carnal pride is the illegitimate offspring of power. It is a lust conceived in the womb of Satan, and though your heart may swell at its birth, it will be to your spirit as Cain to Abel – a deadly foe disguised as your next of kin.

Power is the rightful attribute of God alone. We mortals make a poor showing when we claim it as our own, and so does Satan. The devil, in fact, is the most miserable of all God's creatures, and all the more because he has so much power to misuse. Had he lost all his angelic prowess when he fell, he would have gained by his loss. Tremble, therefore, at any power you have unless you use it for God. A plague of locusts is no more destructive in a field of ripened wheat than prideful power is to a man's grace.

Are you powerful? How do you spend this gift from God? On His work, or on the satisfaction of your own lusts? Here is one of Satan's finest instruments of temptation. Power is a citizen of the world and is equal to the task Satan assigns. It dresses itself first in one fashion, then in another – all designed to impress the rest of mankind. And most are so near-sighted, they are taken in by its false show. Sometimes power parades in the finest silks and jewels, pretending that wealth is the key to greatness. Or it dons the robes of a respected profession and disdains to speak to those of meaner occupations. Then it may dress in military regalia and demand the instant obedience of hundreds and thousands of men beneath its rank. Yet for all its show of strength, power is an iridescent bubble floating on the wind. God need only nod His omnipotent head, and it will disappear into nothing.

Happy would devils be, and happy would worldly potentates be, if at the Judgment they could appear in the garb of some poor slave to receive their sentence. On that day, all their titles and dignity and riches will be read no longer for their honor, but for their eternal shame and damnation.

I do not doubt – nor should you – that Satan's power makes it harder to gain heaven. If the devil is so mighty and the way to heaven so crowded with his mischief-makers, then surely it will cost us something before we can display our banners on the walls of the new Jerusalem. If you see someone taking a long, treacherous journey alone and unprotected, you conclude he expects no thieves on the road and you might well question his wisdom. Many pretenders to Christianity travel in a similar fashion. They tell you they are on their way to heaven, yet they show little inclination to travel in the company of the saints – as if they had no need of fellowship on the journey! Most of them go unfortified, without anything even resembling armour. Others brandish some vain, flighty hopes of the mercy of God, without so much as a single Scripture for ammunition. Such 'hope' is a rusty pistol and will fly in the fool's face when he tries to use it.

These men, many of whom are highly successful by the world's standards, never got their earthly fortunes with so little effort as they expect to get heaven. They know from experience that fortunes are not won while sleeping, nor are families provided for by standing around with their hands in their pockets. The farther along the road to success, the more crooks there are who will try to cheat you. And the closer the Christian gets to heaven, the more there are who will try to cheat his soul and steal his crown of glory if they can. Mark this well: You can never defend yourself alone against Satan; nor with Satan, against God. But align yourself with Christ, and you will be delivered from both self and Satan.

Praise be to God! Satan's power is mighty, but no reason for you to despair. What a marvelous comfort God gives His children in allowing us to see that we do not need to fear Satan. Let them fear him who fear not God. What are his mountains of power before you, Christian? You serve a God who can make a worm thresh a mountain! (*Isa. 41:15*). Surely, then, He can take care of you. The greatest blow Satan can strike at your courage is to cause you to nourish too great a fear of him in your bosom.

I have been told there are wild beasts that, though stronger than the lion, yet tremble when he roars. How many needless hours have you spent trembling at the appearance of Satan when you have th^ power, in Christ, to trample him under your feet! Strive for a proper perspective of Satan's power, and then this lion will not appear so fierce. Three considerations will relieve you when at any time you are in danger of thinking his power is omnipotent.

In the first place, it is a *derived* power. It is not his by right, but by permission from another and that other is God. All power is of God, whether on earth or in hell. Get your faith to embrace this truth and you can walk anywhere with absolute confidence that Satan can do you no permanent harm. Do you think for a moment your heavenly Father would give His archenemy a sword too mighty for you, His own child, to overcome? Since God provides the enemies' arms, you can be sure they will be of little use against you if you place yourself under God's protection.

When Pilate tried to frighten Christ by boasting of his power to pardon or condemn his prisoner, Christ replied that Pilate could do nothing ' . . . except it were given thee from above' (*John 19:11*). In other words, 'Do your worst. I know who sealed your commission.' Satan buffets, man persecutes – but God is the One who gives them both power.

Another thing about Satan's power you should know is that it is *limited*, and that in two ways: Satan does not have enough power to do all he wants to do, nor does he have God's permission to use all the power he possesses.

His desires are boundless, not only here below but in heaven itself. There his fondest wish is to dethrone God and set himself in that sacred place. But he cannot have this desire, nor many of the others that burn within him. He is but a creature and so has a length to his tether. God can and does limit Satan, but Satan can never limit God. And since God is safe, then you are too, for 'your life is hid with Christ in God' (*Col. 3:3*).

Herein is great consolation: Satan cannot command you to sin against your will. Though he can move you faster on your way, as the wind carries the tide more swiftly to shore, he cannot turn the current of your heart contrary to its own course and tendency.

Just as God decides how much power Satan may have, He also controls how much of his power he may expend at any one time. There may be times when you feel that God has left you to fight alone. That is when your faith must do its hardest work. Hold fast to the assurance that God is watching every move of Satan and will not let him have the final victory. He can, when God allows it, rob the Christian of much of his peace and joy, but he is always under command. When God says 'Stay!' he must stand like a dog by the table while the saints feast on God's comfort. He does not dare to snatch even a tidbit, for the Master's eye is always on him. You lose much comfort when you forget that God's hand is always raised above Satan, and His loving eye is always on you.

Not only is Satan's power derived and limited, it is also *subservient* to the overruling power of God. Whatever mischief he devises is appointed by God for the ultimate service and benefit of the saints. It is as true of the devil as of the proud Assyrian, that ' . . . he intendeth not so, neither doth his heart think so' (*Isa. 10:7*), for the devil's heart is always bent toward destroying all men.

But God's intention is otherwise, as many wise saints have learned through the ages. When told what had passed at the Diet of Nuremberg against the Protestants, Luther simply said, 'It was decreed one way there, but otherwise in heaven.' So for the saints' comfort, the thoughts God speeds to them are of peace and preservation, whereas Satan's are of ruin and destruction. Who will doubt that God's thoughts can outrun the devil's?

Know that while Satan is persecuting, God is purging (*Dan. 11:35*). Most of the stains on your graces get there while you feast on peace and prosperity, and they never recover their whiteness as well as when they have come from under Satan's scouring. He sends discouragement, or grief, or despair to swallow up the saint (as the whale swallowed Jonah). But God uses the tribulation instead to sand and polish your faith, so that in the end it is finer and more precious than ever.

We do too little if we do not fear Satan at all. But we flatter him overmuch when we fear him more than we trust God. If you are Christ's, nothing can come into your life without the permission of God. The One who has given life to be yours, has given death also. The One who has given heaven for your inheritance has also given the world with all its afflictions – including the prince of this world in all his wrath and power. This, indeed, is love and wisdom in a riddle. But you who have the Spirit of Christ can unfold it.

III. THE DEVILS' KINGDOM ('THE DARKNESS OF THIS WORLD')

Satan would like nothing better than to convince you that he is 'lord over all,' even though he knows this title belongs exclusively to God. Satan is a ruler of the 'darkness of this world' only and is therefore God's subordinate. The boundaries of his empire are circumscribed and limited. First, the *time* this prince rules is 'in this world,' not hereafter. Second, the *place* he rules is 'in this world,' not heaven. And third, the *subjects* whom he rules are 'the darkness of this world,' not the children of light.

To begin, then, Satan's empire is bounded by time. 'This world' is that little spot of time bounded on either side by vast eternity. On this stage Satan plays the role of a prince. But when Christ calls for the final curtain at the end of this age, Satan will be exposed before everyone, his crown taken off and his sword broken over his head. He will be driven off the stage in utter disrepute, to become the eternal prisoner of hell. No more will he infest the saints or rule the wicked. Instead, both he and all the members of his cast will lie under the immediate execution of God's wrath. The long run of their vile acts will be over for ever.

To this very end Christ has His commission, and His work will not be finished until 'he shall have put down all rule and all authority and power' (*1 Cor. 15:24*). Then, and not until then, He will deliver up His kingdom to the Father. 'For he must reign, till he hath put all enemies under his feet' (*v. 25*). The question is not *whether* Christ will subdue Satan – but *when*.

The fact that Satan's days are numbered is bad news for the wicked. Sinners at present have a merry time of it and seem to think it will go on for ever. On any given day you can hear them laughing while Christ's disciples weep and mourn. They rustle by in their silks, while the saints shiver in rags. The devil is careful to gratify their sensuous nature, as a prince rewards his courtiers with pensions and preferments. 'Am I not able indeed to promote thee to honor?' Balak asked Balaam (*Num. 22:37*).

Oh, it is strange – and yet not strange, considering man's degenerate nature – to see how Satan leads sinners by the nose with his gilded hook. Let him but bait it with honor, or wealth, or pleasure, and their hearts strain after it as eagerly as fish for a worm. He can get them to sin for a morsel of bread. It happened to Demas, who forsook the gospel for the world's pleasures.

An evil heart is so eager to collect the bonuses which the devil promises that it ignores the dreadful wages God threatens to pay for the same work. The men who fall into the devil's snare are those resolved to feast on the fruit of unrighteousness. How it glistens as it hangs on the tree of temptation. One bite, and you want more. But beware! Nothing Satan offers is free of his curse. His rewards are as contaminated as he is. They are poison to the souls of men (*1 Tim. 6:9*).

Would it not be wise, before you barter with the devil, to ask if his promises come with a warranty? Can he secure the bargain and keep you from a lawsuit with God? Can he guarantee that when you die you will not be left destitute in another world? Let the buyer be warned. Time will show how Satan has cheated you. 'Oh, but I have already begun to collect on the pleasures he offers. I am enjoying them right now,' the sinner says. 'And I would have to wait until heaven for most of the things Christ promises.'

Sinner, you are right to say your pleasure is *now*, for you cannot be sure it will last for another moment. Your present happiness is going, and that of the saints, though future, is coming, never to end. Will you, like Esau for a gulp of pottage and immediate gratification, part with the eternal inheritance of God's kingdom? What desperate madness makes sinners refuse a little hardship for the present? They foolishly choose to endure the eternal wrath of God hereafter in exchange for the short feast Satan spreads for them. If Satan keeps you royally entertained for a lifetime, what is that to eternity?

Let this encourage those of you who belong to Christ: The storm may be tempestuous, but it is only temporary. The clouds that are presently rolling over your head will pass, and then you will have fair weather, an eternal sunshine of glory. Can you not watch with Christ for one hour?

Bid faith look through the keyhole of the promise and see what God has laid up for those that love Him. You serve a God who keeps covenant for ever. Having already bathed in the fountain of His tender mercies, how can you stand on this side of eternity, afraid to wet your feet with those short-lived sufferings which, like a little splash of water, run between you and glory?

Besides being bound by time, Satan's empire is also confined as to place. The devil rules 'in this world' only. He cannot ascend to heaven, not even if he marshals all the power of all his demon hosts. The rebel who once shared intimately in God's glory has not dared even to look into that holy place since he was first expelled. So he ranges to and fro here below as a vagabond, excommunicated from the presence of God though not from the saints on their way to heaven.

You can, if you will, take this fact as a source of great joy: Satan has no power where your eternal happiness lies! What do you have of value that is not in heaven? Christ is there, and if you love Him, your heart is there also. Your friends and loved ones who have died in Christ are there, eagerly waiting for you to join them. All your work for the Lord is laid up as treasure inside the walls of that holy city.

Your salvation gives you title to God's kingdom and places you beyond the reach of this low-flying predator if you will but appropriate Christ's power. Such was the case with Job. Let the devil plunder him to his skin and worry him almost out of that as well. Reduced to a bag of bones and boils, he looked death and the devil squarely in the face and did not flinch. He knew Christ was his Redeemer, and he held fast to the promise of a better day when he would be placed beyond the devil's grasp for ever.

Even while confined to this earth, you can be confident that your Father is watching over you. The devil took away Job's purse and left him temporarily destitute, but Job had a God in heaven who replenished his account. As a saint, you have some collateral: your stock of faith, and your deed of inheritance as a citizen of heaven. These are great security both now and for the future. Satan knows it, and will do his best to snatch them away from you. But no matter how hard he tries he cannot blot your name from the Book of Life. He cannot annul your faith, make void your relationship with God, or dry up the spring of your comfort though he may dam up the stream for awhile. Nor can he hinder the glorious outcome of your whole war with sin. God, who is said to preserve us by His power 'through faith unto salvation ready to be revealed in the last time' (*1 Pet. 1:5*), keeps all these things in heaven among His own crown jewels, well out of Satan's reach.

Satan's empire is also restricted as to subjects. The devil's principality is bounded not only by place and time, but also by those he is allowed to govern. They are described as 'the darkness of this world' or, more simply, those who are in darkness.

The word *darkness* is sometimes used in Scripture to express the condition of a person in great distress (*Isa. 50:10*), sometimes to describe the nature of all sin (*Eph. 5:11*), and sometimes to refer to the particular sin of ignorance. It is often compared to the darkness of night or to physical blindness. To enlighten this particular passage, I will take the word in the two following interpretations: first, for the darkness of sin in general; and second, for the darkness of ignorance in particular

Mark this distinction before we begin: The devil's rule is over those who are in a *state* of sin and ignorance, not over those who are sometimes sinful or ignorant. Otherwise, he would take hold of saints as well as unregenerate sinners.

(a) *Why sin is described as darkness*

Over and over in the Scriptures sin is identified with darkness. There are several reasons for using this analogy.

(i) *Spiritual darkness causes sin.* The external cause of sin is Satan, who is its great promoter; the internal cause is the natural darkness of man's soul – the miserable consequence of Adam's fall. When the soul is illumined by the Spirit, the deadly nature of sin is exposed and men flee to God. But when the soul is kept in darkness or hides from the truth, sin goes in disguise and so is welcome.

(ii) *Sin causes spiritual blindness.* While the darkness of our hearts first leads us into sin, it is sin which leads us into greater depths of darkness. Sin drugs the conscience so that what once was noxious becomes palatable and pleasurable. You have perhaps known someone who showed a holy distaste for a certain sin in others, but once he had drunk from the same cup, could no longer see the evil of it or argue against it.

Not only does sin bring darkness to the soul by its very nature, but also sometimes as an express emissary of God. God has warned of the severe consequences of rebelling against the light He offers. His Spirit comes to the black dungeon of your unregenerate soul, carrying the search-light of truth. If you refuse to answer and instead run out at the back door and away to Satan, God has decreed you will 'die without knowledge' (*Job 36:12*) – in other words, in darkness. You flirt with eternal damnation every time you turn your back on Him. Why should He let His candle burn for ever to no avail? Read the edict in His Word: 'My Spirit shall not always strive with man' (*Gen. 6:3*).

(iii) *Sin shuns the light.* To a sinner, the light of truth is more blistering than a desert sun at mid-day (*John 3:19*).

He shuns to walk where it is shining, and when exposed to it, will spare no expense to get relief. Satan is always at his elbow, ready to help him find a way to hide from its penetrating rays.

Does he hear the truth in a powerful sermon? Satan will sit alongside him in the pew and whisper nonsense to distract him. He may ask his plans for dinner, or what is on the docket for tomorrow. And if the sermon gets too hot, the devil will dull his senses and get him to doze until the service is over. Suppose a man's conscience strains toward the truth. Satan may then send him to hear a cool preacher, whose senseless prattle will tickle his fancy rather than prick his conscience. Oh, he may preach from the Word of God, but he does it gingerly. He is too cowardly to use the Sword of the Spirit in all its might and power, lest he 'offend' some members of his congregation. Many who dare to handle the truth and even admire it when encased in a scabbard would faint on the spot to see it drawn and bared.

(iv) *Both sin and darkness cause distress*. What could the Egyptians do under the plague of darkness but sit still and hope it would pass? A man in a state of sin is under the same plague. He can do nothing profitable until God lifts the darkness from his soul. The epitaph of every impenitent sinner could fitly read: 'Here lies one who never did an hour's work for God.'

And if he can do God no service while kept in darkness, neither can he help himself. Pity the man whose darkness hides the disservice he does to his own soul! He is like one who stands helplessly in a dark cellar, supposing himself trapped and doomed to die. But if a candle were lit, he would find the key to the door within easy reach. Christ is the candle that lights the way out of man's darkness. He stands with open arms, offering deliverance. Nothing but

[167]

the prayer of repentance stands between the sinner and his salvation, yet the darkness of his soul keeps him bound in Satan's prison.

This brings us to another cause of great distress: Darkness fills the heart with terror. The wicked have no peace. Even when they sleep, their consciences rest only fitfully. They eat in fear, drink in fear, celebrate in fear. They do not have a single pleasure in this life that is not tainted by its putrid stench.

(v) *Sin leads to utter darkness*. On this earth there is some mixture of darkness and light, even for the vilest sinner – some peace with trouble, some pleasure with pain, some hope of pardon. But in eternity there is darkness to the utmost. There the fire of wrath will burn without slacking, and sin keep pace with utter torment.

(b) *Why those in darkness are under Satan's rule*

Satan is called the 'ruler of the darkness of this world.' All those in a state of darkness are therefore under his rule by God's decree. Scripture tells us sinners are the very dwelling place of the devil. Do you recall the account where the unclean spirit determined to 'return into my house' (*Matt. 12:44*)? It is as though he said, 'I have walked among the saints of God, knocking at this door and that, and no one will let me in. But I know who will. I will go back to my own house, where I am sure to rule with complete control.' And sure enough, when he returns he finds it empty and ready for his enjoyment. Every inclination of the soul is employed to make the house trim and handsome for the master.

Those in darkness have no power to resist Satan. He rules the whole man, shaping his apprehensions and distorting his perceptions. If he reads the Scripture, Satan stands by with his own running commentary, twisting the truth into a maze of lies. If he shows any distaste for sin,

Satan has him view it through the rose-colored glasses of compromise. And while the sinner may think his insight is greatly improved, in truth, he remains under manifold delusions. In fact, Satan is so gracious in lending this or that instrument of unrighteousness, he often is taken for a friend rather than a cruel master. But a man can no sooner cut the tether by which Satan keeps him pastured in sin than the woodsman's axe can chop a tree of its own accord.

Yet here is hope for everyone: Christ the Good Shepherd is standing by. If you will cry out to Him, though it be no louder than the pitiful bleating of the weakest lamb, He will hear and will come to your rescue at once.

Take a long, hard look at the deplorable condition of everyone in a state of sin. What tongue can utter or what heart conceive the misery of this state? What greater abomination than for devils to display their banners in the souls of men and pollute the throne which was made for God to sit upon? No worse pestilence scours the earth than Satan, who greedily devours both heart and spirit. If he is your master, expect nothing for your service but fire and torment.

Look up before it is too late, and behold Christ sent by God to recover His throne and your liberty. If you only knew what the privileges of Christ's servants are, you would say the only happy men in the world are those who walk continually with Him. His laws are written not with His subjects' blood, as Satan's are, but with His own. All His commands are acts of grace. To be commissioned by Him is a privilege, and to be given a present assignment that keeps you in His company is ample reward for past service.

Jesus Christ is a prince who loves to see His people thrive and grow rich under His government. But Satan's fake propaganda is widely distributed among sinners. In

[169]

fact, sometimes when Christ comes to open the doors of their prison and set them free, they shrink back in terror from the very One who has loved them from the beginning.

What a mystery this is that forlorn souls bound by the chains of their lusts and doomed to damnation should, as they are driven to execution, refuse the Lord's deliverance. Surely, dying in their sins, they cannot hope for a better resurrection than they have a death. I am afraid they do not believe they will have any resurrection at all and suppose themselves safe once in the grave. But let sinners know the grave will not hold them when God calls His prisoners to the bar. Death was never intended to be a sanctuary for sinners, but a prison to hold them until the Day of Judgment. Oh, how surprised they will be to see Him become their judge whom they now refuse as king! Renounce the devil's rule while there is still time. Cry out for mercy and grace while they are still to be had. If you save your tears for another world, they will be to no avail.

(c) *Warning to beware of Satan's tricks*

Earlier we considered some of Satan's activities against the saints. Look now at the tasks he undertakes to keep his proper servants, sinners, in subjection to the laws of sin and death.

(i) *Satan intercepts God's messages to the lost.* He knows that contemplation is the first step to repentance. When Pharaoh observed the Israelites' thoughts turning back to God, he knew it was a dangerous sign. He supposed he could hinder their spiritual deliverance by increasing their physical bondage, so he intensified their workload. Satan does the same with his slaves, keeping them too busy to think of heaven or hell. He never leaves them, always working to intercept any thoughts of grace, mercy, peace, or repentance sent by the Holy Spirit.

(ii) *Satan interferes with God's messengers.* When God sent Moses to deliver Israel, Satan sent Jannes and Jambres to resist him (*Ex. 7:11*). When Paul preached truth to the deputy, Elymas countered with lies (*Acts 13:8*). Satan has spies on every corner, watching the activities of the saints. When God sends His children on an errand of mercy to a sinner, these spies race to beat them and block their way.

Sinner, be especially wary of carnal friends and relatives when you decide to follow Christ. Resolve that if your own children grab you by the ankles and try to hold you back from Him, you will drive them away. And if your father and mother throw themselves in front of you, you will step over their backs if you must, to get to Christ. Let those who will, mock and scorn your faith. What is heaven worth if you cannot bear a little shame? If they spit on your face, Christ will wipe it off. They may laugh at you now, but not later. The final outcome has already been declared, and you have sided with the victor.

(iii) *Satan distracts sinners with delays.* He does not fear fleeting thoughts of repentance. I doubt there are many in hell who did not at one time or another give some thought to repenting, but Satan was always able to carry them away on some more urgent business. Sinner, if you ever hope to escape, run for your life – away from Satan, away from your lusts, away from your present joys if they are the handiwork of Satan. The devil says, 'Tomorrow.' God says, 'Today.' Whom will you obey?

(iv) *Satan proposes a compromise.* When a sinner's conscience remains unsettled after all the devil's efforts, Satan will make small concessions. Pharaoh finally agreed to let the Israelites go into the wilderness to offer a sacrifice, but he insisted, 'Ye shall not go very far away' (*Ex. 8:28*). Thus, the sinner may pray, or hear the Word, or make some mild profession, as long as he does not go very far from his sins. But Christ must be king of all your heart, or He is not king at all. Just as Moses declared not a hoof would be left behind when the Israelites left Egypt (*Ex. 10:26*), so the sinner must bid an everlasting farewell to his sin, leaving nothing behind to occasion a return visit.

Deliverance is at your door if you but call on Christ. He that heard the cry of Israel in Egypt will hear yours too, and come at once to your imprisoned spirit. Do not doubt it! Though He is prince of all, yet He chooses you as His bride: 'Thy Maker is thine husband; . . . thy Redeemer the Holy One of Israel' (*Isa. 54:5*). But you must leave Egypt before the wedding takes place. What does Satan have to offer that compares to this?

(d) *The blinding power of ignorance*

Ignorance, above other sins, enslaves a soul to Satan. A knowledgeable man may be his slave by choice, but an ignorant man has no other option. His ignorance may carry him safely past a few sins, but it will drop him at the very feet of more than it saves him from. The escape route from ignorance is well marked, but it is sometimes a rugged path. Perhaps that is why so many live and die ignorant. Where is hope for an ignorant man? Knowledge is the key (*Luke 11:52*); Christ is the way to freedom (*John 14:6*). Ignorance, on the other hand, shuts out Christ but leaves the door wide open for Satan.

(i) *Ignorance opens the door to sin.* An ignorant person is in the same predicament as a sleepwalker who treads barefoot upon an asp and never feels its sting. He falls headlong into sin and never realizes he has been mortally wounded. We read of some 'laden with sins,' who are 'never able to come to the knowledge of the truth' (*2 Tim. 3:6, 7*). Their lives bear nothing but bitter fruit, fed and watered by their own ignorance!

(ii) *Ignorance locks sin up in the soul*. We have already said that ignorance causes darkness. Darkness commonly induces sleep; a blind mind and a drowsy conscience are common bedfellows. An ignorant man will sin and never flinch. Woe to those who are so empty-headed they never even know they are guilty! They face certain death with the complacency of a child who toddles out to play in the very waves that will pull him out to sea and devour him in one thirsty gulp.

If what I say speaks to you, rouse yourself at once. Go quickly and barter with God to exchange your ignorance for His wisdom. Feed your mind on His Word. Conscience is God's alarm to wake the sinner up, but it can only be a witness to what it knows. If not informed of the truth, it will not sound when heresy or sin creeps in and sets fire to your soul. And if you do not wake up and quench the flames with timely repentance, you will burn for ever.

(iii) *Ignorance locks out the means of rescue*. Friends and ministers stand outside and cannot save a burning man if he will not let them in. Neither threats nor promises are of any use if you are counseling a willfully ignorant man. He fears not the one and desires not the other. Write 'Danger!' as large as you can, and paint it red; it will no more serve as a warning to a blind man than to a dumb ox.

Yet there will be times in a sinner's life when, by the grace of God's Holy Spirit, he senses the oppression of his soul and longs for deliverance. So he feels around for an avenue of escape. There are some ways which at first seem right to him, and Satan will lead him on a merry chase down one dead-end street after another to keep him off heaven's road. 'Try good works,' he will say. 'That will lift your spirits.' Or, 'Make some new resolutions and promise yourself to be a better person from now on. What more could God expect from you?' But at last, exhausted and disillusioned by all his misguided meanderings, the sinner looks up to find himself right back where he started – a slave to sin and darkness!

Our omniscient God has known all along that the way to heaven can never be found in the dark; that is why He sent His Son as the Light of the world. There is but one safe exit from your darkened state, one way of escape – through Jesus Christ our Lord. Let your faith join hands with His promise of eternal life for all who believe on Him, and He will lead you out of darkness and into the glorious light of the gospel.

(e) *Warning to beware of ignorance*

(i) *To parents of ignorant children.* Parents, your children have souls which God expects you to nourish with at least as much care as you lavish on their physical needs. Who will teach them if not you? No one is surprised to hear that a ship put out to sea without a compass has sunk or run aground. Why should we be surprised to see children wander far from God, when they have received no spiritual direction?

We see a pattern set for us by the saints of old. David, busy king that he was, thought it his solemn responsibility to instruct his son in the ways of the Lord: 'Know thou the God of thy father, and serve him with a perfect heart and with a willing mind' (*1 Chron. 28:9*). And what need I tell you of Timothy's mother and grandmother, who taught him the Scriptures from the time he was a child? I believe a man calls in question his own Christianity if he does not bother to acquaint his child with God and the way that leads to Him. I will even go so far as to say I have never known a true saint who was not deeply concerned about his child's relationship with the heavenly Father.

You will give a poor account at the Last Day if all you can say is, 'Lord, here are my children. I bred them gentlemen and left them wealthy.' What a mocking witness to your own folly that you would do so much for that which rusts, and nothing for a knowledge of God unto salvation, which endures forever!

A careful study of the principles of God will show how serious this matter is. If we neglect the spiritual training of our children, we fail on three fronts.

You obviously fail your children when you leave them ignorant. Faith and unbelief are fundamentally different, not only by definition but in the way they operate as well. Faith will not grow without planting, and will die even where it is planted unless it is watered and fertilized with the Word of God. Atheism, irreligion, and profanity, on the other hand, not only grow without planting, but will not die without forceful plucking up. Indeed, they thrive best in an untended soul – until simple ignorance and disbelief in the child become willful attitudes in the man.

What a grave injustice is done through your neglect! Your child is not born with a Bible in his heart or in his head. Satan has already done his work by sowing the seeds of unbelief in the womb at conception. Now you must do yours. The strain of faith you plant in your children's hearts must be hardy enough to spring up and choke out the tares of Satan. And the best season for planting faith is in a child's youth.

You also fail yourselves by leaving your children in a state of ignorance, for you heap upon yourselves the consequences of their sins as well as your own. When a child breaks one of God's commandments, it is his sin; but it is also the father's if he never taught the child what the commandment of God was. Wicked children become heavy crosses to their parents. When a father or mother must trace the source of wickedness to his or her own neglect in training the child, cross is laid upon cross and the load becomes unbearable. Can there be a greater heartache in this life than to see your own child running full speed toward hell, and know that you were the one who outfitted him for the race? Oh, do your best while they are young and in your constant care, to win them to God and set them on the road to heaven.

Most important, you fail God when you rear an ignorant child. Scripture tells of those who hold the truth in unrighteousness. Among others, this includes parents who lock up the knowledge of salvation from their children. Where is the parent who will rob his own son's house? Yet this is what you do if you neglect his spiritual education. For you keep in your own pocket the gold talent God intended you to give to your child. If you leave no godly inheritance, what will happen when you die, and the truth of the gospel is buried alongside your rotting bones?

If you are God's child, then your children stand in closer relationship to the heavenly Father than the children of unbelievers. God depends on you to nurture them as you have been nurtured, and to protect them at all costs from the devil's education. Training your children up in the ways of the Lord is no casual suggestion, but a solemn command given to all Christian parents. Your refusal to obey, whether the product of deliberation or neglect, will pay you bitter wages when you stand before the King of kings in the judgment.

(ii) *To ministers – how you become an accessory to ignorance*. Reach out with compassion to those ignorant souls in your congregation who cannot tell their right hand from their left. They are sick unto death and do not even know it. The plague of ignorance is an insidious cancer that silently eats away at the very bowels of their spirits, safe from detection unless the light of knowledge comes in and exposes it.

When knowledge and conscience begin to excise ignorance, the sinner will generally experience some pain leading to conviction. And as physical pain prompts the sick man to go to his physician, so spiritual discomfort drives the sick soul to his minister for counsel. Unfortunately, the ignorant soul shares the leper's curse: he is numb to the pain of his morbid condition. It becomes the minister's duty, therefore, to seek him out and offer a cure.

Do not expect the ignorant to come to you; we have already said they are blind to their own condition. And if by some chance they begin to sense that all is not well in their souls, they are the sort of people who are more afraid of the remedy than of the disease. They will exhaust all their energies to hide their ignorance, rather than have it cured.

To those of you who pastor large congregations, I know how formidable the task of ministering to every ignorant parishioner seems. But let us do for them as much as we can. He who has a large house and only a small income is better off to repair a little now and a little later, than to let the whole thing fall down just because he cannot do everything at once.

It is a blessed thing to be, as Job said he was, 'eyes to the blind' (*29:15*). Such are the ministers God calls 'shepherds according to mine heart,' who feed His people with knowledge and understanding (*Jer. 3:15*). But woe to those who are accessories to their people's ignorance! As a minister, you may aid and abet ignorance in several ways.

First, you may do this by *your own ignorance*. Knowledge is so fundamental to the work and calling of a minister that he cannot fulfill his role without it. 'Because thou hast rejected knowledge, I will also reject thee, that thou shalt be no priest to me; seeing thou hast forgotten the law of thy God, I will also forget thy children' (*Hos. 4:6*). The lack of knowledge in a minister is such a serious defect that nothing else will compensate for it. Be he ever so humble, or patient, or sinless, if he has no skill to divide the Word of truth rightly, he is not cut out to be a preacher.

The usefulness of a thing rests on its ability to perform the task for which it was created. A knife may have a diamond-studded handle, but it is no knife if it will not cut. A bell may be cast in gold, but it is no bell if it will not ring. The primary calling of a minister is to teach others. How, then, can he claim that title if he has not mastered his subject matter?

Ministers are called lights. Now if even the 'light' is darkness, how hopelessly black will be the darkness surrounding the 'light'! Is he not a cruel man who takes a job as pilot for a ship full of passengers, but does not even know how to use a compass? Far worse is the preacher who earns his living by wrecking souls because he is too lazy to study his Bible.

Second, a minister's *negligence* also fosters ignorance. An infant will fare no better with a mother who does not trouble herself to nurse him, than with one who has no milk to give. Pastor, it is not enough for you to know the Word. All your years of training are worthless if you do not use your knowledge to feed Christ's flock. God promises serious consequences to the worthless shepherd (*Zech. 11:17*). It shall be the people's sin if they do not eat when bread is placed before them; but woe to us if we do not give them meat in due season.

Third, *unedifying preaching* fosters ignorance. When a

minister preaches unsound doctrine, he does not perfect the flock's understanding, but corrupts it. Better to leave his sheep in simple ignorance than to color their minds with a false dye.

Some sermons are frothy and flashy, no more nourishing to souls than husks to the prodigal's belly. Other discourses are couched in such complicated theology that they might just as well have been delivered in a foreign language. The latter is a tasty temptation to well-educated ministers: to preach only truths for the mature who have their senses well exercised, and ignore the needs of the greater portion of their hearers. It is true you may find three or four eminent saints who grow spiritually fat on the rich feasts you prepare for them. But in the meantime, most of your congregation will faint for lack of milk because their fragile spirits cannot digest your meaty sermons.

Only an inept builder erects a towering scaffold before he has even laid the foundation for an edifice. The scaffold should rise as the building goes up. The minister, who is to build up the saints, must prepare truths suitable to the level of his hearers. Let the wise have their portion, but let them be patient to see the weaker ones in the family served as well.

Finally, ignorance grows fat on *the scandal of an unholy life*. If the minister's walk is not circumspect, he will undermine the truth of the gospel – like the cook whose dirty apron and unkempt appearance make diners afraid to eat anything he has touched, for fear of becoming contaminated. On the other hand, if the pastor takes carnal pride in his own holiness and walks among his flock with his self-righteous nose lifted high in the air, they will be afraid to come to him for counsel. The one with a true minister's heart must be as careful as a fisherman to see that he does nothing to scare away souls but all to allure and invite, that they may be gently and lovingly trapped in the net of God's grace.

(iii) *To the ignorant.* You who are ignorant, let this stir you from your seats of sloth: Every ignorant soul is the willing slave of Satan!

Are you young? Inquire after God early, while your talents are fresh and your memory is strong. The feet of those lusts which have carried millions of others to perdition stand ready to carry you off the same way. How easy you make their task when you refuse to open the eyes of your understanding and fortify yourself with the knowledge of God.

Perhaps you intend to rouse up from the sleep of ignorance at the eleventh hour, which you suppose is many years away. How foolish! You cannot see the hands on God's clock; therefore, you cannot know how long your stay in the world will be. If you die ignorant of God and His law, what will become of you? The prospect is not pleasant. The small twigs and the old logs – supple young sinners and withered old ones – will meet and burn together.

Are you old and still ignorant? Perhaps you hear nature tolling the passing bell. You know you will shortly come to the end of the road that leads into eternity, but you cannot see what lies in the darkness beyond. The less time you have, the more diligence you must use to gain knowledge. Though knowing the truth of the gospel is no guarantee of salvation, gross ignorance of it is a sure guarantee of damnation.

Are you poor and ignorant? Your sin is not your poverty, but rather your ignorance of where the true treasure lies. 'Better is a poor and wise child than an old and foolish king, who will no more be admonished' (*Eccl.*

4:13). If the princes of the world could only see the end from the beginning, they would beg to trade their ermine robes for the saints' rags. Christian, new robes are being made for you in heaven, which you shall put on – while they shall be left naked in their shame. On that great day you will no longer be sad that you were poor while on earth, but they will be tormented eternally to remember that they who were so rich and great in this world, are made so poor and beggarly in the next.

Are you rich and ignorant? Leave your fields, and labor for the knowledge of the Most High. Solomon had more of the world's treasures than most men will ever see, yet we find him hard at prayer, entreating God for knowledge (*2 Chron. 1:10*). Many wealthy men think themselves privileged and exempt from humbly accepting God's offer of mercy, as if He were bound to save them because they are rich. Oh, the atheism and ignorance that is to be found in those whom the world applauds for their lands and estates! They keep plenty of cash on hand, expecting to purchase a piece of God's kingdom. But their money is not the medium of exchange in heaven. The poorest Christian could teach them a lesson in God's economy if they would only listen. If heaven were to be purchased with houses and lands, then the poor disciples of Jesus would have had a hard time getting through the gates! Praise God, heaven is obtained, not with silver and gold, but with the knowledge that leads to repentance: 'This is life eternal, that they might know thee . . . and Jesus Christ, whom thou hast sent' (*John 17:3*).

(f) *The way to knowledge*

When the light of truth begins to seep into a darkened soul, the sinner can see just enough to realize the seriousness of his dilemma. He may be overwhelmed by the magnitude of his need and ask, 'How can I escape this mire of ignorance?' God provides some simple instructions for the sinking man.

(i) *Acknowledge your ignorance*. Some are blind, like the church of Laodicea, and do not know it (*Rev. 3:17*). Ignorance is a spiritual cataract, but pride keeps this kind of person from seeking a physician. He often considers himself too good to learn from another man, and too bad to be taught by God. Heed this warning if you are such a one: God will accept neither excuse for clinging to ignorance when you stand before Him.

Christ sends out personal invitations to everyone to come and learn at His feet. But the door into His school is low; your pride must stoop to enter. The Master Himself is humble and lowly. How can He teach a haughty student? Therefore, first become a fool in your own eyes. When you hang your head in shame at your own heathenism, then you are ready to be admitted to the school of Christ.

(ii) *Be faithful with your knowledge*. Perhaps you have only a small light to lead you into truth. If so, follow it closely. When it casts a shadow on anything – even the smallest speck – convincing you it is sin, flee from it at once. Or if your light leads you into action for the Lord, follow eagerly and wholeheartedly. How else will your knowledge of the truth grow fat and healthy, unless you exercise it regularly?

Here is a word of caution: use your knowledge properly. God will not bless anyone who uses knowledge as an excuse to sin. Nor will He increase your knowledge of Him if you keep it shut up in your conscience, afraid to confess Him before men. The light of truth in a man's heart is like a candle flame – it must have air to flourish. If you keep it hidden for very long, what little knowledge you have will be taken away. Learn a lesson from what happened to the heathen described in Romans who '[held] the truth in unrighteousness . . . and their foolish heart was darkened' (*Rom. 1:18, 21*).

(iii) *Pray for more wisdom.* God is the repository of all knowledge and wisdom. To excel in the school of divinity, you must study upon your knees. This is the way to place yourself under God's tutelage. You may attend lectures or study in the world's great universities to gain a knowledge of Scripture, but wisdom to apply its precepts comes from God alone. If you wish to be wise, pray, pray, pray! Holy conversing with Him yields *sanctified* knowledge.

Do not hesitate to pray boldly. God gives wisdom to all who ask, and He gives generous, heaping portions. Never be ashamed to go to Him in your ignorance. He is not like those rude, unfeeling teachers we have seen who seem to delight in mocking the ignorance of their pupils. He is a kind teacher, and your desire to learn pleases Him. While everyone does not achieve the same level of understanding in this life, still *all* who come with earnest, open hearts will receive ample instruction to prepare them for the kingdom of heaven. We have this promise from the Psalms: 'Thou shalt guide me with thy counsel, and afterward receive me to glory' (*Ps. 73:24*).

(iv) *Study regularly.* Set aside a regular time to search for truth, which like gold lies deep and must be excavated. When God expelled Adam from paradise, He sentenced him to a life of sweat and toil. From that day to this, man can do nothing without labor (except sin, which unfortunately he comes by naturally). Do not expect the Holy Spirit to transform you miraculously from an ignorant sinner into a learned Christian unless you are willing to burn some late night oil. In John's Gospel, we are admonished to 'search the Scriptures' (*5:39*). The word 'search' implies careful scrutiny and diligent investigation, not an idle curiosity. If you want knowledge, you must be willing to put forth extra effort to get it.

If something is worth this much exertion, will we carelessly toss it aside once it is in our possession? If so, we show our gross ignorance of its true value. If we read the Scriptures – even memorize them – yet show no inclination to use the knowledge for our own or others' good, we suffer serious consequences. Speculative knowledge, like Rachel, is fair but barren. A sick man may learn all that is known about his disease, including the cure. But unless he applies the knowledge and takes the cure, he will die just the same as if he had remained ignorant. Man, whose soul is sick unto death, can study the Scriptures and all the great theologians of the world. But if his faith will not take the precious blood of Christ as remedy for his own personal, morbid condition, he will die in his sins.

Perhaps you have guessed by now that your search for truth should begin with knowledge and lead to wisdom. The Word of God is called a light unto our feet – not to our tongues, merely to speak about – but to our feet, to walk by. Getting knowledge is *your* work; opening your heart to understand is the work of the Holy Spirit. But you must ask Him for wisdom and believe He will give it to you. God has promised wisdom to those who 'ask in faith, nothing wavering' (*James 1:6*). Strive for wisdom, not so that men will respect and admire you, but so that they will celebrate God's greatness. The end of every human effort should be to magnify His name. Go to God with David's prayer on your lips: 'Make me to understand the way of thy precepts: so shall I talk of thy wondrous works' (*Ps. 119:27*).

Do not give up when the lessons are long or hard to understand. Scripture promises, 'Then shall we know, if we follow on to know the Lord' (*Hos. 6:3*). The mysteries of Christ are not learned in a day. Too many read a chapter or two in the Bible, then for lack of interest put it down for weeks at a time and never look at it. Bernard compares the study of the Word and the mere reading of it to the difference between a close friendship and a casual acquaintance. If you want genuine knowledge, he says, you will have to do more than greet the Word politely on Sundays or nod reverently when you chance to meet it on the street. You must walk with it and talk with it every day of the week. You must invite it into your private chambers, and forego other pleasures and worldly duties to spend time in its company.

Do you long for greater intimacy with your heavenly Father? Then meditate often and long on His Word. David likens the Word for sweetness to honey and the honeycomb. Like the honeycomb, the Bible is so rich and full that at first reading some wisdom will now and then drop from it. But unless you press it by meditation, you leave the most behind.

In your study, learn the basic precepts of Christianity before you try to tackle the larger issues. As children, first we go to grammar school, then we go to college; first we learn the facts, then we study concepts. Your spiritual education is not so different. Christians who are not instructed in the fundamentals of Christianity are not likely to mature into solid saints. I sincerely believe a poor foundation is the reason many are not steadfast today. Dear saint, do not be too proud to go back and learn the basic precepts of the gospel if you have not yet mastered them. Too many are more concerned about their reputation than their salvation.

(v) *Wait on the ministry of the Word*. The apostle cautioned the Hebrew Christians not to neglect church attendance (*Heb. 10:25*). If you say you want to know

God's truth, but neglect to go where the Word is preached, you are as insincere as the man who says he wants to watch the sun set but will not bother to turn his chair toward the west.

To know God, you must come to where He has appointed you to learn. If there is a church, go. If there is none, study your Bible diligently and wait on the ministry of the Spirit at home. You can trust your heavenly Father to use extraordinary measures to honor your demand for spiritual food. He is like a father who, if there is no school in town, teaches his child at home and turns him into an excellent scholar. God, Paul tells us, ' . . . maketh manifest the savour of his knowledge by us in every place' (*2 Cor. 2:14*).

God's Word is filled with good things for your soul. He wants you to have them all, so see to it that you are a wakeful and attentive student. Strive to be like Lydia, who 'attended unto the things which were spoken by Paul' (*Acts 16:14*). When you go to church, try to fix your quicksilver mind and set yourself to hear the sermon. Above all, make sure your heart is consumed with love for God, and your will is in submission to His desires. The mind goes on the will's errand; we spend our thoughts on what our hearts propose.

IV. THE NATURE OF EVIL SPIRITS ('SPIRITUAL WICKED-
NESS')

The inherent nature of the devils themselves, as well as the character of their works, is included in the description, 'spiritual wickedness.' A literal rendering of the passage reads, 'against the spirituals of wickedness.' Some interpret this to mean 'against wicked spirits.' That is true, as far as it goes. But it overlooks an additional truth, in that the passage refers not only to the spiritual nature of devils but also – in fact, chiefly – to the nature and kind of sins they perpetrate. These sins are the apples of temptation which they most often use to poison the saints. Such sins are the 'spirituals of wickedness.' Not gross, fleshly sins which ignorant sinners, like swine, wallow in – but *spiritual sins*, which are much more subtle and perhaps even more despicable.

This brief phrase, 'against spiritual wickedness,' when taken in context, presents us with three doctrinal conclusions: (1) The devils are spirits; (2) The devils are consummately wicked spirits; and (3) These wicked spirits use spiritual wickedness both to persecute the saints and to provoke them to sin.

(1) The devils are *spirits*. The word *spirit* has several meanings in Scripture. It is often used to describe angels, both good and evil ones (*Heb. 1:14; 1 Kings 22:21*). Frequently the devil himself is called a spirit: the 'unclean spirit,' 'foul spirit,' 'lying spirit.'

What, then, are spirits? And, more particularly, what are the special characteristics of evil spirits?

First of all, they are *immaterial* – not made of matter like humans. 'Handle me, and see,' Christ said to His disciples, who thought they had seen a spirit, 'for a spirit hath not flesh and bones, as ye see me have' (*Luke 24:39*). We have no evidence to indicate that sin altered Satan's basic substance. As Lucifer, son of the morning, his essence was immaterial; as Satan, prince of darkness, he is immaterial still. If devils were not immaterial – i.e., spirits – how could they enter into bodies and possess them (*Luke 8:30*)?

While spirits do not have bodies, they are nonetheless real, created beings. Do not make the mistake of thinking they are mere qualities, or evil emotions – as some have absurdly supposed. Such an assertion denies Scripture, for there we find their creation recounted (*Col. 1:16*), the

[187]

fall of some from their first estate (*Jude 6*), and the standing of others – called the elect angels (*1 Tim. 5:21*). Scripture also records the happiness of the spirits who live in God's court and serve the saints (*Heb. 1:14*), and the misery of those spirits 'reserved in everlasting chains under darkness . . . ' (*Jude 6*).

All this evidence points to the fact that spirits, both good and evil, are personal beings. But fallen man, helplessly immersed in the flesh, will not readily believe what he cannot see with his mortal eyes. On the same grounds, we might deny the existence of God Himself, because He is invisible.

What a clever trick on the part of Satan, to make us think that if we cannot see something, it does not exist! A sinner may carry Satan in his heart and walk all day long in his company, yet never notice him. Like a horse with blinkers, he feels the crack of the whip that drives him to selfish ambition or lustful desires, but never sees the face of the driver. But Satan is there – whether you see him or not. When your passions are on a runaway course, hell-bound for destruction, you can be sure it is the devil himself who spurs them on.

Another characteristic of spirits is that they are highly *intellectual*. They are smarter than other creatures because they come closest by creation to the nature of God. By diligent study, men have accumulated vast stores of scientific knowledge. Still, the wisest human being is as far from the angels' intelligence as the earth is from the heavens.

No doubt the fallen angels lost the use of much of their celestial knowledge – all their wisdom as holy angels, in fact. What they now know of God has lost its savor, and they have no power to use it for their own good. Jude's assessment of wicked men applies to them: They misuse the knowledge they have been given to corrupt themselves further (*v. 10*). They know the holiness of God, but do not love Him for it. They know the evil of sin, and do not love it the less. And though they are utter fools with regard to their own destiny, evil spirits are more than a match for all the saints on earth – except for one thing: We have Almighty God to play our game for us!

In addition to being immaterial and highly intellectual, spirits gain a distinct advantage by being *immortal*. Of other enemies, you may hear at last that 'they are dead which sought [thy] life,' as the angel told Joseph concerning Herod (*Matt. 2:20*). Wicked men walk a turn or two upon the stage, then are called off by death; so end their plots. But devils do not die. They will track you to your grave, and if you die Christless, they will meet you in another world to accuse and torment you there also.

These wicked spirits are indefatigable. When the fight is over among men, even the conqueror must sit down and catch his breath. His strength has a limit. Other men, successful by human standards but deprived of their own personal goals, lose their will to fight and give up in despair. Tertullian said of Diocletian that he threw down his scepter in a fit of pique when he was unsuccessful at stamping out Christianity. He could not kill Christ's followers as fast as they were being born into the kingdom, so at last he gave up altogether and sought some other fiendish amusement.

But the devil never becomes dispirited, nor does he tire of doing mischief to the souls of men. He has not stood still for a moment since he first began to walk to and fro in the earth (*Job 1:7*). Indeed, God Himself must bind him hand and foot to stop his feverish activities.

(2) Not only are devils spirits, but they are *extremely wicked* spirits. God is called the Holy One because none is

[189]

as holy as the Lord. The devil is called the 'wicked one' because he is uniquely evil (*Matt. 13:19*). What we know of him from Scripture gives us a measure of the height of his wickedness, and can be used to judge the degrees of sins and sinners among men. The formula is simple. The more we are like God, the holier we are; the more like the devil, the more wicked.

These fallen angels are the *inventors of sin*. They were the first to sound the trumpet of rebellion against their Maker, and led the dance to all the sin that ever was or ever will be. There is not a language on earth with adjectives strong enough to describe the magnitude of such sin!

God had set Lucifer at the pinnacle of creation, nearest Himself. He kept nothing from this beloved angel but His own royal diadem. Yet this favorite of the court, without any cause or solicitation from anyone else, initiated his bold and blasphemous attempt to snatch God's crown and place it on his own head. The gravity of Satan's rebellion rests in the fact that *he sinned without a tempter*. It gives him the shameful distinction of being called the father of lies (*John 8:44*), in the same tradition that men who have founded an art or profession are called the 'father' of it. And while men are not in danger of Satan's supreme act of treason, they come close to it when they become 'inventors of evil things' (*Rom. 1:30*).

Sin is an ancient trade. But, like other trades where ingenious men build upon others' inventions to create new and better products, in every generation infamous men are spawned who think up new sins by adding to old wickednesses. Sexual perversion is an ancient sin, but the Sodomites were filthy in a new way and the sin they invented carries their name to this day. Some invent new heresies; others, new oaths. Those with a thirst for blood invent new devices for persecuting the righteous. To the end of the world, every age will exceed the previous one in its degree of sinning. Ishmael and the mockers of the old world will look like children and bunglers compared to the scoffers and cruel persecutors of the last days.

Think twice before you use your intelligence to invent new sins! You may provoke God to new punishments. Sodom devised a new way to sin, so God devised a new way to discipline them: He sent hell from above upon them.

These same demons who invented sin are likewise the *chief promoters* of it. The apostate angels were not only the inventors of sin, but are also its chief enterprisers. These spirits are therefore called 'the tempter,' and sin is called 'the work of the devil,' no matter who commits it – just as the credit for the design of a house goes to the architect, even though other men do the actual construction.

When you cause anyone to sin, you take the devil's office out of his hands. Let him do it himself if he can, but *never* allow him to use you as his hireling. Tempting someone else to sin is worse than sinning yourself. Those who tempt others plant their own wickedness in fertile fields and raise up new seed to the devil. To cultivate the devil's crop of sin with the evil in your own heart shows sin is mighty in you indeed. Parents, especially, must guard against such a heinous act. What are they but devils incarnate who, by their own example, teach their children the devil's catechism – to swear and lie and drink?

Do you not know what you do when you tempt? I will tell you. You do that which cannot be undone by your own repentance. You contaminate your family and friends with error, and send them rushing to join the devil's throng. Later, you may see your mistake and turn from your wicked way. But can you force those you have led

[191]

astray to fight against the press of the worldly crowd to get to Jesus at all cost? You may plead and weep, and prostrate yourself before them. Your heart may break, like Lamech's, with the weight of your sorrow. But unfortunately their rescue is out of your hands. What a grief to your spirit to see them on the road to hell and know you paid the toll, yet not be able to call them back! Even after you are dead and gone, your sins may be perpetuated in those who are alive, generation after generation.

Devils are *maliciously and incessantly wicked*. Fallen angels are not just incidentally or occasionally wicked, but willfully and constantly wicked. The devil's name, 'wicked one,' denotes his spiteful nature, his desire to vex and harass others. He draws souls to sin, not because he tastes any sweetness or finds any profit in such enterprise. He has too much light to have any real joy or peace in sin. He knows his doom, and trembles at the thought of it. Yet his spiteful nature drives him mercilessly. He is as bloodthirsty for souls as a mad dog for sheep. The difference is that the dog will finally drop in exhaustion, whereas Satan never tires of his work as a butcher of souls.

Though he toils for the eternal damnation of every soul, the devil's open vengeance is most often directed toward the saints. If he could, he would not leave one of Christ's flock alive. Such is the height of his malice against God, whom he hates with a perfect hatred. And because he cannot reach Him with a direct blow, he strikes at Him secondhand through the saints. He knows that the life of God is in a very real sense bound up in theirs. If you are even now feeding in God's green pastures and drinking from the well of His mercy, beware. Satan is sure to attack. He knows the honor God receives on this earth is directly related to the flow of His mercy. He therefore labors to build a dam with his wicked deeds that will stop the flow of mercy to the saints. This is the worst that can be said of these wicked demons: They maliciously spite God, and in God, the glory of His mercy.

(a) *The importance of understanding the nature of devils*
What is the point of knowing the height of the devil's wickedness? Several things, among others, come to mind.

(i) *To convict a self-righteous sinner*. If the measure of a man's own good works compares favorably to everyone else's – i.e., if they are not noticeably meaner or viler than his neighbor's – he thinks he can pass God's inspection. Before the Holy Spirit can convict such a person of his need of Christ, he must agree with God that all his righteousness is but filthy rags. It may help him understand his own wickedness if he sees how utterly polluted the spring is that incessantly feeds it.

Can you somehow get a mental picture of the monstrous intensity of Satan's wickedness? Then you have an idea of every man's potential for evil. The finest human being – the most sincere philanthropist or moral crusader – has within him the same seeds of corruption, the same potential for wickedness as the devil himself. If his true nature has not yet shown through, it is because God's grace is intervening. For until you are made a new creature in Christ, you are of the same brood as the Serpent; his seed is in you. And the devil can only beget a child like himself.

Sinner, if you do not blossom into Satan's likeness here on earth, you can be sure you will in hell. There the flames will wash off the paint that hides your true complexion. In heaven, the saints will be like the angels in alacrity, love, and constancy to God; in hell, the damned will be like the devils, in sin as well as in punishment. Before you excuse yourself by claiming 'good intentions,' know this: If your heart is good, then so is the devil's! His nature is wicked,

[193]

and so is yours! The blemishes which you think are so small and insignificant are symptoms of a deadly disease within. Without gospel medicine – the blood of Christ – applied to you personally, you will die a leper. Sin is a hereditary disease that increases with age: a young sinner will be an old devil. And the malady is always passed on to the next generation.

(ii) *To humble a self-righteous saint.* The saint whom Christ has redeemed at an early age needs to recognize the potential wickedness of his own heart. He can get a clear picture by looking into the mirror of the devil's nature. Really to understand the significance of the Cross in your life, you must realize you are as great a debtor to the mercy of God as the worst of sinners. Until you accepted Christ's pardon, the same sentence of death lay upon your soul as upon Judas'. If you have not sinned as grievously as someone else, it does not mean you are a better person; it means that God has been gracious. Our old nature (whose residue is not cast off until heaven) has the devil's stamp of 'traitor' on it from the day we were born. Our sovereign God had every right to crush us for it then and there – just as we destroy a nest of poisonous snakes, not for any harm they have yet inflicted, but because we know their potential danger.

Can you honestly say that when God first came to you your thoughts were pure and your intentions holy? Were you not already armed with the weapons of rebellion – a covetous spirit, a deceitful heart, a lying tongue? Oh, yes, you had a nature fully charged with enmity against God. It lay like unfired gunpowder, waiting for a flame! Fall on your knees in humble gratitude to the One who sent His Spirit and grace to stop you, even while your nature meditated on nothing but war against God and His laws.

(iii) *To uncover Satan's design in perpetrating sin.* One

reason we are so easily persuaded to sin is because we do not understand Satan's purpose. He does with men in sinning as generals do with them in fighting. Captains beat their drums for volunteers, promising pay and promotions to all who enlist. The guarantee of such excellent benefits makes soldiers come streaming in, with little or no thought as to whether the ground of the war is just. Satan entices to sin by giving golden promises of rewards for entering his service – power, fame, or fortune. Many foolish souls are won by his clever arguments and the prodding of their own greedy natures. Few bother to ask, 'Why is the devil so eager to have me join his ranks?'

Shall I tell you? Do you think *your* pleasure or profit is his goal? Not likely! His aspirations are all for himself. He has a personal grudge against God, and he brings you, by sinning, to join in his quarrel. What he fails to mention is that you jeopardize your very soul to defend his pride and lust. But he is hardly worried about your welfare. He loses no more sleep over your certain damnation than a demented general does over the men he sends on a suicide mission. Knowing this, why would you ever join Satan in his fight against God? He sends you on a suicide mission! This bloody Joab will order you where no one ever came off alive. If you stand where God's bullets fly, you are a dead man, unless you throw down your arms and surrender at once.

(b) *Spiritual wickedness in the saints: the cause and the cure*

These wicked spirits are chiefly responsible for provoking the saints to spiritual wickedness. No sin can be committed that does not have spiritual consequences. But some sins are more specifically 'spiritual sins' than others. Two kinds stand out especially: (1) sins kept within the confines of the heart; and (2) sins directly related to spiritual topics – idolatry, spiritual pride, atheism, heresy, and the like. Paul calls them 'filthiness of the spirit' and sets them apart from filthiness of the flesh (*2 Cor. 7:1*).

(i) *First sort of spiritual wickedness – sin in the heart.* When the spirit or the heart is the stage whereon sin is enacted, it is a spiritual sin; such are all impure thoughts, vile affections, and desires which do not break forth into overt action but are nonetheless real acts of the inner man. As with all sin, Satan is the great, unseen instigator of every sin of the heart.

When thoughts and feelings overtake you that you know are not pleasing to God, what can you do? You do not want to be critical – but you are; you do not want to covet – but you do. How can you take these stones of offense and rocks of stumbling Satan hurls into the path of your thoughts, and use them to build a monument of glory to the Father? In two ways in particular: by keeping a close watch on your heart and by steadfastly resisting its sins.

First, keep a close watch on your heart. What welcome does Satan find when he comes with these 'spirituals of wickedness' and asks you to dwell on them? I do not ask whether such guests step inside your door. If we had God's ability to look into man's heart, we would see the worst of sins stirring in every Christian. That they have been scattered on the field of our hearts, we already know, and by whom – the grim sower, Satan. What is important is whether he finds our hearts a fertile field or whether, with holy thoughts and earnest prayer, we pour oil upon them and light a match to them, so that they are consumed in a holy fire.

Now Satan is insidious. Many who would turn away in horror to see spiritual sins operating in broad daylight as fleshly lusts, have been deceived into welcoming them into their private chambers as honored guests. What upstanding church member would be seen walking through town arm-in-arm with a prostitute? Yet he may, in the inner sanctum of his heart, spend his desires on an unclean lust at his leisure. Most of us would never commit murder, but how often have we taken a neighbor into some dark alley of our thoughts and there torn him limb from limb with a desire for revenge over some petty quarrel?

Christian, this is imperative for you to realize: When wicked or unclean thoughts first force their way into your mind, you have not yet sinned. This is the work of the devil! But if you so much as offer them a chair and begin polite conversation with them, you have become his accomplice. In only a short time you will give these thoughts sanctuary in your heart. Your resolve – not to yield to a temptation you are already entertaining – is no match for Satan and the longings of the flesh.

Your confidence must rest on this fact: Unclean thoughts will not stay where the love of Christ reigns supreme. They are as panicked by overhearing your conversations with Christ as an escaped murderer would be upon realizing he has been spotted in town. And well they should be – for your holy thoughts will track down these evil thoughts and kill them on the spot. Both the trial and the sentence will be speedy.

Secondly, steadfastly resist sins of the heart, thereby showing where your loyalties lie. We need to be constantly reminded that heart sins are sins as much as any: 'The thought of foolishness is sin' (*Prov. 24:9*). Every point of hell is hell! Lust, envy, and murder are sins when committed in the heart, the same as in the outward act. Such thoughts cannot run rampant in a Christian without serious consequences. Your spirit is the dwelling place of

[197]

the Holy Spirit; He takes up the whole heart for His lodging. When He sees you have leased out rooms to the lusts of the devil, it is time for Him to be gone. If you cherish His presence, declare your loyalty to Christ at Satan's first knock by renouncing every thought that is not a willing captive of God.

Do you see why sins of the heart may be even more wicked than sins committed by physical means? The more the heart and spirit are involved in any evil action, the worse it is. And the more the heart and spirit are involved in any holy action, the more real goodness there is in it – even though men may not think so. The widow's two mites was the best gift, according to Christ. Why? Not because the outward act exceeded that of the other givers, but because the inward act of her heart surpassed them all!

Let Satan buffet your heart with his vile imaginations. You cannot stop his puffing any more than you can halt a hurricane headed for shore. But you can take timely precautions when the storm of evil thoughts approaches.

First precaution: Seal the windows of your heart with *prayer*. If the tongue is so unruly and hard to tame, then what is the mind – where thoughts fly as thick and fast as bees from an upset hive? Here lies the secret: to control your thoughts, ask Christ to control your heart.

How often David cried out in this respect. He knew the management of his heart was beyond his skill or power. But he had God's promise to help him and so have you, if you are His child (*Ps. 37:23; Prov. 30:5*). How would you feel, as an earthly parent, to see floodwaters rushing into your home, and have your trapped child refuse to let you carry him to safety? That must be how our heavenly Father feels when the floods of temptation threaten to overwhelm us, and we refuse to grab hold of His promise to carry us above the tumult.

You will need to pray more and harder than ever when you are called to a duty that brings you in closer contact than usual with the world. This is where Satan's thoughts attack like a plague of locusts. First, be sure you are going on God's business and not your own. God's promise to protect you is conditional: 'Commit thy works unto the Lord, and thy thoughts shall be established' (*Prov. 16:3*). Do not try to stave off the onslaughts of Satan in your own strength. Tell God you are afraid of what may happen if He does not intercept these wicked imaginations. Make Him the censor of your thoughts, and you will not need to worry. The devil's arm is not long enough to reach you when by earnest prayer you place yourself under the shadow of the Almighty.

Second precaution: *Set a strong guard around your outward senses*. Satan flies overhead, looking for a landing place such as your eyes or ears, which give him easy access to the inner man. As stagnant air pollutes everything around it, so unwholesome thoughts corrupt the whole person. Be sure to breathe clean air! As for your eyes, keep looking heavenward. Lustful objects cause lustful thoughts. Will not holy objects, then, cause holy thoughts?

Third precaution: *Inspect your heart daily*. Take time every day to reflect on the thoughts that have shaped your attitudes and actions for that day. A teacher does not call the class to order, then leave the room for the rest of the school term. How long do you think the students would stay at their desks or busy themselves with productive work? The noise from their antics would soon fill the halls of the whole school. Your heart tends to be an unruly pupil. Much of the unholy noise that erupts (anger, envy, impatience, bitterness, and all the rest) is because you have left it to its own devices. The mind is the classroom of the body; the heart is the student. Be mindful of what kind of learning is going on.

Here is a quick way to check your heart. Are your thoughts good or evil? When good, do you give credit to Christ? When evil, are you appalled and determined to expel these nasty urchins? If so, you show that these spirituals of wickedness are more Satan's than your own.

Besides evil thoughts, there are others that should also be unwelcome. These are empty, frothy, vain imaginations. Though you may not find them so abominable in themselves, still they keep you from something better. And who among us has time to waste in this life? Like the water that runs beside the mill, every thought that does not help you do God's work is wasted. The bee will not sit on a flower that has no nectar. Neither should the Christian entertain a thought that does not feed his spirit.

Even your good thoughts are not impervious to Satan's tampering. For instance, you may be overcome with the guilt of your sins and honestly mourn before the Lord. Yet if you become consumed with remorse, you are in danger of losing your faith in God's glorious promise of redemption by His grace. Or perhaps your thoughts turn to the needs and care of your family. Providing for your own is certainly scriptural. But if you worry so much about this responsibility that you forget God is the real provider, you again show a serious deficiency of faith.

We are instructed to learn and observe the whole counsel of God. What will it profit to light upon one of God's commandments and show it to be your favorite, if you slight all the rest? You will be in as much trouble as the person whose surgeon restores the flow of blood in a minor vein, but in the process severs a major artery. Such carelessness is likely to maim the man, if not kill him outright. Your soul is a delicate creature, and requires the utmost skill to maintain its equilibrium. Be constantly on your guard against concentrating so hard on one or two of God's ordinances, that you have no time for all the others.

(ii) *Second sort of spiritual wickedness: sins about spiritual topics*. Sins may be labeled spiritual sins because of the topics they address. Like sins which are committed in your heart, these 'spiritual wickednesses' corrupt the inner man rather than the body. Satan enjoys great success with them. For your edification, study the following two, which are favorites of his: errors involving spiritual principles, and errors resulting in spiritual pride.

First let us consider errors involving *spiritual principles*. Satan was at work at the first sowing of the gospel, scattering his weeds among Christ's wheat. Notice how often the apostle had to root out pernicious errors that cropped up among the early Christians.

Why is Satan so obsessed with perverting God's principles? For one thing, God highly honors His truth (*Ps. 138:2*). He is more scrupulous about it than all His other works. Jesus declared, 'Heaven and earth shall pass away, but my words shall not pass away' (*Matt. 24:35*). God can make new worlds whenever He pleases, but He cannot make another truth. Therefore, He will not lose one iota of it. Satan knows this, and sets his whole heart on disfiguring that which is so precious to God.

It should also be precious to us. The Word is the mirror in which we see Christ and, seeing Him, are changed into His likeness by the Holy Spirit. If the glass is cracked, our conception of Him will be distorted, whereas the Word in its native clearness sets Christ out in all His glory. You can see, then, that not only does Satan strike at God when He attacks the truth, but he also strikes at the saints. If he can lead them into error, it will weaken – if not destroy – the power of godliness in them.

[201]

The apostle joins the spirit of power and of a sound mind together (*2 Tim. 1:7*). We are exhorted to 'desire the sincere milk of the word, that [we] may grow . . . ' (*1 Pet. 2:2*). Like milk diluted with water, the Word mixed with error is not very nutritious. All error, no matter how innocent it seems, is a parasite. And as ivy saps the strength of the tree it intertwines, so error saps the strength of truth. The soul that feeds on tainted truth cannot grow fat and healthy.

To use another analogy, Paul talks about believers being wedded to Christ. When you receive an error, you take a stranger into Christ's bed and commit spiritual adultery. One of the horrible things about adultery is that it turns the adulterer's heart from the true spouse. It turns his thoughts and attentions toward the illicit affair, and away from his first love. We see this happening in the church today, where a faction embraces some doctrinal error or flaming heresy, and contends for it with more zeal than for the simple gospel truths that led them to Christ in the first place. The loss in such instances is great, for Christ can never share true, conjugal love with a soul that is coupling with error.

By now I hope you realize that error is not so innocent a thing as many think. It not only disrupts the relationship of the individual saint with the Beloved, but it also disturbs the peace of the Bride – the church. 'I hear,' Paul writes, 'that there be divisions among you; and I partly believe it. For there must be also heresies among you' (*1 Cor. 11:18, 19*). The implication here is that divisions are the bastard offspring of an adulterous affair with error. When Christians walk in truth, they also walk in unity and love; when they walk in error, the antithesis prevails.

Here is a word of exhortation for all who will hear – especially those who call themselves Christians. Are you so proud that you think all this talk about polluting God's truth with error does not apply to you? If so, what a dangerous position you are in! Doctrinal error is the disease of the times! What makes you so sure you have been inoculated against it? I must tell you, it is one of those afflictions for which there is no one-time cure.

The more knowledge we accumulate, and the more sophisticated we become in our study of the faith, the more careful we must be to guard against error! That great preacher Paul felt compelled to press the point home repeatedly. He hardly gave a sermon or wrote a letter without begging believers to beware of those things which would adulterate the gospel. He thought his warning indispensable for the saints at Galatia, at Corinth, and Philippi. Have we come so far in our day that we no longer need his admonition? Satan has not grown tired of perpetrating his lies; we dare not grow complacent about seeking God's truth.

But how will you prepare yourself for this task?

First, make sure you have experienced a thorough change of heart. See that your heart has been properly prepared, so that your faith in Christ takes root and grows. Then it will choke out error as fast as it springs up. If you are firmly established in Christ, you will be kept from serious error. I do not say from *all* error, but of this I am sure – free from *damning* error. It is one thing to know a truth, and another thing entirely to know it by the unction of the Holy Spirit. Even the devil may do the former; only the saint can do the latter. The anointing is what gives your soul the savor of Christ's knowledge. It is the anchor that will keep you from being set adrift and carried away from the truth by the winds of 'divers and strange doctrines' (*Heb. 13:9*).

Once you have experienced a true change of heart,

crucify the flesh daily. I will be so bold as to say that never have any turned heretic, but flesh was at the bottom. Either they have served their carnal appetites, or a lust for pride. Christian, if you can once and for all break your engagement to the flesh and become a free man in Christ, truth will be your steadfast friend.

Study God's Word faithfully as well. Satan has a habit of stopping the ears from hearing sound doctrine before he opens them to listen to corrupt. He will, as often as he can, pull a saint away from God's Word and talk him into rejecting some point of truth. But he who rejects the truth of one doctrine, loses the blessing of them all. Paul predicted how this would happen: 'They shall turn away their ears from the truth, and shall be turned unto fables' (*2 Tim. 4:3, 4*).

Do not pretend you want to be led into truth if you will not bother to study the whole Word of God. You are no different from a child who says he wants to learn, yet plays the truant. Such a child must be disciplined. Because your heavenly Father loves you, He will bring you back to the Word with shame and sorrow, rather than leave you trapped in Satan's lies.

As you study and grow, be wary of new doctrine. Do not hastily accept everything you hear, even from the pulpit. Now I admit that to reject a doctrine simply because we have never heard it before is foolish. But we have every right to wait and inquire before embracing it. When you hear a new notion about the truth, go to God in prayer and seek His counsel. Search the Scriptures. Discuss it with your pastor and with other Christians whose wisdom and maturity you trust.

The truth will stand up under scrutiny. It is a fruit that never bruises or spoils from handling. But error, like fish, begins to stink after a few days. Therefore, let new ideas sit before you make a meal of them. You do not want to poison your soul with rotting mackerel when you could be feasting on manna from heaven!

A second type of error Satan sows among saints is *pride*. Pride was the sin that turned Satan, a blessed angel, into a cursed devil. Satan knows better than anyone the damning power of pride. Is it any wonder, then, that he so often uses it to poison the saints? His design is made easier in that man's heart shows a natural fondness for it. Pride, like liquor, is intoxicating. A swallow or two usually leaves a man worthless to God.

One of the perilous things about pride is that it uses both our good and our bad inclinations to draw its chariot. On the one hand, it works companionably with other sins. In fact, a multitude of sins will slave all day long and into the night, supposing they are their own masters, when all along they are the hirelings of pride. Watch someone cheating, deceiving, lying, oppressing others. What is his motive, if not to acquire an estate to maintain his pride?

Even worse than teaming up with other sorts of wickedness, this rascal pride will also harness itself to that which is good, and work alongside God's ordinances. When this happens, we see a person zealous in prayer or faithful in church attendance, and suppose him to be a mighty saint. But all the while pride is the master he serves, though in God's livery. Pride can take sanctuary in the holiest of actions and hide itself under the very skirt of virtue. Thus you may hear of someone giving generously to the poor, and be moved to admire his charity. Yet pride – not compassion – may be the reason he lavishes out his gold so freely.

Another may steadfastly resist every appearance of evil and be respected as a model Christian. And all the while, pride – not true heart conviction – may be the promoter of his circumspect walk. This was the case with the Pharisee, who flaunted his spirituality and bragged because he was not like the publican. Christ showed us in a word or two how He felt about that kind of pride!

Of the two strains of pride, I think spiritual pride must be far more odious to the nostrils of God, for it is on a higher plain than carnal pride. The life of a Christian, as a Christian, is superior to the life of a man as a man. And as the natural man is proud of those things which make him seem superior in the natural state (i.e., wealth, honor, beauty), so the Christian is prone to puff himself up when he perceives that he has superior spiritual attributes. There are three areas I wish to explore. First, pride of gifts; second, pride of grace; and third, pride of privileges.

First, *pride of gifts*. By *gifts* I mean those spiritual abilities the Holy Spirit dispenses to Christians for the edification of the body of Christ as a whole. The apostle tells us of the great diversity of gifts (*1 Cor. 12:4*). Just look around you at the different species of plants and flowers, and you will have some idea of God's love for infinite variety. He has been no less creative with the human personality. Every child of God is unique and important for the proper functioning of the body of Christ. But when pride creeps in, we begin to create hierarchies among the brethren and among gifts. This inevitably leads to divisions and disputes. Satan knows it and labors to taint every single gift with pride. In so doing he can hurl two stones at once. With one, he strikes the unity of the body as a whole; with the other, he cripples the individual saint.

Consider the possibility that pride is the reason we do so little good for others with our gifts. When pride prevails, we pray, preach, comfort, or console to be thought good by others, rather than to do good to others. We set ourselves upon a spiritual pedestal and, in a manner of speaking, expect those we serve to worship at the shrine of our good works. Will God honor such efforts? He has told us in no uncertain terms that He will not share His glory with anyone else (*Isa. 48:11*). The humble man may have Satan at his right hand to oppose him, but the proud man will find himself in a worse fix. God Himself will be there to resist him. If you doubt it, read His Word: '[He] resisteth the proud, but giveth grace unto the humble' (*James 4:6*).

Our pride is also the reason we receive so little good from the gifts of other Christians. Pride fills us with notions of our own spiritual sufficiency. We think we are too good (or too holy) to need the help of most other saints. We find few preachers who are 'spiritual' enough to minister to us. And if someone offers a word of correction, we close our ears. Pride fools us into thinking we 'are rich, and increased with goods, and have need of nothing' (*Rev. 3:17*). Alas for us! How long can a soul thrive if it steadfastly refuses wholesome nourishment, and will only sit down to a 'choice dish' of high-sounding theory? Just as simple food is healthier for our physical bodies than an elaborate feast, so a steady diet of plain truths and God's ordinances is better for our souls than dipping in the lordly dishes of theological supposition.

If you are one who holds yourself in high spiritual esteem, hear this: Many humble Christians, of low estate by the world's standards, have much to offer you if you are not too proud to receive spiritual food at their hands. Pride always destroys love and separates saints. Without love for all the brethren, we are bound to lose much that God wants to give. The Bible says *every* saint has been given gifts to benefit the body of Christ.

Here is a word to you who think your gifts are inferior to

those of other members of the body: *Be content with your condition*. Great gifts lift a saint up a little higher in the eyes of men, but they also tempt him to pride. Do not envy those with great gifts; instead, pity and pray for them. It is hard for them to escape the error of supposing that God's grace in them is their own doing. You have a real advantage over them, for you have the help of their gifts but not the temptation of their pride.

Here, now, are some words of caution for you to whom God has given more or better gifts than ordinary.

Pride wants to grow where the best gifts have been bestowed. So beware of pride! The only thing that will keep you from it is your humility. Remember whom you wrestle with – spiritual wickednesses. Their ploy is to lift you up high in order to give you a harder fall. They will try to convince you that your spiritual accomplishments are a result of your own efforts and that you deserve the credit for them. Surely you know this is not true! In case you have forgotten, think back to what you were like before the Holy Spirit came to you with gifts from God's storehouse. How can you be proud of another's bounty? You may be able to impress other men with your gifts, but you will not impress God. He knows where they all came from.

Where pride flourishes, the body of Christ suffers. Had God given you gifts merely for your own pleasure or edification, the sin of pride would not be quite so bad. But when you use your gifts to lift yourself up, you tear down the body of Christ. Your gifts are necessary to the health of the whole body, but they must be administered properly. You must be careful to acknowledge that Christ is the Great Physician; you are only the assistant who uses His instruments and carries out His orders.

Where pride grows, grace withers. Here is another reason

to be humble if you have great gifts: Every proud thought you entertain costs you a measure of grace. There is not room for both to prosper in the Christian's heart. Indeed, when grace and pride sit down at the same table, pride shows itself a glutton, and grace leaves the table unfed. Pride must have the most and best of everything to satisfy its appetite. This voracious lust will devour your spirit of praise. When you should be blessing God, you will be applauding yourself. It will eat up Christian love, and cause you to disdain the fellowship of other Christians. It will keep you from acknowledging the gifts of others, because that would take away some of the glory you want for yourself. Ultimately, pride so distorts our taste that we can relish nothing drawn from another's dish.

Where pride reigns, God chastens. God will not allow such a weed as pride to grow in His garden without taking some course or other to root it up. He may let you fall into a sin that will humiliate you before men and God, and force you to come crawling home in shame. Or He may use a thorn in the flesh to prick the balloon of your pride. If your pride has placed His honor in jeopardy, expect to feel God's rod of correction. Most likely it will be applied to the very spot where your pride is rooted. Hezekiah boasted of his treasure; God sent the Chaldeans to plunder him. Jonah was proud of his gourd; God sent a pestilence to destroy it. Can you expect Him to wink at this sin in your life when He has dealt so firmly with it in His other children?

Where gifts are bestowed, God calls an audit. Suppose a friend died and named you executor of his estate. But instead of dividing his inheritance according to the instructions left in his will, you took the money and put it in your own bank account, then went around town bragging about how rich you were! How long could you fool people with your false prosperity? Sooner or later the rightful heirs would show up and not only take what is theirs, but probably sue you as well. In a spiritual sense, you are only God's executor. He has given you gifts, and specific instructions on how to dispense them. By the time you have paid all the legacies, you will see little left for yourself to brag or boast of. Never forget for a moment that you will be held accountable for the talents left in your care.

Now perhaps you do not keep your gifts from others, but serve the church tirelessly. That sounds commendable. But let me ask you this: Who gets the credit for your activities? Suppose a man who was named executor of an estate paid out the legacies as instructed but he pretended they were gifts from himself. Would we not label him a thief and a swindler? A proud soul who takes the credit for his good works is just as much a thief. What is worse, he steals from God Himself!

How can you know when you are in danger of committing the sin of spiritual pride with respect to your gifts? Here are some warning signals.

You are in danger of spiritual pride if you catch yourself dwelling on the thoughts of your gifts with *a secret kind of contentment* – always taking them out to look at and admire. A proud man is consumed with love for himself. He is the apple of his own eye. The great subject and theme of all his thoughts is who he is and what he has that is better than someone else's. Before you protest that you could never fall into the hands of pride, let me tell you that no one is beyond its pale. Bernard, that great old saint, confessed that even in the middle of one of his sermons, pride would be whispering in his ear, 'Well done, Bernard, well done!'

How can the Christian escape those persistent self-promoting thoughts? Run from them as you would from an enraged bear. Do not stand still to listen to these lies, or soon the devil will have you erecting a monument to yourself with the glory of your God-given gifts. Remind yourself daily how weak you are and how utterly depen-dent on God for every good and perfect gift.

Another indicator that you are caught in the trap of spiritual pride is *envy of others' gifts*. Keeping our hearts and envy separated is as difficult as keeping two lovers from meeting. It is the sin that shed the first blood: Cain's envy hatched Abel's murder.

Envy is an affront to the character and person of God. When you envy, you are questioning God's right to administer His gifts as He sees best. You are also maligning the goodness of God. You are angry that God wants to bless someone besides you. Would you not have God be good? You might as well say you would not have Him be God, for He can no more cease to be good than He can cease to be God! When your envy prods you to belittle the gifts of other Christians, you are really belittling God who gave them.

Envy, like its mother, pride, is the scout for a whole host of other sins. This sin of the heart goes before and sets the stage for all kinds of sins of the flesh. Saul, Israel's first king, fell so low as to plot the murder of the very man who had saved his kingdom. From the day he heard David preferred above himself in the women's songs, he could not get the sound out of his head. Envy brought him to hate, which carried him on to plot David's death.

Later on, what did envy do to David's own heart but make him covet the wife of his trusted soldier, Uriah, and lead him through a maze of lust, lies, adultery, and murder? Not one of these would have been committed had it not been for that rabble-rouser, envy. It is a bloody sin the womb wherein a whole litter of other sins is formed (*Rom. 1:29*). Therefore, unless you are willing to welcome the devil and his whole train, resist the sin of envy.

To gain mastery over this sin, you must call in help from heaven. We have a sure promise that the foundation of our grace is stronger than that of our lust, but only if we enlist the Holy Spirit in our behalf: 'The spirit that dwelleth in us lusteth to envy. But he giveth more grace' (*James 4:5, 6*). Do not challenge envy to a duel with your own resolve; you are not strong enough or smart enough to win. But God can give you more grace than you have sin – more humility than you have pride. If you are humble enough to ask for His grace, He will make sure you are not so proud as to envy His gifts or grace in others.

The second kind of spiritual pride that grows like tares among wheat and which Satan uses to assault the Christian is *pride of grace*. Gifts equip us to *do*; grace equips us to *be*. We are talking now about the measure of grace, or godly attributes, God gives a person. We know everything we possess in this life is subject to decay – nothing the Christian has or does, but this worm of pride will breed in it. Pride is most often responsible for the soft spots in our graces, which are highly perishable. It is not the nature of our grace, but the salt of God's covenant, that preserves the purity of it.

In what ways, then, can a saint become proud of his grace?

First, *by relying on the strength of his grace*. To trust in the strength of your own goodness is to be proud of grace. In this way you refuse the poverty of spirit Christ so often commended (*Matt. 5*). We are called to acknowledge our own spiritual beggary and so to lean on Him for every need. Paul was such a man. He was not ashamed to let the whole world know that Christ carried his purse for him: 'Our sufficiency is of God' (*2 Cor. 3:5*).

What happened to Peter when he bragged of the strength of his own grace? 'Although all shall be offended, yet will not I,' Peter boasted (*Mark 14:29*). He set himself up to contest a race with the devil, and he fouled before he was even out of the gate. Christ in mercy let Satan trample Peter's own grace to show him its true nature and to dismount him from the height of his pride.

Pray that He will be as merciful to you if He sees you climbing the ladder of your own spiritual successes. Joab said to David, when he saw him growing proud of the strength of his kingdom and wanting to take a census, 'The Lord add to the number of thy people an hundredfold, but why doth my lord the king delight in this thing?' (*2 Sam. 24:3*). Can a groom be proud when he rides his master's horse, or a garden boast because the sun shines on it? Should we not say of every dram of goodness, as the young man of his hatchet, 'Alas, master! for it was borrowed' (*2 Kings 6:5*)?

Count on the strength of your own godly attributes, and you will grow lax in your duties for Christ. Knowing you are weak keeps you from wandering too far from Him. When you see that your own cupboard is bare and everything you need is in His, you will go often to Him for supplies. But a soul who thinks he can take care of himself will say, 'I have plenty and to spare for a long time. Let the doubting soul pray; my faith is strong. Let the weak go to God for help; I can manage fine on my own.' What a sad state of affairs, to suppose that we no longer need the moment-by-moment sustaining grace of God.

Not only does overestimating the strength of our own goodness make us shun God's help, but it also makes us foolhardy and venturesome. You who boast about your spirituality are likely to put yourselves in all kinds of dangerous situations, then brag that you can handle them.

You think you are so established in the truth that a whole team of heretics could not draw you aside. You will go where no Christian ought to go, listen to what no Christian ought to hear – all the while insisting that though others may betray Christ in those circumstances, you never will. Peter showed this same foolish confidence on the eve of our Lord's crucifixion and how he came off, you know. His faith would have been slain on the spot if Christ had not rescued him with His look of love.

An arrogant confidence in the strength of your own grace will also make you critical and unsympathetic toward fellow Christians who are admittedly weak – and this is a most uncomely sin. 'If a man be overtaken in a fault,' says Paul, 'ye which are spiritual, restore such an one in the spirit of meekness' (*Gal. 6:1*). And if you wonder why you, who think you are so far above reproach, should stoop to help a fallen brother, here is an excellent reason: ' . . . considering thyself, lest thou also be tempted.'

God warns you against overconfident spirituality. What makes men unkind to the poor? They think they will never be so themselves. What makes Christians judge others harshly? They trust too much in their own goodness, thinking they could never fall. Bernard used to say, when he heard any scandalous sin of a brother, 'He fell today; I may stumble tomorrow.' Oh, that we all could have such a spirit of meekness!

A second way to become proud of our grace is *by relying on the worth of our grace* – thinking we can be good enough to please God. Scripture calls inherent grace 'our own righteousness,' and sets it in opposition to the righteousness of Christ, which alone is called the 'righteousness of God' (*Rom. 10:3*). When we trust in our own grace, we exalt it above the grace of God. If it were in fact superior, then a saint could say when he gets to heaven, 'This is the city which I built, which my grace purchased.' This would make God a tenant, and His creature the landlord! Ridiculous? Yet this is the very attitude we disclose when we set about to win God's acceptance through our own efforts. How does the God of the universe so patiently endure such pride in His lowly creatures!

If you understand God's Word at all, you know God has cast the order of our salvation into a method far different from working for it. It *is* a method of grace – but never our grace. Rather, it is God's divine grace. Any grace inherent in us has its place and office to accompany salvation (*Heb. 6:9*), but not to procure it. That is Christ's work, and His alone.

When Israel waited on the Lord at Mount Sinai, they had their bounds. Not a man was to come up the mountain to talk to God, except Moses. They were not even to touch the mount, or they would die. Here is a spiritual metaphor of our grace. All the graces are given to enhance our service to God, but none comes up to challenge *faith* as the basis for God's acceptance. Faith – unencumbered by works – is the grace that must present us to Christ for salvation and cleansing.

This doctrine of justification by faith has had more assaults made against it than any other teaching in Scripture. Indeed, many other errors were but the enemy's sly approaches to get nearer to undermine this one. When Satan cannot hide this truth, he works to hinder the practical application of it. Thus you see Christians who speak in defense of justification by faith, yet their attitude and actions contradict their profession. Like Abraham, when he went in to Hagar, they try to accomplish God's purpose by a carnal plan. All these efforts that seem so noble are really baseborn, for they are rooted in pride.

[215]

At bottom, pride in your own abilities is what keeps you working for righteousness. You keep trying to pray harder, working to be a better Christian, laboring to have more faith. You keep telling yourself, 'I can do it!' But you will soon find your own grace insufficient for even the smallest task, and your joy will run out at the crannies of your imperfect duties and weak graces. The language of pride hankers after the covenant of works. The only way out of this trap is to let the new covenant cut the cord of the old one, and acknowledge that the grace of Christ supersedes the works of the law.

Satan uses two types of pride to keep us trusting in the worth of our own grace. One I call a *mannerly pride*; the other, *a self-applauding pride*.

Mannerly pride tiptoes in, disguised as humility. This is the soul that weeps and mourns for its vile condition, yet refuses to be comforted. It is true – not one of us can paint our sins black enough to do them justice. But think how you discredit God's mercy and Christ's merit when you say they are not enough to buy your pardon! Can you find no better way to show your sense of sin than to malign the Savior? Are you unwilling to be in Christ's debt for your salvation, or too proud to beg His forgiveness?

It is horrible pride for a beggar to starve rather than take alms from a rich man, or for a condemned criminal to choose death rather than accept pardon from the hand of a compassionate ruler. Yet here is something worse – for a soul pining and perishing in sin to reject the mercy of God and the helping hand of Christ to save him. God says there is not a soul He cannot save. If you continue in your self-effacing way, you call Him a liar. You have been tricked into believing your tears are a stronger purgative than Christ's blood.

Another form of spiritual pride that shows you are depending on the worth of your own grace is *self-applauding pride*. This is when the heart is secretly lifted up and says of itself, 'I may not be perfect, but I'm certainly better than most Christians I know.' Every such glance of the soul's eye is adulterous – in fact, idolatrous. Any time you give your own righteousness the inward worship of your confidence and trust, this is great iniquity indeed. You come to open heaven's gate with the old key, when God has put on a new lock.

If you are truly a Christian, you must acknowledge that your first entrance into your justified state was by pure mercy. You were 'justified freely by his grace, through the redemption that is in Christ Jesus' (*Rom. 3:24*). Having been reconciled, to whom are you now indebted – to your own goodness, to your obedience, to yourself – or to Christ? If Christ does not lead in all you do, you are sure to find the door of grace shut to you. 'The righteousness of God [is] revealed from faith to faith . . . [for] the just shall live by faith' (*Rom. 1:17*). We are not only made alive by Christ, but we live by Christ. Heaven's way is paved with grace and mercy from beginning to end.

Why is God so insistent that we use His grace instead of our own? Because He knows our grace is inadequate for the task. The truth is this: Trusting in our own grace only brings trouble and heartache; trusting in God's grace brings lasting peace and joy.

In the first place, trusting in your own goodness will eventually destroy it. Inherent grace is weak. Force it to endure the yoke of the law, and sooner or later it will faint by the wayside, unequal to the task of pulling the heavy load of your old nature. What you need is Christ's yoke, but you cannot take it until you shed the one that harnesses you to works.

How is this done? By renouncing *every* expectation from yourself. If you are one of those who have claimed for years to be a Christian, but you see little fruit in your life, perhaps you should dig down to the root of your profession and find out whether the seed you planted was cultivated in the barren soil of legalism. If so, pull it up at once, and replant your soul in a fertile field – God's mercy. David gave an account of how he came to prosper when some who were rich and famous suddenly withered and died: 'Lo,' he said, 'this is the man that made not God his strength; but trusted in the abundance of his riches. . . . But I am like a green olive tree in the house of God: I trust in the mercy of God for ever and ever' (*Ps. 52:7, 8*).

Not only do you crush your grace by making it carry the burden of your salvation, but you also deprive yourself of true comfort in Christ. Gospel-comfort springs from a gospel-root, which is Christ. 'We are the circumcision, which worship God in the spirit, and rejoice in Christ Jesus, and have no confidence in the flesh' (*Phil. 3:3*). The first step to receiving gospel comfort is to send away all comforters of our own. A physician asks his patient to stop going to every other doctor who has been tampering with his health, and trust him for a cure. As your spiritual physician, the Holy Spirit asks your soul to send away all the old practitioners – every duty, every other course of obedience – and lean only on Him.

Does your soul cry out from its depths for inward peace? Then check to see what vessel you are drawing your comfort from. If it is the vessel of your own sufficiency, the supply is finite and will soon run dry. It is mixed, or diluted, and therefore not very nourishing. Above all, it is stolen if you claim it as your own and do not acknowledge it as God's gift to you. Now how much comfort can you expect from stolen goods? And how foolish to play the thief when your Father has so much more and better to give than you could pilfer in a lifetime! What clever deceit of Satan – to make us willing to steal, but too proud to beg mercy at God's hand.

The third kind of spiritual pride is *pride of privileges*. This is the third kind of pride which wicked spirits use to puff up the Christian. Three sorts of privilege are especially useful for their purposes: the privilege of eminent place; the privilege of persecution; and the privilege of special blessing.

Pride of prominent place. To keep the heart low when the man stands high takes a great measure of grace. Christ perceived a budding pride in the seventy missionaries He commissioned during His earthly ministry. They came back from their journeys, obviously impressed by their achievements and eager to spread the news about the miracles they had performed. Our Lord stepped in with a word of caution, saying, 'Rejoice not, that the spirits are subject unto you; but rather rejoice, because your names are written in heaven' (*Luke 10:20*).

In other words, 'Don't get blinded by your own glory when your ministry flourishes, or think that the merit of your works is in any way a measure of your own worth. There will be souls in hell who will say, "Lord, Lord . . . in thy name [we] have cast out devils" (*Matt. 7:22*). Value yourselves, therefore, not by the works you have done in My name, but by the evidence of My saving grace in your souls.'

Pride of persecution. Suffering for God's truth is indeed a tremendous privilege: 'Unto you it is given in the behalf of Christ, not only to believe on him, but also to suffer for his sake' (*Phil. 1:29*). Faith is a great gift; we cannot get to heaven without it. But perseverance is greater, because without it faith would not last long nor be worth much. And if perseverance is a valuable thing in itself, how much more honorable it is when applied in the case of suffering.

We sometimes imagine martyrs to be men so godly they are beyond Satan's reach. But as long as there is the feeblest breath of life in any saint, Satan will be on hand to try to destroy his faith. The greater the faith, the greater Satan's wrath. If he cannot keep a zealot from suffering for Christ, he will then spend his energies trying to pollute by pride this act of love and obedience.

To keep yourself humble if God should allow you the privilege of persecution, write the following admonitions on the tables of your heart.

1. 'I deserve to suffer.' Though you may not deserve to suffer at the hands of other men, still you cannot say you do not deserve to suffer. Did not your sins, as well as any, nail the Savior to the cross? None have suffered without sin except Christ, and therefore none can glory in suffering except Him. We must all cry out, with Paul, 'God forbid that I should glory, save in the cross of our Lord Jesus Christ' (*Gal. 6:14*). The English martyr, John Careless, who died in prison for the cause of Christ, made this humble statement: 'Such an honor it is, as angels are not permitted to have; therefore, God forgive me my unthankfulness.'

2. 'I can endure only by God's grace.' When you are called to suffer, is it your own grace which bears you up, or Christ's? Are they your words or His you speak when called to bear witness to the truth? And how is it that you happen to be a sufferer, and not a persecutor? You owe everything to God! He is not indebted to you, not if you had a thousand lives to give! He could have left you alone to live and die in your lusts. He could have let you perish at the gallows as a martyr in the devil's cause – for murder,

rape, or some other horrid crime. Or He could have withdrawn His grace and left you to face your persecutors alone. How long do you think you would endure in the presence of a Nebuchadnezzar without God's sustaining power? You had better follow Stephen's example, who 'looked up stedfastly into heaven' (*Acts 7:55*). If you need the Holy Spirit's strength to live daily for Christ, how much more will you need it if you are called to die for Him?

3. 'If I take the credit for suffering, I cannot say I suffer for Christ.' Not the act of suffering, but the frame of heart in suffering is what makes a person a martyr for God. You may give your body to be burned, but if you stand in the fire with a proud heart, you are dying for yourself – not for Christ! If your secret goal is to raise up a monument to your own memory so that people will praise your faith and courage long after you are dead, your offering is unacceptable to the Lord. God will receive no gift the proud heart offers; He will refuse no gift extended with a humble hand.

Pride of blessing. If on the one hand Satan stands at the door of persecution and offers pride as a consolation, you can be sure he will be at the fountain of blessing as well, extending the same lust.

When God flows in with more than ordinary manifestations of His love, then the Christian is in danger of having his heart secretly swell in pride. Because God appears to be paying extra attention to him, he begins to think he is a 'favorite' child. The proper response to God's special blessings should be humility and a deep sense of love and gratitude. If our hearts are somewhat hard and frozen by the cares of this life, they should soften and melt in the sunshine of His love. But as usual, Satan tries to thwart God's purpose, and he finds pride the easiest way to spoil His gift.

Truly, God lets us see our proneness to this sin of pride by the short stay He makes when He comes to us with greater-than-usual discoveries of His love. The Comforter abides for ever in the saint's bosom, but that exhilarating feeling of joy in the Holy Spirit comes and is gone again with the speed of a gazelle. A brief glimpse of heaven and a vision of love now and then cheer the spirit of a discouraged Christian as he trudges up the mountain of a duty or trial. But if the Lord let him build a tabernacle there and dwell under the constant shine of such an exhibition of His favor, he would soon forget where it all came from and begin to think he was lord of his own comfort.

If the apostle Paul was in danger of falling into the trap of spiritual arrogance after his short rapture – to prevent which, God gave him a thorn in his side – do you not think Satan is more than likely to catch us, too? Therefore, Christian, if you ever had need to watch, this is the time – when God dandles you most on the knee of His love.

Here are some precautions you may take.

1. Do not measure your grace by your comfort. God does not necessarily send you an extra measure of comfort as a reward for being good. Such discoveries of His love do indeed bear witness to the truth of His grace in you, but they say nothing about the degree and measure of your inherent grace. The weak child may be – in fact, generally is – oftener in his parent's lap than the strong one.

2. Do not grow lax when you are being comforted. Rather, use this time of blessing to work harder than ever for the Lord. The manifestations of God's love are to fit us for our work. Basking in the light of His comfort is one thing; going forth in the power of the Spirit's comfort is quite another. How foolish is the man who spends all his time counting his money but never invests it; how wise is the one who puts his money to work for him and earns

dividends. Spiritually speaking, the one who hoards his comforts will lose what he has, while the one who puts his comforts to work for Christ will increase his stock five, ten, even an hundredfold.

3. Do not think you are the source of your own comfort. Remember that you depend on God for your continued peace and joy. The smiles you had yesterday will not make you happy today, any more than the bread you ate then will keep you satisfied if you do not eat again. You will need new draughts of God's love every day to keep you satisfied. Let God hide His face just for a moment, and you will quickly forget the taste and lose sight of the comforts you had just a short time earlier.

How we would ridicule the man who, when the sun shines in at his window, tries to trap the sunbeams indoors by closing the shutters. But we are just as foolish to take our present joy, then turn away from God's presence, suppos-ing that we have all we need. You can feel the heat from the sun only when you stand beneath its rays; you can feel God's comfort only as you keep your face turned toward Him.

The believer's comfort is like Israel's manna. It is daily rained, as that was, from heaven. We are told God gave His people manna to 'humble' them (*Deut. 8:16*). Do not suppose it humbled them because it was poor man's food, for it was in fact 'angels' food' (*Ps. 78:25*). Rather, the manner of dispensing it kept them meek. God held the key to their cupboard. They were forced to wait upon Him and con-tinually acknowledge that He and He alone was the source of their need. God communicates our spiritual comforts in the same way and for the same purpose – to humble us

(c) *A final thought on spiritual wickedness*

Satan strains every nerve to engulf you in spiritual

[223]

wickednesses above all others. They are the ones that sear your conscience, blind your mind, and petrify your heart. If ever you perish, it will be by the hand of these sins. Other sins are preparatory to spiritual sins. Satan therefore draws you into carnal sin to bring you ultimately into spiritual sin.

Carnal sins pave the way for spiritual sins in two ways. First, the soul engulfed in carnal sin is more naturally disposed to spiritual sin. Any kind of sin by its very nature hardens the heart: 'Lest any of you be hardened through the deceitfulness of sin' (*Heb. 3:13*). You may have seen a bridle path that has been beaten hard by the hooves of many horses. Though you cannot see it with your natural eyes, carnal sins do the same thing to a heart. God's Holy Spirit stands by the lane, entreating the sinner to leave his sins and come to Him for forgiveness. He can make the heart soft again. But if the sinner steadily refuses and lets these sins race across his heart, God will finally give him up to his lusts. This is the second way carnal sins prepare the heart for spiritual sins. When God removes His restraining power, the devil has a sinner under lock and key. If God leaves your heart hard and unbroken, it is a sad sign He does not intend to sow the seed of grace there. Pray that none of these things will come upon you. And to assure that they do not, be careful not to reject any offers He makes to soften you.

God's hardening is a consequence of our hardening our own hearts. Though you may lose your earthly estate against your will, you cannot lose your spiritual estate against your will. God will harden none, damn none, unless they willfully reject His grace. Here is a sobering thought: If you enter eternity with a hard, impenitent heart, you have no one to blame but yourself.

v. THE GROUNDS OF WAR ('IN HIGH PLACES,' OR 'FOR HEAVENLY THINGS')

The last phrase in the description of our grand enemy is somewhat ambiguous in the original text. Most translators read it 'in high [i.e., heavenly] *places*' as though the apostle wanted to stress the advantage of place which our enemy has by being above us. Yet some interpreters, both ancient and modern, read the words not 'in heavenly places,' but 'in heavenly *things*.' This would mean that Paul is saying, in essence, 'We do not wrestle for small or trivial things, but for heavenly things – in fact, for heaven itself!'

This seems to me to be the preferred interpretation for several reasons:

First, the same word used in other passages of Scripture is translated to mean 'things.' It appears almost twenty other times in the New Testament and is never interpreted to mean an aerial place, but always to mean things truly heavenly and spiritual. If the word did mean *place*, then it would signify a supercelestial location, and would therefore be an area where the devil cannot go.

Second, what would be the purpose in pointing out that Satan is above us in place? If we know anything about spirits at all, we know that by their very nature they are 'above' us. Being immaterial – not confined to flesh and bone – gives them this advantage. But if we interpret the word as meaning *things*, then it adds weight to all the other branches of the description we have been studying in depth. Now it means we wrestle against principalities and powers and spiritual wickedness for the greatest prize of all – for that which heaven itself holds forth. Such an enemy and such a prize make it a matter of our greatest care how we manage the combat.

(a) *The saint's heavenly calling*

What, then, is Paul's premise? Simply this: that we are in

a life-or-death struggle with Satan himself; all our hopes are fixed on heaven. In other words, Satan's main design is to plunder the Christian of all that is heavenly, which is the same as to leave him destitute. The Christian as a Christian is an alien on earth. All he has or desires is heavenly. So whatever happens here below is quite apart from his being or true happiness, and interferes with neither his joy nor his grief.

Heap all the riches and honors of the world upon a man – they will not make him a Christian. Heap them on a Christian – they will not make him a better Christian. Again, take them all away. When stripped and naked, he will still be a Christian, and perhaps a better one.

Satan could do the sincere saint little harm if he directed his forces only against his outward enjoyments, because they mean nothing to him in comparison with his spiritual inheritance. Indeed, Satan's attack on a Christian's earthly possessions should do him no more harm than a robber does to a man if he strips him naked and then proceeds to beat the man's clothes as they lie on the ground in a heap! Insofar as the spirit of grace prevails in a saint's heart, he has put off his desire for the things of the world. Therefore, his heavenly treasure is the booty Satan waits for: his nature, his occupation, and his hopes.

(i) *The Christian's nature is heavenly*, born from above. As Christ is the Lord from heaven, so all His offspring are heavenly. The holiness of Christ in you reminds Satan of his own first estate. He has lost the beauty of holiness for ever, and now, like a true apostate, he endeavors to ruin it in you.

God stamps His image of holiness on the face of your soul. This attribute of beauty is what makes us most like God. How God longs to see His clear likeness reflected in

His children, and His true children long to be like Him! Satan knows this and works tirelessly to disfigure the divine image. Marring the Christian's nature brings shame to the saint and pours contempt upon God in distorting His likeness. Is it not worth risking life and limb against this enemy who would annihilate that which makes us like God Himself?

(ii) *The Christian's occupation is heavenly.* That is to say, God is our overseer. We may plant our seeds here on earth, but our crop will be harvested in heaven. This keeps our hearts and desires on a celestial plane. In a spiritual sense, the Christian's feet stand where other men cannot even see. He treads on the moon and is clothed with the sun. He looks down on earthly men as one from a high hill looks upon those living in a swamp. While he breathes in pure heavenly air, they are suffocating in a fog of carnal pleasures and profits. He knows one heavenly pearl is worth infinitely more than the earthly accumulation of a whole lifetime.

The great business of a saint's life is to be doing things that enlarge the kingdom of heaven. Not only is he interested in his own welfare, but he eagerly recruits his friends and neighbors to join in his eternal enterprise. Now this alarms hell. What! Not content to go to heaven himself, but by his holy example and faithful work will he try to carry them along with him also? This brings the lion raging out of his den. Such a Christian, to be sure, will find the devil in his way to oppose him.

(iii) *The Christian's hopes are all heavenly.* He does not expect lasting satisfaction from anything the world has to offer. Indeed, he would think himself the most miserable person to have ever lived, if the only rewards he could expect from his religion were on this side of eternity. No, it is heaven and eternal life that he anticipates. And though he is so poor that he cannot leave one cent in his will, yet he counts himself a greater heir than if he were a child of the greatest prince on earth.

Hope is the grace that shows us how to rejoice in the prospect of promised glory. It sits beside us in the worst of times. When things are so bad that we cannot imagine how they could possibly get worse, hope lifts our eyes from our immediate troubles and places them on our future eternal joys. We can smile even in the face of our persecutors, knowing that in only a short time the cross will be lifted from our shoulders for ever – and the earthly crowns will be lifted from the heads of those in the devil's service. Their portion of joy will all have been spent, but the Christian will be given an endless supply.

An understanding of this truth fills the Christian with such joy, he will not listen to the devil's lies about God's faithlessness or lack of concern. Shutting his ears to Satan's taunts, he opens his heart to the promises in God's Word and rests on them. His peaceful attitude torments the devil, who cannot bear to see the saint under full sail for heaven, filled with the sweet hope of a glorious celebration when he reaches that port. So he raises whatever storms and tempests he can, hoping to cause a shipwreck or at the very least force the saint to cripple into heaven's harbor empty-handed.

(b) *A call worth fighting for*

We see, by considering the intensity of Satan's attack on our spiritual inheritance, the necessity of the saint's perseverance in wrestling against him. Now a word of reproof to four sorts of persons:

(i) *To those who refuse to wrestle.* There are many who, instead of taking heaven by force, keep it off by force. How long has the Lord been crying in the streets, 'Repent, for the kingdom of heaven is at hand!'? Yet to this day millions drive madly on toward hell and will not turn back. They willfully refuse to be called the children of God. They choose the pleasures of sin over the riches of heaven, preferring to die in their sins rather than admit they need Christ's pardon.

What foolish pride! A historical parallel illustrates the stupidity of such thinking. Cato and Caesar were bitter enemies. When Caesar came to power, Cato knew he would have to appeal to his arch-rival if his life were to be spared. Rather than humble himself, he committed suicide. Upon hearing the news, Caesar cried, 'Oh, Cato, why did you begrudge me the honor of saving your life!'

Do not many walk as if they were begrudging Christ the honor of saving their souls? What other reason can you give, sinner, for rejecting His grace? Are heaven and happiness repugnant to you? Can you honestly say you do not want them? Why, then, do you not accept them? For the love of God, think what you are doing! You are fighting against eternal life and in so doing, you judge yourself unworthy of it (Acts 13:46).

(ii) *To those who neglect to wrestle.* You would be hard pressed to find a person who would not rejoice for his soul to be saved at last. But where is the Christian who by his vigorous effort shows he is in earnest? For most, if wishing could bring eternal life, they would be happy to enter heaven's gates. But if it means wrestling and fighting, and making their faith top priority, then they are not so sure.

Too many people waste their lives away, wishing the way to heaven were easier, but unwilling to get busy and seek the grace they need for such an enterprise. They need to see that wrestling *for* the Lord promises a sure victory, while wrestling *against* Him is a guarantee of defeat.

The misery of the damned will be compounded when

[229]

they fully understand what they have lost in losing God, and when they remember all the means once offered them which could have gotten them eternal life. When it is too late, they will regret they had no heart to take Christ's offer.

(iii) *To those who only pretend to wrestle.* I am speaking now of those individuals who make a lot of noise about their religion, but who secretly have their hearts set on earthly goals. They pretend to be heaven-bound, but their hearts are full of hypocrisy. Such deceivers are like the eagle who, when he soars highest, has his eye fixed on some carnal prey on the ground.

Hypocrites have always been and ever will be a part of the crowd thronging into the church and mingling with the true saints of God. Their speech is pure, their service admirable; but their hearts are lined with deceit. Worst of all, they fool even themselves. The world may mistakenly call them saints, but Christ knows they are devils. What did He say about the master hypocrite, Judas? 'Have I not chosen you twelve, and one of you is a devil?' (*John 6:70*).

Truly, of all devils, none is as bad as the professing devil – the preaching, praying devil. God has repeatedly shown His severe displeasure when His so-called people have prostituted sacred things to worldly ends. Of all men, God strikes with greatest speed the one who gilds over worldly and wicked business with holy pretensions. God has made a solemn promise: 'I will set my face against that man, and will make him a sign and a proverb, and I will cut him off from the midst of my people, and ye shall know that I am the Lord' (*Ezek. 14:8*).

(iv) *To those who keep others from wrestling.* Among thieves, there is often a scout who searches out where the booty is to be had. He is the brains behind every illicit operation, but he never risks his own neck by actually committing a crime. The devil uses this same tactic by watching how a Christian walks, where he goes, whose company he enjoys. Then he decides the best way to rob him of his grace. When the plan is set, he sends someone else to carry it out. Thus he sent Job's friends and even Job's wife to tempt him; he sent Potiphar's wife to entice Joseph.

Friend, ask yourself whether or not you have ever done the devil some service of this kind. Have you ever had a child whose heart was tender toward God, but you were too busy to take him to church or teach him the ways of the Lord? Perhaps now he is grown and has no time for the things of Christ at all. Or perhaps your spouse was full of enthusiasm and faith, but living with your cold spirit and bitter attitude has doused the flame that once burned so brightly.

How do you suppose the indictment will read when you are brought before the bar on Judgment Day? It was not enough for you to reject Christ yourself; you had to intimidate those who wanted to wrestle their way to heaven. A terrible offense indeed! You thereby lay up to yourself wrath against the day of wrath! (*Rom. 2:5*).

(c) *A word of caution to those who desire a heavenly prize*

(i) *In getting earthly things.* If heaven and heavenly things are the prize you wrestle for, then you will have a holy deportment of heart even in your secular pursuits. Take every precaution that you do not do business like the rest of the world. If you, as a Christian, resort to the world's ways in your drive for material possessions, you cost yourself two valuable commodities: the glory of God, and the happiness of your soul. Many a dear servant of God has rejected wealth or fame because the price was too high. Moses tossed aside all the privileges of court because he refused to be called the son of Pharaoh's daughter.

Abraham refused gifts from the king of Sodom for fear someone might accuse him of covetousness or self-interest. Every child of God should be as conscientious as this. Never forget: Nothing you can get on earth is worth exchanging for God's glory or your own peace of mind.

A true saint will be zealous in his daily affairs, but all his energies will be tuned to heaven. While his hands are busy at his tasks, his heart and head will be taken up with higher matters – how to please God, grow in grace, enjoy more intimate fellowship with Christ. The carnal man, in contrast, spends long, hard hours in his shop and then goes home and spends half the night plotting how to get ahead in business. He sweats in the shop, but grows cold in the prayer closet. No weather is bad enough to keep him from market, but if the road to church is a little slippery or there is a chill in the air, he begs his leave from the services. No inconvenience is too great if it fattens his pocket, but let the preacher keep him a minute or two past the hour, and he complains. In short, at work he keeps his eyes on the till; at church, he keeps them on his watch.

If anything I have said speaks to you, go quickly to God and petition for a thorough change of heart.

(ii) *In using earthly things.* Perhaps you have a heavenly spirit in getting earthly things. But do you have the same spirit when you use them? The good wrestler uses his earthly estate for heavenly ends.

What do you do with the fruits of your labor? Do you bestow them on your own overstuffed paunch, your hawks, and your hounds – or do you share them with the poor? If you are a prominent member of your community, how do you use your influence – for good or for evil? For selfish or selfless ends? To pray for 'things' without a heavenly end in mind is close to idolatry. Use your material wealth with a holy fear, dear saint, lest earth should rob heaven, and your temporal enjoyments endanger your heavenly interests. As Job sanctified his children by offering a sacrifice out of fear that they might have sinned, so the Christian must continually sanctify his earthly enjoyments by prayer. In this way He will be delivered from the snare of them.

(iii) *In keeping earthly things.* The Christian must practice the same indifference in keeping his earthly possessions as he did in getting them. God never signs the title of anything over to us, but merely gives us things to keep in trust. All will be left behind when He calls us home. If He sees fit to let us keep them until then, we bless and thank Him for His generosity; and if He takes them away sooner, we bless Him still.

God never intended, by His providence in bringing Moses to Pharaoh's court, to leave him there in worldly pomp and grandeur. A carnal heart would have reasoned that Moses could best help his people – slaves under Pharaoh – by using his position and power to influence the king, or perhaps even by aspiring to the throne. But when Moses renounced his place of privilege, his faith and self-denial were made more eminently conspicuous. It is for this obedient faith that Moses is given such honorable mention in the New Testament (*Heb. 11.24, 25*).

Sometimes God lavishes us with things, not so we can hang on to them, but so we will have something to let go of to show our love for Him. Was there anything better in the whole world Mary could have done with her precious oil than to anoint her Lord? What enterprise will pay more lasting dividends than to invest what you possess in the cause of Christ?

Christian, keep a loose grip on the material possessions you value most highly. Be ready at a moment's notice to throw them overboard, rather than risk the shipwreck of your faith. You cannot labor for heavenly possessions if your hands and heart are loaded down with earthly pursuits. In the end, if you can save anything, it will be your soul, your interest in Christ and heaven. If you should lose all your worldly goods, you should still be able to say with Jacob, 'I have enough [all things]' (*Gen. 33:11*).

(d) *A practical note – on the folly of pursuing earthly things*

(i) *Earthly things are unnecessary.* Something is indispensable only when it cannot be replaced by any other thing. Though Satan often convinces us to the contrary, there is nothing we enjoy that Christ cannot make provision for, should it be taken away. In heaven there will be light but no sun, a rich feast and yet no meat, glorious robes and yet no clothes. Not one thing will be missing – yet none of the earthly things we esteem so highly will be there.

But you do not have to wait for heaven to be recompensed. You may be under great physical affliction here, your health taken away. God will provide better comfort than if you had your health. You may be so insignificant by the world's standards that no one even knows you exist; nevertheless, in the midst of your obscurity you may be receiving an excellent report in heaven by virtue of your faith. You may be so poor you do not have a dime in your pocket; God can make you rich in His grace. Remember what Paul wrote to Timothy: 'Godliness with contentment is great gain' (*1 Tim. 6:6*).

Suppose you do die penniless. What will it matter at all? But suppose you die graceless! Heaven and heavenly things are the kind that cannot be recompensed by anything else. Do not let Satan distract you with baubles and toys. While he is entertaining you with his clever illusions, his other hand is in your treasure, robbing you of that which is irreplaceable. It is more necessary to be saved, than to be; better not to be, than to have a being in hell.

(ii) *Earthly things are uncertain.* No matter how hard you work for material gain, there is no guarantee of success. Men have been doing business for thousands of years, yet no one has come up with a fail-proof plan for getting rich. How few carry away the prize in the world's lottery! Most have only disillusionment and bitter memories for their trouble.

But now for heaven and the things of heaven, the plan is quite clearly laid out in the Bible: 'As many as walk according to this rule, peace be on them . . . ' (*Gal. 6:16*). If anyone pursues heavenly things and does not get them, it is because he did not follow God's instruction in the right manner.

If you want heaven but you also want your sins, do not expect to succeed. You must part company with one or the other. If you will not let go of your sins, God will have to let go of you. If you want heaven but insist on purchasing it with your own righteousness, you will fall short of the price. You are like the near kinsman in *Ruth* who wanted to buy Elimelech's land but was not willing to marry Ruth as the law required (*4:2–4*). All the good you do, all the duties you perform, are admirable if they are acts of love that follow your act of repentance. But if you offer them as the price you are willing to pay for heaven, God will not deal with you. You must close with Christ and Him alone, or lose the whole bargain.

How can you be sure you will gain heaven and eternal life? Only be persuaded to renounce your lusts and throw away any confidence in your own righteousness. Then run to Christ and present yourself to Him in need of salvation. Long for Him more than for life itself. He is already

[235]

standing outside your heart's door, calling you by name, and has promised not to turn away any who come to Him with a contrite heart. Then, though you continue to dwell on earth, your eternal life is as certain as if you had already taken up residence in that holy city.

How sad that so few will trade their uncertain hopes in this life for the promise of heaven. What account can be given for this, except the desperate atheism of men's hearts? They cannot be convinced to believe what the Scripture says. May God open the eyes of the unbelieving world so people can see that the things of the spirit are real and not fictitious. Faith and faith alone can make the invisible visible to them.

(iii) *Earthly things are uninsurable*. Though God may have blessed you with wealth, you could be rich today and poor tomorrow. You could be in good health when you go to bed, but seized by pangs of illness or death before morning. Can you take enough precautions to guarantee that nothing will happen to wipe out your fortune? Can you become rich enough to buy good health or add one day to the span of your years?

Scripture compares the world's population to a mighty ocean. Kings and rulers sit upon this ocean. As a ship floats upon the waves, so their lives float upon the favor of the multitude. And what kind of security is there in riding the waves? For a while they will be lifted up to the heavens, only to fall down again into the deep. David knew how fickle the world's preferments are: 'We have ten parts in the king,' said the men of Israel (*2 Sam. 19:43*); and in the very next verse the tide had already turned: 'We have no part in David, neither have we inheritance in the son of Jesse' (*2 Sam. 20:1, 2*). Thus was David tossed up and down, almost in the same breath.

But heaven is a kingdom that cannot be shaken. Christ

is an abiding portion which changes not. His graces and comforts are sure waters that spring up into eternal life. The quail that were food for the Israelites' greed soon ceased, but the rock that was drink for their faith followed them. This rock is Christ. You may lose every temporal comfort, including family and friends, but if your treasure is secure in Christ, you are a rich man still. Christ will come to you in your darkest hour with peace and a promise: 'Fear not death nor devils. I will stay right here beside you until you breathe your last breath. My angels are waiting with Me. As soon as your soul is breathed out of your body, they will carry it to heaven and lay it in the bosom of My love. Then I will nourish you with those eternal joys that My blood has purchased and My love has perfected for you.'

(iv) *Earthly things are unsatisfying.* No matter how much we have of this world's goods, it will never be enough. A man's wealth often breeds misery, but never contentment. How foolish to suppose it ever could! Our spirits are immaterial; they will not be satisfied with the perishable delights of flesh and blood. The earthly prizes we strive to win are far inferior to the nature of man. Therefore, we must look far beyond them if we want to be blessed – even to God Himself, who is the Father of spirits.

The possessions God allows us to have are intended for our use, not our enjoyment. Trying to squeeze something out of them that was never in them in the first place is a futile endeavor. A cow's udders, gently pressed, will yield sweet milk, nourishing and refreshing. Applying more and more pressure will not produce greater quantities of milk. We lose the good of material things by expecting too much from them. Those who try hardest to please themselves with earthly goods find the least satisfaction in them.

All our frustrations could be easily avoided if we would turn away from things and look to Christ for happiness. Here is what you can expect when you do:

First, the guilt of your sins all gone. Guilt is the pin that constantly pricks our joy. When Christ takes away your sins, He also takes the guilt.

Second, your nature renewed and sanctified. Holiness is simply the creature restored to the state of health which God intended when He created him. And when is a man more at ease than when he is healthy?

Third, adoption into the family of God. Surely this cannot help but make you happy – to be the son or daughter of so great a King.

Fourth, an eternal inheritance with Christ. We cannot begin to comprehend what this means in terms of everlasting joy. Our present conceptions of heaven are no more like heaven itself than an artist's painting of the sun is like the orb in the sky. But we can cling to the promise that what God has prepared for us is beyond our most extravagant dream (*Isa. 64:4; 1 Cor. 2:9*).

(e) *A final word about our heavenly prize*

Find out for yourself whether you are devoted to heavenly or earthly things. You cannot pursue both. Earthly things are like trash, which not only does not nourish, but takes away the appetite from that which would. Heavenly things have no appeal for one corrupted by such trash. Only when you come to the end of yourself, like the prodigal, will you make the judgment that heavenly things are better. Then you will know bread is better fare than husks, and your Father's house a better place to dwell than with hogs in the field.

If you will have heaven, you must have Christ, who is all

in all. And if Christ, you must accept His service as well as His sacrifice. No holiness, no happiness. Take the whole offer, or take nothing. One can compare holiness and happiness to those sisters, Leah and Rachel. On the surface, happiness, like Rachel, seems more desirable. (Even a carnal heart will fall in love with that.) But holiness, like Leah, is the elder and has a special beauty also, though in this life it appears at some disadvantage – the eyes red from tears of repentance and the face furrowed with the work of mortification.

Here is heaven's law: The younger sister cannot be bestowed before the elder. We cannot enjoy fair Rachel – heaven and happiness – until we first embrace Leah – holiness – with all her demanding duties of repentance and mortification. Will you live by this law? Marry Christ and His grace, then serve a hard apprenticeship in temptations both of prosperity and adversity. Endure the heat of the one and the cold of the other. If you will be patient, at last the fairer sister will be handed over to you. This is the only way to win the prize of heavenly things.

4: Third Consideration: A Second Exhortation to be Armed

1. The Exhortation and the Implication

Wherefore take unto you the whole armour of God, that ye may be able to withstand in the evil day, and having done all, to stand (Eph. 6:13).

I N this verse, the apostle's words, ' . . . take unto you the whole armour . . ,' seem to repeat his instructions in verse 11: 'Put on the whole armour. . . . ' No doubt he uses repetition to emphasize a point. In his intervening statement (*verse 12*), he gives a full report of Satan's power and malice, and discloses his evil design against the saints. Now he sounds an alarm to battle and bids them, 'Arm! Arm!' But if we look more closely at the verse, a new revelation of truth will unfold to us.

First we will discuss why the apostle repeats the exhortation so soon; second, the results that will follow: (1) 'that ye may be able to withstand in the evil day' – i.e., be able to fight; (2) 'and having done all, to stand' – i.e., be able to conquer.

FIRST OBSERVATION: THE IMPLICATIONS OF A REPEATED ADMONITION

When your child is finally old enough to cross the street alone, do you send him off with a wave of the hand and a casual reminder to be careful? Of course not! You tell him over and over again exactly what he needs to know to ensure his safety. Paul knew all too well the dangers these young Christians faced; he longed to have them forewarned and forearmed. Out of the depth of his conviction that God's armour was their only hope came the compelling need to remind them once more – 'Put it on!'

Paul was like the conscientious workman who drives one nail squarely home with repeated blows before he takes up a second. Too many preachers resemble the carpenter who, in a rush to finish a job, uses tacks instead of screws to fasten the legs of a chair. True, he will be done sooner but how long will his workmanship hold? Impatient preachers, before they have nailed down the last truth securely, are already off on another. If they were more sensitive to their congregations, they would realize that unless they hit the truth squarely on the head, they are not likely to penetrate the consciences of their hearers. Most of us are spiritually hard-headed. We need to have the truth hammered home with repeated blows.

Not only that, but we generally retain best those truths which are simplest and least cluttered with extraneous ideas. In shopping for clothes, I am more likely to make a purchase if the salesman shows me only a few choice items from which to choose. If he pulls everything off the racks and piles it in a heap, I am only confused, unable to get a good look at anything. To know one foundational truth well is better than to have heard them all but understand none.

IMPERATIVE TRUTHS

A preacher should not apologize for preaching the same truth over and over. Paul himself says, 'To write the same things to you, to me indeed is not grievous, but for you it is safe' (*Phil. 3:1*). Three sorts of truth should be preached regularly from the pulpit.

(a) *Primary (fundamental) truths*

These are the truths everyone must know and believe for

[241]

salvation, the verities upon whose shoulders the whole weight of Christianity rests.

The fundamental truths of the gospel are landmarks to keep us safely within the boundaries set by God. Suppose your grandfather owned some property which at one time had been carefully surveyed. He was there when they set the stakes and could have paced it off blindfolded. But he never took the time to show anyone else the markings. Over the years, the markers rotted, were rooted up, or washed away. Now your grandfather has died and left the land to you. But a dishonest neighbor claims it is his, and as proof of ownership points to the burgeoning crop of corn he has planted. You discover that the deed and land description have been lost. Since you do not really know the proper boundary lines yourself, how will you defend your case in court? You will probably end up losing your property because no one ever told you where it ends and your neighbor's begins.

The spiritual parallel is this: Every fundamental truth has some evil neighbor (i.e., heresy) butting up against it, eager to plant a crop of lies upon the sacred ground of God's Holy Word and thus fool the saints. And the very reason that a spirit of error has encroached so far upon the truth in the last few years is because ministers have not walked the boundaries of the gospel with their people and acquainted them with these primary truths.

We have both staples and luxuries in our religion, just as in our homes. Luxuries are wonderful and often enhance our appreciation of the staples, but they quickly lose their appeal when our basic needs go unmet. What pleasure is there in dining from fine china if you have no food to put on the plate? Of what value is a silk blouse in winter if you have no coat?

(b) *Precarious truths*

A preacher should preach not only fundamental truths, but also those truths he observes to be most frequently undermined by Satan. These are often the ordinances of God that should dictate the Christian's response to controversial issues of faith and practice.

To know which doctrines are under greatest attack among his own congregation, a pastor must read and study his people as diligently as any book in his library. From the personal tone of Paul's letters, we can surmise that he frequently paced the boundaries of the young church, looking for encroaching errors. When he discovered that false apostles had infiltrated the Galatian church and were preaching the law again, how he pounded home the gospel truth of justification by faith. When word came to him of divisions and strife among the Corinthians, what poured forth from his heart but that peerless exhortation on love?

Pastor, your flock may sometimes grow restless and complain that you keep them in the same pasture too long by preaching on one sin. The fault is not yours, but theirs, if they keep straying away from the Shepherd every time your back is turned. Who can blame a dog for continuing to bark when the wolf is still prowling about the fold?

If you long to grow in the likeness of Christ, do not pray for a preacher who will entertain you with a clever new topic each Sunday. Plead instead for a man of principle who will preach against sin and for truth without compromise, until his people repent and turn from their evil ways.

(c) *Practical truths*

These are the 'bread and salt' truths. Whatever else is on the table, they must be present at every meal. Peter put it this way: 'I will not be negligent to put you always in remembrance of these things, though ye know them' (2 *Pet. 1:12*). He was speaking specifically about those things we need to know to live a Christ-like life from one day to the next.

You should never grow weary of hearing practical truths preached. When a man loses his taste for meat and vegetables and wants nothing but dessert at every meal, we know something is seriously wrong. How sad that our present age is far advanced in this spiritual disease that spoils our appetites for anything but honeyed phrases and sugar-coated doctrines.

If you love God, love His truth! Receive gladly the doctrines that equip you for the task God calls you to. Faith and repentance will be good doctrines to preach and hear to the end of the world. You may as well quarrel with God for making only one way to heaven, as to quarrel with the minister for preaching the message of faith and repentance again and again. Both babes in Christ and mature Christians need to hear this truth.

If your heart were humble and your palate spiritual, old truths would be new to you every time you heard them. In heaven the saints draw all their wine of joy at one tap – Christ. Yet it never tastes flat. God is the one object that fills their souls, and they never weary of Him. It shall be so for all eternity. And how can we weary of anything here on earth that speaks of God and His love?

Having said all this, let me make one thing clear. I am not excusing any slothful servant in the work of the gospel who wraps up his talent in idleness, or buries it in the earth while he plays all week long. Such a minister has nothing to set before his people on the Lord's day but one or two moldy loaves which were kneaded many years before. This is not good stewardship! Yes, we need to hear the old truths, but that does not mean we should never hear new.

If the minister does not study and pray to increase his stock of knowledge and wisdom, he is the worst thief in town.

It is inexcusable for a man entrusted with the care of an orphan to let the child's estate lie dormant because he is too lazy to invest the funds. Much more for a preacher not to improve his gifts, which I may call his people's estate, and which he should invest for the good of their souls. Woe to the man of God who wastes his days in frivolous activities, or spends more time figuring out how to line his own pockets than how to add to his people's gifts and graces!

SECOND OBSERVATION: THE NEED TO IN-SPECT AND REPAIR YOUR GRACES

The second observation regarding Paul's repeated exhortation in Ephesians 6:13 is taken from the verb, which means not only 'to take', but 'to take again.' In other words, to recover something which was lost, or to resume an undertaking that up to the present has been abandoned.

Considering that Paul was writing primarily to the Christians at Ephesus, we may assume he was not telling them to put on God's armour by a conversion to the faith. This they had already done. Rather, Paul was exhorting them to pull their armour more closely to their bodies in the places where it was hanging loose, and to repair any holes in their graces.

I. WHY YOUR GRACES MUST BE KEPT IN GOOD REPAIR

Who wears armour in times of peace? Armour is designed for those going into battle! Do not think simply putting on the grace of God will frighten the enemy away. He is not impressed by a show of force. On the contrary, the very sight of God's armour upon your back is like waving a red flag at Satan. So to have it on for show is not enough; you must have it securely fastened at every point.

Satan is not challenging you to a mock battle; this war is a life-or-death struggle. If you do not believe me, look what he has done to God's servants in times past. Charging full speed ahead at many a dear saint, he has battered their armour until the grace of God in them was almost unrecognizable. All this he does when he catches a saint off guard.

Do you remember what happened to Jacob when he unbuckled his girdle of truth and sincerity, and used a trick to get his father's blessing? He got the blessing all right, but he also was repaid in kind when Laban switched Leah for Rachel. Think how much suffering he might have saved himself by keeping his whole suit of armour in place!

What about David? Oh, the battering he took by removing his breastplate of righteousness in the matter of Uriah! He sustained a dreadful wound, being shot right through the heart. And Jonah, when God wanted to send him to Nineveh, got caught without his shoes on. By that I mean he lacked the preparation and readiness with which his mind should have been shod, to have gone at the first call. Then there was poor Hezekiah. He had his helmet of hope knocked askew and so badly dented that he cried, 'I shall not see the Lord . . . in the land of the living' (*Isa. 38:11*). Even Abraham had fits of unbelief and distrustful qualms that crept in at some rusty spots in his graces.

This war is a spiritual holocaust. Either you destroy the power of Satan in your life by putting on the whole armour of God and keeping it on, or Satan will destroy you. The great saints of every century have been tried in the fires of temptation. And to a man they have been singed whenever Satan found the smallest chink in their graces. Do not disregard what history has repeatedly shown to be true.

Satan will watch and wait; sooner or later, he will catch you with this or that grace laid aside for the moment. Then he will attack. This hour of intense battle is the very time you need all your resolve to get your armour repaired – and to do it at once! Do not give up in despair; Christ is an excellent workman. He can make new all that is broken in you.

II. WHO SUFFERS WRONG WHEN YOUR GRACE DIMIN-
    ISHES

When you decline in grace, the negative effects go far beyond your own situation – even to God Himself. Let us examine the serious consequences of neglecting your spiritual welfare.

(a) *You wrong God*

God's honor is more dependent on His saints' graces than on any other single thing. Even the flagrant sins of the world do not discredit Him the way a saint's careless conduct does. When men of the world use the talents God has given them to increase their own bank accounts, they rob Him only of His oil, flax, and wool. But when the Christian misuses or neglects his grace, he takes away God's glory! Letting God's glory leak out at the holes in your graces is serious indeed. It shows utter disregard for His will. He intends for His glory to be magnified by your attitudes and actions not diminished!

Suppose a man entrusts one person with his money, and another with his child. Which would grieve him more: to have his money mismanaged and wasted, or to have his child neglected and injured? Grace is God's child in you, the new creature in Christ. When it comes to any harm because of your negligence, it cuts deeper into God's heart than when a sinner wrongs Him, because He has never trusted that individual with such a precious gift as He gave you.

(b) *You wrong other Christians*

by neglecting to repair your broken armour. When the physical body is sick in one part, all the others are somehow affected. The same principle is at work in the spiritual body (*1 Cor. 12:26*). When we ignore God's commandments, which always results in diminished grace, we show our indifference toward the entire body of believers. We are told to 'love one another' (*2 John 5*). And how do we demonstrate our obedience to this commandment? John tells us in the very next verse: 'And this is love, that we walk after his commandments' (*v. 6*). There is a cause-effect relationship between grace and sin: Whenever the former declines, the latter inevitably increases.

(c) *You wrong yourself*

When you see that the grace of God in you is taking a turn for the worse, but do nothing to reverse the process, you will suffer for your negligence. A declining Christian is always a doubting Christian. Your grace is like a tree: As long as it is healthy, it never stops growing. But if it begins to wither, you know something is very wrong. Satan is quick to spot the first signs of blighted faith. Your weakened condition makes you highly susceptible to his lies.

Here is what he tells you: 'If you were really a Christian, you would be growing. True saints go from strength to strength; but you – you go from strength to weakness! You say you are saved. Then why are you so much further from God than on the day of your alleged salvation?' Satan's lies do contain an element of truth. When your graces are in a state of decline, you *do* feel far from God and heaven; you *do* begin to wonder whether you were ever really saved.

Imagine that you held an estate because of having custody of a child, upon whose death the estate would be taken away from you. I have no doubt that the child would be well looked after. You would never let him out of your sight, and the slightest headache would send you running for a physician. The only claim we have to our heavenly estate is the child of grace that comes to dwell within us when we accept Christ as Savior and Lord. So when this 'child of grace' is sick or weak, we had better use every means to make it well again.

If God's grace in you is sickly, you will find little joy in life, present or future. A person with a chronic illness gets no pleasure from anything he does. His food is tasteless; he sleeps fitfully; he has no energy to work or play. If the image of Christ in you has faded, you are chronically ill. You will not taste the sweetness of the promise, nor enjoy any rest in Him. You will limp painfully to every duty, wondering whether you have strength enough to see it through. All the while, your disconsolate heart will be crying out at the heavy load you make it carry.

How sad that our own carelessness so often gives Satan the advantage! By our own spiritual complacency we put a staff in his hand and an argument in his mouth which he uses to question our salvation. But how sweet is the promise to our faith when it is active and vigorous! How easy the yoke when the Christian is not galled with guilt, nor his strength enfeebled by declining grace! When your relationship to Christ is set aright, you and your brothers and sisters in Christ are alike benefited, and your heavenly Father is glorified.

III. HOW TO KNOW WHETHER OR NOT YOUR GRACE IS DECLINING

Having shown why the Christian should make every effort to restore his declining graces, it will be appropriate to give a word of counsel on early detection of this spiritual disorder. As with most diseases, the sooner you isolate the cause, the more quickly you can effect a cure.

(a) *False or misleading symptoms*

Before we get to the root cause, let me first advise you of some false symptoms that may lead you mistakenly to think your grace is in a state of decline.

(i) *An increased sense of sin.* Christian, do not necessarily think your grace has gotten weaker because your sense of personal sin has grown stronger. This common error often causes great distress to a saint. All of a sudden he becomes acutely aware of pride, or hypocrisy, or some other corruption that seems to break forth in hideous boils within his own nature. He is horrified at the sight of this sin. Satan piles on the guilt, and before long the saint is almost overcome with the pain of remorse.

If this is the case with you, let me ask you something: Is it not quite possible that the sin which is weighing you down has been present for years, but you never noticed it until now? If so, rejoice to know that your grace is not fading, but flourishing and choking out some perennial weeds that Satan may have sown long ago. If you are still distraught, reassure yourself in knowing that sin cannot be getting the upper hand when a person's horror at its presence is growing stronger. (Do be careful not to use this as an excuse for newly hatched sins. Deal honestly with yourself and with God!)

None are so full of remorse at the presence of the least sin as those whose love for Christ is increasing. As winter passes and spring approaches, the sun grows stronger and melts the frost earlier each day. A sure sign that the love of Christ is shining stronger in your heart is when sin cannot lie long without being melted into sorrow and genuine repentance. The decaying soul is the one where sins lie hard and frozen, and where little awareness or sense of sorrow for them appears.

(ii) *A decreased sense of comfort*. Grace may be hard at work within you when you least feel its presence. Did faith ever triumph more than when our Savior cried in utter despair, 'My God, my God, why hast thou forsaken me?' (*Mark 15:34*)? Here faith was at its zenith, though it was midnight with respect to joy. Perhaps you have just performed an act of obedience and are returning home without those sheaves of comfort you are accustomed to gathering after working in the Father's fields. Do not feel because of this that something was wrong with the work you did. Feelings are not always an accurate measure of your spiritual state.

Comfort is not essential to duty; it is a bonus which God may or may not give. How well you performed the task He assigned you has nothing to do with it. A traveler may go as fast and cover as much ground when it is cloudy as when the sun shines its brightest. Sometimes, in fact, he can go faster on a dreary day. The warm sun may make him sleepy and cause him to stop and rest, whereas when it is dark and cold, he will spur his horse to reach his destination more quickly. Some graces, like some flowers, grow best in the shade – perseverance, humility, and dependence on God, for instance.

(iii) *Increased temptation*. If you should hear someone say that he has grown weak, because he cannot run as fast today with a hundred-pound weight on his back as he could yesterday without it, you would soon tell him where his mistake lies. You can make the same mistake with regard to temptations. They do not always lie with the same heaviness upon your conscience.

You may overcome one temptation with very little conscious effort, while another weighs you down day in and day out. It is easy to grow discouraged and conclude that you are lazy or insincere. Yet grace may be acting stronger in you while it struggles against this stubborn temptation, than when it overpowers a lesser one. A ship, lightly ballasted and sailing with the wind, goes flying across the waves. That same ship, heavily loaded and fighting the wind, may hardly move forward at all. But the crew will have to expend all its energy in the latter situation, whereas in the former, half the men may be in their quarters taking a rest.

(b) *Genuine symptoms of declining grace*

(i) *A careless attitude toward temptation.* Has your conscience become so inattentive and drowsy that you give little thought to the devil's snares? David's heart cut him to the quick when he only tore Saul's robes. But later he did not seem to feel a twinge when he cast his eye on Bathsheba and lust filled his heart. Being so easily led by Satan from one horrid sin to another shows that godliness in David had become heavy-eyed and his heart less holy than it once had been. When a person's conscience is numb to temptation, his graces are in a critical condition.

If your conscience is alert to temptation but heartless to fight against it, your graces must still be listed as very ill. A man who lets temptation loiter along the borders of his conscience proves himself a poor guardian of his godliness. If you do not take up arms against your enemy and seek God earnestly and fervently for deliverance, you may be sure that lust will soon gain the advantage over grace.

Being able to resist temptation does not guarantee that God's grace in you is strong, however. Lest you grow complacent, ask yourself why you are resisting the devil's trap. Perhaps you remember a time when your love for Christ would have spit fire in Satan's face for tempting you to sin. But now that holy fire is so nearly extinguished that some base motive is the only thing that keeps you from sinning. If all you care about is your own reputation, for instance, and you have little or no regard for God's reputation, your grace is at a low ebb. After all, He is the one most offended by your sin. Every act of grace must be a building stone in the monument to His glory, or it becomes a stone of offense.

(ii) *An inattentive attitude in worship and service*. Perhaps at one time your heart eagerly answered the call of the Holy Spirit, bidding you to seek God's face: 'Thy face, Lord, will I seek' (*Ps. 27:8*). You longed as much for the season of worship to come as the sinner does for it to be gone. You cherished time alone with your heavenly Father. To hunger and thirst after righteousness is a sign of health, for a craving soul is a thriving soul. On the other hand, the soul that does not constantly cry out to God for spiritual food will grow weaker by the day.

Those who commune most with God know best how to serve Him. A captain can lead his soldiers only if they stay within the sound of his voice. Your frequent retreats into the secret places of God assure that you will hear Him when He speaks and receive your orders direct from Him. It is not frequency of duty but spirituality in duty that causes a Christian's graces to thrive. Just to be busy doing something for the Lord is not enough; you must make certain your work is stamped with faith, zeal, and love. If you find yourself going about your spiritual tasks out of habit rather than love, it is time to repair your armour.

[253]

Does your heart still receive the same generous portions of spiritual nourishment when you go to commune with God? This communion should strengthen both your faith and your obedience. Or do you listen and pray, but no longer find strength to keep a promise or power to win over temptation? How you dishonor the Lord when you come down from the mount of communion and break the tables of His law as soon as you are off the place! To find no renewed faith and no renewed strength in your communion with Him is a sure sign of spiritual decline.

(iii) *An obsessive attitude toward your work.* How easy it is to let the responsibilities of job and family leave us in a less spiritual frame of mind than we once possessed. If we let them, the cares of this world will follow us into our prayer closets and cleave to our spirits, giving a stale, earthly odor to our prayers and meditations.

One way to become weighed down by the cares of this life is to put too much stock in your worldly estate. Perhaps you work diligently but receive little remuneration, or you preach and receive little recognition. When you first became a Christian, all you cared about was getting to know Christ better. Estate and rank meant nothing to you, and life's disappointments only drew you closer to God. But now, this hankering of your heart after the world's treasures and esteem drives you relentlessly. How urgently you need to have your grace restored! If you will labor less to promote your earthly account and pray harder to improve your fund of grace, you will soon find your soul at peace with God's providence.

IV. HOW TO RECOVER FROM DECLINING GRACE

The Christian's armour becomes damaged in two ways. The first is by violent assault – when you are overcome by temptation to sin. The second is by neglect – when you fail to perform those duties which, like oil, keep your armour polished and shining. So inquire which has been the cause; it is likely the two agents have concurred.

(a) *How to recover when sin is the cause*

(i) *Renew your repentance.* Here is Christ's counsel to the church at Ephesus: 'Repent, and do the first works' (*Rev. 2:5*). In essence He is saying, 'Repent, so that you may once again do your first works.' A repenting soul is promised healing (*Hos. 14:2–4*). Therefore, go and search your heart as diligently as you would your house if you suspected a murderer was hiding, waiting to cut your throat in the night. When you have found the sin that has done the mischief, fill your heart with shame for it and indignation against it. Cast it before the Lord in a heartbreaking confession.

(ii) *Reaffirm your faith.* When you have renewed your repentance, then renew your faith in God's promise to pardon (*1 John 1:9*). Repentance is a purgative to remove the tendency to sin; faith, a tonic to restore strength. Even if your godly character has wasted away to almost nothing, faith can quickly restore its strength. Faith infuses you with peace from the promise, called 'peace in believing' (*Rom. 15:13*). From peace flows joy, and joy provides strength, according to the scripture, 'The joy of the Lord is your strength' (*Neh. 8:10*).

(iii) *Renounce your lusts.* Having repented and claimed God's promise of forgiveness, back up your actions by rooting out sin wherever it threatens to crop up. Where weeds thrive, flowers die. Grace that does not grow vigorously and blossom profusely is most likely being choked out by some contrary lust. You know the hardy constitution of your lusts! If you do not mortify them daily by the Spirit, they will spring up overnight. So chop at the root of every sin with this axe of mortification. Then watch God bless and improve the character of your grace.

[255]

(b) *How to recover when neglect is the cause*

When the armour of God which girds your soul is rusty from disuse, rather than tarnished by willful sin, follow God's instructions for the strengthening of grace. If a fire goes out for lack of wood, the only solution is to lay on more wood. Likewise with grace; if neglect of your Christian duties causes its decline, you must restore those duties which kindled a fire under your grace in the first place. I refer you to four principal duties:

(i) *Read your Bible*. Perhaps you say, 'Oh, but I do read God's Word.' Then read it more! The Word shows your graces a perfect picture of the object of their affections – Christ. And just as a young man's heart leaps at the sight of his beloved, so your graces come to life when they behold the Christ who loved you and gave Himself for you. At the same time, when you see what your sins cost Christ, it should produce in you a godly sorrow and a hatred for sin.

(ii) *Meditate*. Meditation is to grace as bellows are to a fire. It revives the languishing soul with fresh thoughts of God. As you ponder over them, a holy fire will burn and your heart will grow warm within you. Resolve to spend time every day thinking about what has passed between God and you.

Think, first of all, about the mercies you have received from the Lord. Do not be like Pilate, who asked a question but did not wait for a reply (*John 18:38*). Stay until you have received a full report of God's gracious dealings with you, and you will find memories of mercies, both new and old, flooding your soul. Meditating often on the magnitude of God's goodness teaches us to rejoice even in times of trouble, for the little evil that is our portion is drowned in the sea of His abundant mercies on our behalf.

Second, reflect upon yourself and your own behavior. What has it been toward God and toward man during the day? Ask yourself, 'Soul, where have you been? What have you done for God, and how?' In this reflection, do not make excuses for yourself nor pamper yourself, for ultimately, God will judge you with full justice.

(iii) *Pray*. A soul in meditation is on its way to prayer. The two duties join hands to bring the soul into close communion with God. Meditation lays the wood in order, but the spark to kindle it comes from above and must be fetched by prayer. How can your soul flame with love for God if you never get close enough to Him to catch that heavenly spark? As it is with your love, so also with your faith, your joy, your patience – indeed, all your graces.

Astronomers say the planets have the greatest influence when they are in conjunction with the sun. In a spiritual sense, the graces of a saint never work more perfectly than when aligned with prayer, for this puts them in closest conjunction and communion with God. How often in the Psalms (*e.g., Psalm 56*) do we see a dark cloud upon David's spirit at the beginning of his prayer. But before he has finished talking with the Father, his spirit has soared to new heights of faith and high acclamations of praise!

(iv) *Fellowship with other Christians*. It is no surprise to hear a house has been robbed when it is miles from the nearest neighbor. If you keep your distance from the saints, Satan can more easily sabotage you. But if you walk in fellowship, you have the added protection of their graces surrounding you and ministering to you in times of trial. The apostle harnesses two duties to the same plow, to 'hold fast the profession of our faith . . .' and to ' . . . consider one another to provoke unto love and to good works: not forsaking the assembling of ourselves together' (*Heb. 10:23–25*). When you forsake the communion of saints, you take a dangerous step toward apostasy. Do not forget what happened to Demas in this regard. Paul said of him, '[He] hath forsaken me, having loved this present world' (*2 Tim. 4:10*).

2. Reasons for the Exhortation

Paul continues his exhortation with a twofold reason for the Christian to put on God's armour: 'that ye may be able to withstand in the evil day, and having done all, to stand' (*Eph. 6:13*). The first reason has to do with the hour of battle – 'in the evil day.' The second reason has to do with what is required for the glorious outcome of the war, which is certain victory if we are properly clad for the conflict.

FIRST REASON: THE HOUR OF BATTLE

What is 'the evil day' to which Paul refers? Bible scholars have given this brief phrase careful consideration.   Some take 'the evil day' to encompass the whole life of a Christian on earth. With this interpretation the exhortation runs something like this: You must cover yourself with the whole armour of God in order to persevere to the end of your life, which is just one day of trouble and trial after another. Jacob confessed to this attitude as he looked back over his life: 'Few and evil have the days of the years of my life been' (*Gen. 47:9*). To some it seems there is never a day when the sun shines so brightly that rain does not come before nightfall. Every day has its proportion of evil; we do not need to borrow the sorrows of tomorrow to make up today's load!

The Scriptures speak of daily bread; they also speak of a daily cross, which we are told to take – not make (*Luke 9:23*). The reference here is not to those crosses we fashion for ourselves; God in His providence will always provide a cross of His choosing for us. And though He tells us explicitly to take it up, He never tells us to put it down.

The span of our lives and the span of our trials measure the same distance.

Much has been made of Job's lament during his time of testing. But listen to what he says about his former prosperity: 'I was not in safety, neither had I rest, neither was I quiet, yet trouble came' (*3:26*). Even when his bed was as soft as a man could wish, Job tossed and turned, unable to sleep under the weight of a heavy spirit. He tells us from his own experience that earth's finest rewards will not satisfy the longing in a man's soul. As Christians, even the best of times becomes a cross to bear because it detains us from our crown. Every day spent in this wicked world is one less day spent in the presence of Christ.

The only consolation in this evil is that it is short. Our life is, in fact, only an evil *day*. A few steps, and we will be out of the storm. There is an ever-widening chasm between the saint and the sinner in this respect. They are like two travelers riding in the same country but in opposite directions, both caught in a rainstorm. The saint, however, is riding away from the storm and will soon be out of the rain. When death comes, he will have eternal fair weather. But the wicked man rides into the eye of the storm. The farther he goes, the worse it gets. What he is facing on earth is but a sprinkle compared to the great tempest he will face when he dies. The flood of God's wrath will be in hell – both from above of His righteous fury, and from beneath of the sinner's own accusing and tormenting conscience.

Another explanation of the term 'evil day' is that it does not encompass the whole span of our lives, but rather that time which is particularly and especially fraught with suffering. Though certainly our whole life is evil when compared with heaven's blissful state, still one part of our life, when compared with another, may be called good and the other evil. Earth is a middle place between heaven and hell; it partakes of both. We go uphill and downhill before we reach our journey's end. Inevitably we find the deepest slough nearest our final destination – death, I mean – and into this slough all the other troubles of life pour, like streams winding down to some great river. Death being the comprehensive evil, I conceive that it is primarily what Paul meant by 'the evil day.'

I. THE NATURE AND QUALITY OF EVIL AND 'THE EVIL DAY'

To grasp Paul's meaning, we must first understand in what sense affliction is evil, and in what sense it is not. Since God credits Himself with devising the 'evil' of affliction, it can be neither morally nor intrinsically evil. The Lord Himself declared, 'Against this family do I devise an evil' (*Micah 2:3*). Again, in Amos, we read that there was no evil (i.e., affliction) in the city except that which was of God's doing (*Amos 3:6*).

If affliction were intrinsically evil, then it should never be the object of our desire, as it sometimes may be. Affliction may take the form of persecution, for example. In that case, when the choice is to disobey God or to suffer persecution, one must certainly choose the latter. When put to the test, we are to submit to the greatest affliction rather than succumb to the smallest sin. Moses chose persecution with the people of God rather than the 'pleasures of sin for a season' (*Heb. 11:25–27*).

Another type of affliction is temptation, which, according to James, is cause for rejoicing (*James 1:12*)! How could we 'count it all joy' to fall into something morally or intrinsically evil?

If the term 'evil' when applied to the day of affliction does not mean sin or moral wickedness, what does it signify? In what respect can the day of affliction for the saints be termed evil?

(a) *It is a day when joy deserts us*

Affliction is evil, or bad, in the sense that it may rob us of our joy. Like bitter medicine, affliction has an unpleasant effect on the senses. Therefore, Solomon, speaking of the evil days of sickness, declares them to be so distasteful that we shall say, 'We have no pleasure in them' (*Eccl. 12:1*). Natural joy is a flower that flourishes in the sun of prosperity and withers when that sun is hidden by a cloud of trials.

Nevertheless, the saints can have their greatest portion of joy in affliction, for the source of their joy is outside themselves. God sends it, or else they would be as miserable as others are when trouble strikes. For comfort to spring from affliction is no more natural than for grapes to grow on thorns or for manna to appear in the wilderness. But God chooses this season to make the omnipotency of His love the more conspicuous. When Elijah challenged the prophets of Baal, he first had the wood and sacrifice drenched with water and the trench around the altar filled to the brim. Then he prayed and brought fire from heaven to lick it up. In like manner, God may allow a flood of afflictions to pour upon His children; He then kindles that inward joy in their bosoms to consume all their sorrows. The very waters of affliction add a further sweetness to their spiritual joy. Still, it is God who is good and affliction that is evil.

(b) *It is a day when past sins are remembered*

The day of affliction brings unwelcome reminders of what sinful evils have passed in our lives. Old sins which were buried many years ago in the grave of forgetfulness come back to haunt us. Their ghosts walk in our consciences. And as the darkness of night heightens our fear of the unseen, so the day when death approaches adds to the terror of our sins, then remembered. Never did the patriarchs' sin look so ghastly to them as when it recoiled upon them in their distress (*Gen. 42:21*).

(c) *The day of affliction is a day when present sin is revealed*

Affliction troubles the waters of our souls. If any sediment of sin is at the bottom, it will rise to the surface. The agitation of affliction washes off the hypocrite's paint, which may be the very reason for a time of testing. Some lose their faith when persecution comes; others ' . . . curse their king and their God' (*Isa. 8:21*). A false heart cannot think well of an afflicting God. Yet even when a person appears to be full of God's grace, affliction can reveal that corruption is stronger and grace weaker than they were thought to be. One example is Peter, who stepped so fearlessly out of the boat and on to the water, but then began to sink. In an instant he saw there was more unbelief in his heart than he had supposed.

Sharp afflictions are to the soul as a driving rain to a house. We do not notice the leaks in the roof until we hear the drips and watch the puddles form on the floor. When tribulation beats down upon your soul, it soon discloses the weak spots in your graces. This is the reason none are so humble and compassionate toward other aching souls as those who are most acquainted with afflictions. They have been buffeted so sorely themselves that they keep the sails of self-esteem low, more ready to pity than condemn fellow sufferers who are weak.

(d) *It is the day Satan comes to tempt*

That which Matthew called the time of 'tribulation' (*Matt. 13:21*), Luke refers to as the time of 'temptation' (*Luke 8:13*). Indeed, they both meet. God seldom afflicts us without Satan adding temptation to our wilderness. Christ's sufferings from man and His temptation from the devil came together. 'This is your hour,' Christ said to the chief priests and elders, 'and the power of darkness' (*Luke 22:53*). Esau, who hated his brother for the blessing, said in his heart, 'The days of mourning for my father are at hand; then will I slay my brother Jacob' (Gen. 27:41). Times of affliction are the days of mourning; Satan waits for them to do us mischief.

(e) *It is the day of trouble*

'All is well that ends well,' the saying goes. Though the day of affliction is troublesome, sincere saints always benefit from it. God's rod of correction yields the peaceable fruits of righteousness. In the wicked, however, the result is evil. The day of affliction leaves them more impenitent, hardened in sin, and outrageous in their wicked practices. Every plague on Egypt added to the plague of hardness on Pharaoh's heart. Many are not purged, but poisoned, by their afflictions. Although the affliction may pass, the poison remains and breaks out in more hideous sins than before. Every affliction on a wicked person produces another, greater affliction, until the greatest comes at last. The wicked man finds himself in hell, where all his afflictions meet in one that is endless.

II. THE CERTAINTY OF AN EVIL DAY

We can no more escape the hour of darkness that is coming upon us all than we can stop the sun from setting at its appointed hour. 'There is no man that has power over the spirit to retain the spirit; neither has he power in the day of death; and there is no discharge in that war' (*Eccl. 8:8*). When called to active duty in war, a man may sometimes be excused because of his age or a physical weakness. Or he may try to bribe an official or obtain someone else to take his place. But in this personal war with death, the rules are so strict that there is no escape. We must in our own person come into the field and look death in the face.

Some live as though they think they will never die.

Others are so foolish as to say they have made a covenant with death and an agreement with hell. When the plague passes through, they expect to be spared. So for now, like debtors who have paid the bailiff, they walk around boldly and fear no arrest. But God tells them, 'Your covenant with death shall be disannulled, and your agreement with hell shall not stand' (*Isa. 28:18*).

Regarding the day of death, there is a divine law which came into force with Adam's first sin, that fatal knife to the throat of mankind. God, to prevent all escape, has sown the seeds of death in our very nature; we can as soon run from ourselves as from death. We need no woodsman to come and hew us down. There is in the tree a worm which grows out of its own substance that will destroy it; we have in us those infirmities of nature which will bring us down to the dust. Our death was bred when our life was first conceived. And as a woman cannot stop the hour of her travail, which is a natural consequence of conception, so neither can man hinder the bringing forth of death with which his life is impregnated. Every physical pain you endure is a groan from your dying nature, warning you that death is at hand.

God owes a debt both to the first Adam and to the second. To the first He owes the wages of his sin; to the second, the reward of His sufferings. The place for full payment of both is the other world. So unless death comes to convey man there, the wicked – who are the posterity of the first Adam – will miss the full pay for their sins. The godly also – who are the seed of Christ – cannot receive the whole purchase of His blood until they leave this frame of dust. Before the world began, God promised the Son that His shed blood would purchase eternal life for all who trust in Him. This is the reason why God has made the day of death so sure. In it He discharges both bonds.

III. THE NECESSITY OF ARMOUR TO WITHSTAND THE EVIL DAY

Since death is inevitable for every person, it behooves us, first of all, to prepare for this evil day in regard to *our duty*. Your faithful allegiance to God is what keeps you safe. Suppose a subject, entrusted with the care of one of his prince's castles, should hear a powerful enemy was coming to lay siege to the castle. Yet he took no precautions to lay in arms or provisions for its defense, and so it was lost. How could he be cleared of treason? Did he not through negligence betray his prince?

The soul is a castle which we are each one to keep for God. We have been warned that Satan will lay siege to it. The time when he intends to come with all his powers of darkness is that 'evil day.' Now in order to be found true to our trust, we must plan for our defense and equip ourselves for a vigorous resistance. We cannot, without shameful, ingratitude to our God, waste those aids He provides for that evil day.

What would you say of a prisoner who was sent money for his release, but used it instead to amuse himself while in prison? This is in essence what we do when we take the talents God expects us to use in preparation for the hour of death, and instead bestow them upon our lusts. What profit will we find in our Bibles or our ministers if we do not use them to equip ourselves with God's armour?

In a word, why does God lengthen our days in the land of the living? Is it that we might have time to revel in the pleasures of this vain world? Are we to be chasing such butterflies as earthly riches and honor? It cannot be. Wise masters do not give their servants such tasks as will not pay for the candles they burn in doing them. And truly nothing less than glorifying God and saving our souls at last can be worth the precious time we spend here.

The great God has a greater goal than most think. To understand it, read His own interpretation of His actions. The apostle Peter bids us 'account that the longsuffering of our Lord is salvation' (*2 Pet. 3:15*). Paul states it thus: 'Or despisest thou the riches of his goodness and forbearance and longsuffering; not knowing that the goodness of God leadeth thee to repentance?' (*Rom. 2:4*). From both scriptures we are taught what is the mind of God: He speaks to us by every moment's patience and inch of time we are given. Since it is God's mercy that grants us every day we spend on earth, this lays upon us a strong obligation to spend every moment of our time wisely.

Second, we must prepare for this evil day in regard to *wisdom*. A prudent man expends most of his energy on that which is of greatest importance to him. Only fools and children are intent on toys and trifles. They are as earnest in making a house of cards as Solomon was in making his temple. Now such is the importance of the evil day, especially that of death, that a man proves himself to be either wise or foolish by the way he prepares for it. If the counsels and projects we have pursued prepare us for a blessed death, then we shall appear to be wise men indeed. But if, after all our sincere plans and efforts for other things, we are not prepared for that hour, we shall be exposed as fools at last.

Whoever you are and whatever you have to glory in – even if you seem to be the saintliest person on earth – know that there is no salvation from the flood of death but Christ. Hanging on to the outside of the ark by a false profession of faith will not save. Imagine how those in Noah's day ran for their lives, some to this hill and others to that high tree; but the waves pursued them until at last they were swept into the devouring flood. Such will your end be if you turn to any other way for help than Christ.

Yet the ark waits for you, comes up close to your gate to take you in. Noah did not put forth his hand more willingly to take in the dove, than Christ does to receive those who fly to Him for refuge.

Ask your soul soberly and solemnly, 'Have you provided for this day, this evil day? Can you part with what that day will take away and welcome what it will certainly bring?' Death comes to carry away all your carnal enjoyments and to bring you a reckoning for them. Can you take your leave of the one, and with peace and confidence read the other? Think what answer you will give to God when you appear before Him. What will you say when He asks, 'Why should I not pronounce the sentence of eternal damnation against you?' Do not doubt for one moment that your day of reckoning will come.

IV. DIRECTIONS FOR PREPARING FOR THE EVIL DAY

Are you wise enough to prepare for the day when you must stand before God? Would you like to live now without dreadful anticipation of that day? Then take these directions:

(a) *Establish a covenant relationship with Christ*

You cannot expect to face death without fear unless you have solid ground that Christ will claim you as His. The heirs of heaven are those who are in covenant with God. And how do you get into this covenant relationship? By breaking your covenant with sin! You are by nature a covenant servant to sin and Satan. If ever you are to be taken into a new covenant with God, you must break the old one. A covenant with hell and heaven cannot stand together.

(b) *Betroth yourself to Christ*

God bestows the covenant of grace only upon Christ's spouse. Rebekah did not receive the jewels and costly

[267]

raiment until she promised to become Isaac's wife (*Gen. 24:53*). 'All the promises of God in him are yea, and in him, Amen, unto the glory of God by us' (*2 Cor. 1:20*). When you receive Christ, you also receive the promises. He who owns the tree has a right to all the fruit it bears. See to it that there is found in you what Christ expects in every soul that He espouses.

Consider whether you can heartily love the Person of Christ. Look fondly on Him again and again, as He is set forth in all His spiritual perfection. Do His holy nature and perfect grace make you desire Him? Can you find it in your heart to forsake all others and cleave to Christ? Will you put the life of your soul in His hands, to be saved by the sole virtue of His blood and by the strength of His omnipotent arm? If you have sufficient faith in His care to provide for you now and in the life to come, you can be sure His promises are for you.

One thing more, if you have Christ, you must love not only Him but your new kindred by marriage as well – that is, all the saints. Can you love them heartily, and forget all the old grudges you have had against them? If you find it in your heart to answer 'Yes', I pronounce Christ and you husband and wife. Go and comfort yourself with the expectation of the Bridegroom's coming for you. And when the evil day approaches and death itself draws near, do not look upon it with terror. Instead, revive, like old Jacob, when you see the chariot which will carry you over into the embraces of your Husband. Be assured He is able to make you welcome when you arrive there.

(c) *Labor to die continually to this life and its enjoyments*
The desire to resist death is not so strong in one who has long been ill and wasting away, as it is in the one who has been sick only a few days and still has strength to fight. The same tendency is found in the saint. That Christian

whose love of this life has been wasting away for many years will more easily part with his earthly life than he whose love for it is stronger. All Christians are not mortified to the world in the same degree. Paul tells us he died daily. He was always sending more and more of his heart out of the world, so that by the time his evil day had come, all his affections were packed up and gone! How eager he was to follow: 'I am ready to be offered up' (*2 Tim. 4:6*). When a tooth must be extracted, the deeper the roots, the more pain for the patient. If you will loosen the roots of your worldly affections, your life will fall more easily and with less pain in the day of your affliction.

Remember this: If you are a Christian, you have no reason to fear the evil day. Bring your heart up close to it. Show your soul what Christ has done to take the sting out of it, what sweet promises He has given to help you overcome your fear. Here you will find all the comfort you need.

SECOND REASON: THE REQUIREMENTS FOR A HAPPY OUTCOME OF THE WAR

We come now to the second argument the apostle uses to press his exhortation home. It is taken from the glorious victory which hovers over the head of the believer as he fights, and which shall surely crown him in the end. Stated in these words, 'and having done all, to stand,' the phrase is short but full.

Heaven is not won with good words or a bold profession, but with 'having done all.' Sacrifice without obedience is sacrilege. His religion is in vain whose profession brings no letters of testimony from a holy life. The doing Christian is the one who shall stand when the boasting Christian shall fall. Such braggarts rob God of that which He values most. A great captain once smote one of his own soldiers for railing at the enemy, saying that his orders were not to rant and rave, but to fight and kill him. To cry out against the devil, to rail against him in prayer or conversation, is not enough. You must take action against him and mortify him if you want to please God.

Is claiming sonship to the King of heaven so small a matter that you think you can obtain it without giving a real proof of your zeal for God and hatred of sin? 'Not a forgetful hearer, but a doer of the work; this man,' says the apostle, 'shall be blessed in his deed' (*James 1:25*). Notice he does not say *by* his deed, but *in* his deed. He shall meet blessedness as he walks obediently. The hypocrite disappoints others who, seeing the leaves on his tree, expect fruit but find none. And at last he disappoints himself. He expects to reach heaven, but will miss it entirely.

Observe also that God's mercy to His children is so great that He gladly accepts their weak efforts to please Him as long as those efforts are joined with sincerity and perseverance. When the heart is right, God accepts the works as if they were done in full obedience. This is why the saints are said to have 'done all.' Oh, who would not serve such a God! You hear servants sometimes complain that their masters are so unreasonable they can never please them, even when they do their best. Such a charge can never be brought against God. Only do your best, and God will pardon your worst. David knew the indulgence of the Lord when he said, 'Then shall I not be ashamed, when I have respect unto all thy commandments' (*Ps. 119:6*). The heart that labors always to come nearer and nearer to full obedience to God's will shall never be put to shame.

Here in the short phrase 'and having done all, to stand' four distinct doctrines are to be found, pertaining to the following issues: the necessity of perseverance, the necessity of divine armour to persevere, the certainty of persevering and overcoming if armed, and the promised result of perseverance.

I. THE NECESSITY OF PERSEVERANCE

Perseverance is the mark of a true soldier of Christ. 'Having done all' includes our conflict with death. We have not done all until that pitched battle is fought. The word means 'to finish a business, and bring a matter to a full issue.' Do not be a half-hearted Christian, but a thorough one. Not he that takes the field, but he that keeps the field; not he that sets out, but he that holds out, deserves the name of saint. There is no such thing as an honorable retreat; no such word of command in all Christ's military discipline as, 'Fall back and lay down your arms.' Your order is, 'Forward, march!' from the day you take up arms until you are called off by death.

(a) *Our covenant and oath demand perseverance*

Soldiers used to take a military oath not to flinch from their colors, but faithfully to follow their leaders. The obligation to take such an oath lies upon every Christian. It is so essential to being a saint that they are identified by it: 'Gather my saints together, those that have made a covenant with me' (*Ps. 50:5*). We are not Christians until we have subscribed to this covenant without reservation. When we profess Christ, we enlist ourselves in His regiment and promise to live and die with Him in opposition to all His enemies. Christ tells us upon what terms He will enroll us among His disciples: 'If any man will come after me, let him deny himself, and take up his cross, and follow me' (*Matt. 16:24*). He will not accept us until we resign ourselves freely to His disposal, that there may be no disputing His commands afterwards.

(b) *The persistence of the enemy requires perseverance*

The devil never retreats or declares a truce. If an enemy

repeatedly assaults a city and those within cease to resist, you know who will win. The prophet who was sent to Bethel did his errand well and withstood Jeroboam's temptation. But on his way home he was drawn aside by the old prophet and at last slain by a lion (*1 Kings 13*). Thus many flee from one temptation, only to be vanquished by another. Many precious servants of God, not making such vigorous resistance in their last days as in their first, have fallen miserably, as we see in Solomon, Asa, and others.

You know it is hard to hold anything in your hand for very long and not have your fingers grow numb. This is also true in a spiritual sense. Therefore, we are frequently admonished to hold fast the profession of our faith. And surely when we see our enemy always keeping watch to catch us when we fall, we will be challenged to strengthen our grip, not loosen it.

(c) *Our eternal reward is contingent upon perseverance*
The saint's crown stands at the goal; he who comes to the end of the race wins it. 'To him that overcometh will I grant,' says Christ (*Rev. 3:21*). In his letter to Timothy, Paul said, 'I have fought a good fight . . . henceforth there is laid up for me a crown of righteousness' (*2 Tim. 4:7, 8*). Why 'henceforth'? Was it not laid up before? Yes, but having persevered and come within sight of home, ready to die, he now takes surer hold of the promise. Indeed, in this sense, a gracious soul is nearer his salvation after every victory than he was before, because he approaches nearer to the end of his race, which is the time for receiving his promised salvation (*Rom. 8:10*). Then, and not until then, the garland will be placed on his head.

II. THE NECESSITY OF DIVINE ARMOUR TO PERSEVERE
There can be no perseverance without true grace in the

heart. A soul without divine armour cannot persevere. The sanctifying grace of God's Spirit is this armour. Anyone without it will never endure to fight all the battles necessary before the victory is won.

Common gifts of the Spirit, such as enlightenment, conviction, affection, may for a time help someone to appear zealous for the Lord, but the strength these afford is soon spent. John the Baptist's hearers got some light and heat by sitting under his burning ministry, but how long did it last? 'Ye were willing for a season to rejoice in his light' (*John 5:35*). His words imbued their consciences with beautiful colors, but they were not laid in oil and therefore were soon washed off again. The foolish virgins made as great a blaze with their lamps as the wise virgins, but their lamps went out before the Bridegroom appeared. The stony ground was more responsive than the other soil. The seed sprouted quickly, as if a crop should soon be ready for harvest. But a few nipping frosts turned its hue, and the day of harvest proved a day of desperate sorrow.

All these instances and many more in Scripture show that nothing short of solid grace, and a principle of divine life in the soul, will persevere. Free-thinkers and flighty professors of faith promise themselves hopes of reaching heaven, but they will find it too long a step for their short-breathed souls to attain.

III. WHY THE UNREGENERATE CANNOT PERSEVERE

(a) *Their source of strength is fragile*

The gracious soul perseveres because of the continual supply of strength it receives from Christ, just as the arm and foot are kept alive by the vital nourishment they receive from the heart. 'I live,' says Paul, 'yet not I, but Christ liveth in me' (*Gal. 2:20*). That is, 'I live, but at Christ's cost. He holds my soul, and also my grace in life.'

Without this union a man will waste away; he has no root to sustain him. A carcass, once it begins to rot, never recovers. The process of decay continues until it returns again to dust. No salve will reverse the process of death. But where there is life, then nature sends help to work with the salve for a cure.

The difference between the Christian and the non-Christian is as great as the difference between life and death. The righteous man 'falleth seven times and riseth up again: but the wicked . . . fall into mischief' (*Prov. 24:16*). That is, in falling, the wicked fall farther and have no power to recover. When Cain sinned, see how he fell farther and farther like a stone rolling downhill, never stopping until he came to the bottom of despair. He went from envying his brother to malice, from malice to murder, from murder to impudent lying and brazen-faced boldness to God Himself, and from that to despair.

The Scriptures promise, 'Evil men shall wax worse and worse' (*2 Tim. 3:13*). When a saint falls, he gets up again because he has strength to cry out to Christ. 'Lord, save me,' cried Peter, when he began to sink. And at once Christ's hand was put forth. Though the Lord chided him for his unbelief, still He helped him.

(b) *Their gifts are impermanent*

An unregenerate soul has no guarantee that he can keep the common gifts of the Spirit which he may possess at one time or another. Even when his table is most sumptuously spread, he cannot show any word of promise from God that he will be provided with another meal. God gives these things to the wicked as we might give a crust or a night's lodging to a beggar in our barn. And all that God chooses to give, He can also choose to deny. If you are not a Christian, you may have some knowledge of the things of

God, but, even so, you may die without *saving* knowledge at last.

(c) *Their resolve is weak*

A man engaged to the world may profess faith in Christ, but he will quickly show his true colors when forced to make a choice between Christ and Satan. When Satan bribes him with worldly treasures to abandon his profession of the Savior, he will, like Demas, show where his love lies. Or if his lusts call him, he must go, in spite of profession, conscience, God, and all. Herod feared John the Baptist, but love is stronger than fear. His love for Herodias overcame his fear of John, and made him cut off not only John's head but the hopeful buddings of his conscience as well. If the complexion of the soul is profane, it will finally show itself, though for a while there may be some religious color in a man's face from some external cause.

The lack of a thorough change of heart is the root of all final apostasy. The apostate does not lose the grace he had, but only discovers he never had any. Many take up their sainthood upon a false pretense, and use the credit they have gained from others' opinions of them to establish their trade among God's true saints. These false professors assume they are Christians because others suppose them to be. Their whole reputation is built on an outward show of religion. The fact that they have no stock of solid grace within to maintain them in their profession proves their undoing at last.

Let us therefore consider upon what basis we take up our declaration of faith. Is there anything within us that is proportionate to our outward zeal? Have we laid a good foundation? Is the superstructure top-heavy, jutting too far beyond the weak foundation? The roots of a tree spread as far underground as the branches do above; so does true grace.

IV. THE CERTAINTY OF PERSEVERING IF ARMED

There can be no perseverance without true grace in the heart. But if Christ's grace reigns in you, victory is assured! That is why putting on the armour of God is so important – it guarantees you will persevere and overcome at last. True grace can never be vanquished. Scripture promises that everyone ' . . . born of God overcometh the world' (*1 John 5:4*). Victory is sown in our new natures – the very seed of God, which keeps us from being swallowed up by sin or Satan. As Christ rose never more to die, so He lifts the saint's soul from the grave of sin, never again to come under the power of spiritual death. Hence he that believes is said in the present tense to have eternal life (*1 John 5:13*).

The law came four hundred years after God's covenant with Abraham, yet it could not nullify the promise God had made. Likewise, nothing that intervenes in the saint's life can nullify the promise of eternal life that was given to Christ before the foundation of the world. If it were possible for a child of God somehow to miss the mark and lose the eternal life promised him, it would have to be from one of these causes: because it is possible for God to forsake the Christian and withdraw His grace from him; because the believer can forsake God; or because Satan has the power to pluck him out of God's hands. But none of these will stand, for the following reasons:

(a) *Because God can never forsake the Christian*

He Himself has said, 'I will never leave thee, nor forsake thee' (*Heb. 13:5*). He has also promised that He will not change His mind with regard to the love and special grace He awards His children: 'The gifts and calling of God are without repentance' (*Rom. 11:29*). Even when you sin, you do not provoke God to disinherit you. Instead, He is prompted to win you back to fellowship with Him. Hear His words through the prophet Isaiah: 'For the iniquity of his covetousness was I wroth, and smote him: I hid me, and was wroth, and he went on frowardly in the way of his heart. I have seen his ways, and will heal him' (*Isa. 57:17, 18*). Never doubt for a moment that whom He loves, He loves to the end.

To give further proof to our doubting hearts, God seals His promise with an oath: 'With everlasting kindness will I have mercy on thee, saith the Lord thy Redeemer. For this is as the waters of Noah unto me: for as I have sworn that the waters of Noah should no more go over the earth; so have I sworn that I would not be wroth with thee' (*Isa. 54:8, 9*). He continues, 'The mountains shall depart' – meaning at the end of the world, when the whole frame of the heavens and earth shall be dissolved – 'but my kindness shall not depart from thee, neither shall the covenant of my peace be removed' (*v. 10*). Now before you argue that the promise was given to the Jews alone, read the rest of the passage: 'This is the heritage of the servants of the Lord, and their righteousness is of me, saith the Lord' (*v. 17*). So we see that all God's children are included.

As Christ came from heaven on an errand of mercy for us, so He returned there to take possession of the promised inheritance which He purchased with His death. How can there be any doubt concerning God's love standing firm when we see the whole covenant already performed to Christ on our behalf? God not only called Christ, sanctified and upheld Him in the great work He was to finish for us, but also justified Him by His resurrection. Then God welcomed Him back to heaven, where He sits on the right hand of the Father on high as advocate and intercessor for every saint. Thus He not only has possession for Himself, but full power to give the inheritance to all believers.

(b) *Because the believer can never forsake God, according to the provision made in the covenant*

Knowing the journey to heaven is long and arduous and our grace is weak, we may often be afraid that we will forsake God before we reach our eternal destination. But God's covenant scatters this cloud of doubt by making provision for our weakness.

The Spirit of God is given to ensure our safe arrival in heaven. 'I will put my Spirit within you, and cause you to walk in my statutes, and ye shall keep my judgments, and do them' (*Ezek. 36:27*). Notice the verse does not say the saint will have His Spirit *if* he walks in God's statutes, but that the Spirit will *cause* him to do it. The Holy Spirit is both teacher and guardian of the saint. Perhaps you fear that if you grieve the Holy Spirit He may get angry and leave you to perish in your sins. It is true the Spirit of God is sensitive to disobedience and may draw back from your sins, just as He withdrew from Samson and let him fall into the Philistines' hands. But He did not abandon him permanently. When Samson cried out in his distress, the Spirit responded and put forth His strength in him again. It should put your fears to rest to know the office of the Spirit is to abide for ever with the saints: 'He shall give you another Comforter, that he may abide with you for ever' (*John 14:16*).

While the Spirit is dwelling within the saint to keep and protect him, Christ is interceding in heaven on his behalf. 'I have prayed,' Christ told Peter, 'that thy faith fail not' (*Luke 22:32*). If He prays for one, surely He will pray for all the others as well. In this same passage our Lord instructed Peter, 'When thou art converted, strengthen thy brethren' (*v. 32*). In other words, 'When you feel the force and effectiveness of My prayer for your faith, tell all your friends about it. Hearing how I care for My own should strengthen their hearts.' As long as Christ is interceding for us, how can we perish? Do you suppose He will ever grow weary of this act of love? His Word assures us that 'he ever liveth to make intercession . . . ' for all who belong to Him (*Heb. 7:25*).

(c) *Because Satan cannot pluck the believer out of God's hands*

If you are a saint, you are wrapped up in the everlasting arms of almighty power. The devil, however, is wrapped up in chains of everlasting condemnation and cannot shake them off no matter how hard he tries. If he cannot free himself from God's chains, how can he tear you from God's grasp? The devil can tempt a saint only by God's permission. If you believe God loves you, then surely you can trust His wisdom when He releases Satan to assault you. Will it not be when he can be repulsed with the greatest humiliation?

To know that Satan's power is limited, and God's grace is limitless, should restore the spirits of weak believers who fear they will not hold out to the end. God has given Christ the life of every soul within the ark of His covenant. If you are His, your eternal safety is provided for. Was He not able to make you willing to march under His banner and join His quarrel against sin and hell? The same limitless power that overcame your rebellious heart will overcome all your enemies within and without. The God who can make a few wounded men rise up and overthrow a city can also make a wounded spirit triumph over sin and Satan (*Jer. 37:10*). The ark stood in the midst of Jordan until the whole camp of Israel was safely over into Canaan (*Josh. 3:17*). So does Christ's covenant, which is typified by the ark. Christ, covenant and all, stand to secure the saints a safe passage to heaven.

A word of caution must be given. There is a great danger of believers falling from this comfortable doctrine into a careless security and presumptuous boldness. Although the Christian is secure from a total and final apostasy, yet he may suffer a grievous fall which bruises his conscience, weakens his grace, and brings reproach to the gospel. To know these dangers lurk in the shadows of this doctrine should be enough to keep the Christian upon his watch at all times.

Be careful that you do not misuse your liberty in Christ as a license to sin. Shall we sin because grace abounds? 'God forbid!' says Paul (*Rom. 6:2*). To what towering heights has sin grown when a man draws his encouragement to sin from the everlasting love of God! We may surmise that true grace does not dwell in the heart that draws such a cursed conclusion from the premises of God's grace. The genuine Christian will draw quite the opposite conclusion: that is, that God's grace is given not so he can wallow in sin, but so he can overcome it! The only acceptable response to the magnitude of God's love and grace is to cleanse ourselves from all filthiness of flesh and spirit (*2 Cor. 7:1*).

Just as a child should be motivated to please his father by a force stronger than the fear of being disinherited, so we should rise above performing our Christian duties out of fear of falling away. We are under the law of a new life. This should cause us as naturally to desire communion with God, as a child's love causes him to desire to see the face of his dear father.

It is the nature of faith – the grace that trades with promises – to purify the heart. And the more certain the report of God's love which faith brings back to the soul from the promise, the more it purifies the heart, because faith fueled by love inflames the heart toward God. If once this affection takes fire, the room becomes too hot for sin to stay there.

V. THE PROMISED RESULT OF PERSEVERANCE

The phrase 'having done all, to stand' includes the blessed result of the saints' perseverance. *To stand* at the end of this war will abundantly recompense all the hazard and hardship endured in the war against sin and Satan.

In earthly wars, not everyone who fights shares the spoils. The gains of war are commonly put into a few pockets. The common soldier, who endures most of the hardship, usually goes away with little of the profit. He fights to make a few that are great yet greater, and is often discharged without enough to pay for the cure of his wounds. But in Christ's army, the only soldier who loses is the one who runs away. Every faithful soldier receives a glorious reward, which is spelled out in this phrase, 'having done all, to stand.' *To stand* implies three things:

(a) *It means 'to stand conquerors.'*

An army, when conquered, is said to fall before its enemy, and the conqueror stands. At the end of this spiritual war, every Christian shall stand a conqueror over his vanquished lusts and Satan who headed them. Though the Christian enjoys many sweet victories here over Satan, still the joy of his conquests is interrupted by fresh alarms from the rallied enemy. He wins a victory one day, only to be confronted with still another battle on the next. And often, even his victories send him from the conflict bleeding. Though he repulses the temptation at last, yet the wounds his conscience receives in the fight cast a shadow on the glory of the victory.

For your eternal comfort, Christian, you can look forward to a day when there will be a full and final decision in the quarrel between you and Satan. You will see your enemy's camp completely scattered, with not a weapon left in his hand to use against you. You will tread upon the very fortresses from which he fired so many shots. You will see them dismantled and demolished, until there is not one corruption left standing in your heart for the devil to hide himself in. On that glorious day, the enemy who has made you tremble will be trampled under your feet.

    (b) *It means to stand justified and acquitted at the great day of judgment*

Scripture uses the term 'stand' frequently in this sense: 'The ungodly shall not stand in the judgment' (*Ps. 1:5*); that is, they shall not be justified. 'If thou, Lord, shouldest mark iniquities, O Lord, who shall stand?' (*Ps. 130:3*); that is, who can be justified?

    The great God, upon whose errand we come into the world, has appointed a day when He will judge the world by Jesus Christ. It will be a solemn day when all who ever lived – high and low, good and bad – shall meet in one assembly to appear personally before Christ, and from His mouth to receive the eternal verdict. The Lord shall be attended by an illustrious guard of angels ready to carry out the sentence He pronounces. I do not wonder that Paul's sermon on this subject caused an earthquake in Felix's conscience. Rather, I am amazed that any should be so far gone in numbness of conscience that the thought of this day cannot restore them to their senses.

    Do you not count them happy who will be acquitted by Christ on that day? Do you not wish to know who these blessed souls will be? To find out, you do not need to go to heaven and search the rolls. You may know here and now that those who shall *stand* in the judgment are those who fight the Lord's battles on earth against Satan, wearing the Lord's armour. They are Christians who have 'done all.' The proceedings of that day will utterly discredit Satan, who was their accuser to God and their consciences, always threatening them with the terror of condemnation at the judgment seat of Christ. How confounded will the wicked world be to see the dirt they threw on the saints' faces wiped off with Christ's own hand. Would this not be sufficient recompense for all the scorn and conflict the Christian endures in this life? But this is not all!

(c) *It also denotes the saints' rank in heaven*

When princes wish to reward subjects who have distinguished themselves in service to the crown, they award them a place of honorable service at court. Solomon indicated that one of the highest honors a man could receive was to stand before the king. Heaven is the royal city where God keeps His court. The joy of angels is to stand there before God: 'I am Gabriel, that stand in the presence of God' (*Luke 1:19*). That is, 'I am one of those heavenly spirits who wait on God, and stand before His face, as courtiers wait upon their prince.' Every faithful soul is promised this honor.

Nothing should have a more powerful effect upon a saint's spirit than to consider his blissful estate in heaven as being the reward of all his conflicts here on earth. This sword should cut the very sinews of temptation and behead those lusts which defy whole troops of other arguments. How can sin co-exist with the hope of such glory? It is when the thoughts of heaven are long out of the Christian's sight, and he forgets his hope of that glorious place, that he begins to set up some idol as Israel set up the calf and worshipped it in the absence of Moses. Only let heaven come into view, and the Christian's heart will be well warmed with thoughts of it. You may as soon persuade a king to throw down his royal diadem and wallow in the mud with his robes on, as convince a saint to sin when his heart is filled with the expectation of heaven's glory.

Sin is a devil's work, not a saint's. The saint waits every hour for the summons that will call him to stand with angels and glorified saints before the throne of God. How this should cheer and sustain his heart when the fight is hottest and the bullets fly thickest! If he must go through fire and water to reach it, what is that discomfort compared to the eternal comfort of heaven? Keeping the joy of heaven always before you will help you run your race with patience. It will help you endure your short scuffles with temptation and affliction. What is more, it will make you reckon also that these afflictions 'are not worthy to be compared with the glory which shall be revealed in us' (*Rom. 8:18*).

5: *Fourth Consideration: The Position to be Maintained in the Fight*

Stand therefore . . . (Eph. 6:14)

In verse 13 of Ephesians 6 the Apostle Paul clearly states the kind of armour you as a Christian must use – God's armour. Next, so you will not be tempted to fashion counterfeit armour in your own private forge and call it the 'armour of God,' Paul describes the true armour piece by piece, beginning in verse 14. (Roman Catholics and Protestants alike have often been guilty of devising their own weapons to fight the devil – weapons God never appointed.)

Later we will discuss the pieces of armour in the order the apostle names them. But first, we will explore another matter. Notice in verse 14 that Paul specifies the necessary posture for a Christian soldier: '*Stand* therefore. . . . ' What good will it do to be properly armed if we do not stand in valiant opposition to the enemy?

1. Stand – Do Not Flee or Yield

To stand is the opposite of *to flee* or *to surrender*. A captain who sees his men retreating or on the verge of surrender gives the order, 'Stand!' and every soldier worthy of his calling responds at once to his captain's voice. In like manner, every Christian is to respond to God's command to 'Stand!' – or, in other words, steadfastly to resist and never yield to the attacks of Satan. Four reasons are sufficient to show why this is so important.

SCRIPTURE EXPRESSLY COMMANDS IT

Peter says of Satan, ' . . . whom resist steadfast in the faith' (*1 Pet. 5:9*). As the word 'steadfast' implies, hold the line in battle against Satan; fight him whenever he advances. Soldiers are to adhere strictly to their orders even if it costs them their lives. When Joab sent Uriah to the front line of battle at David's command, no doubt Uriah saw the danger he would face. Yet he did not argue with his general; obey he must, though he lose his life in the process (*2 Sam. 11:14–17*).

Among soldiers, cowardice and disobedience are among the most damning sins. How, then, can they be considered slight offenses by those who have Christ for their captain and sin and the devil as their enemies? To resist some temptations may cost us dearly. 'Ye have not yet resisted unto blood, striving against sin,' the apostle said (*Heb. 12:4*). He implies that spiritual warfare may well come to that – and if it should, it does not alter the case nor give us an excuse to choose to sin rather than to suffer.

When is it ever permissible for a Christian to shirk his duty because it is accompanied by danger? If we are to be successful soldiers, the preservation of God's honor must always take precedence over our fears. Just as an earthly soldier represents his country's honor in battle, the Christian represents God's honor whenever he is called to contend with temptation. Such testing quickly reveals how far we are willing to go in defending our Sovereign's reputation. David's subjects valued him as worth ten thousand of their own lives; every one of them would die rather than endanger their leader. Surely God deserves as much from His subjects. How dishonorable to expose His blessed name to any reproach rather than expose ourselves to a little scorn, temporal loss, or trouble!

The Roman general Pompey boasted that a nod of his

head would send his soldiers scrambling up the steepest rock on their hands and knees, though they were knocked down as fast as they advanced. This is the kind of loyalty God wants from us. And while He is never reckless with the blood of His servants, sometimes He tests our loyalty in hard service and sharp temptations, so that through our faithfulness and bravery He may triumph over Satan.

Perhaps you recall the time Satan impudently accused God of 'bribing' Job, charging that this choice servant really only served himself in serving God: 'Doth Job fear God for nought?' (*Job 1:9*). He dared God to take away His blessing, insisting that Job would curse God to His face rather than submit to suffering. So God let the devil have his way – and what was the result? Because Job remained steadfast in adversity, we find the Lord boasting to Satan, 'Still he holdeth fast his integrity, although thou movedst me against him' (*Job 2:3*). In essence, God said, 'You see, I have some who will serve Me without a bribe, who will hold fast to their commitment when they can hold on to nothing else. You took Job's estate, his servants, and his children, and still he stands his ground. You have neither captured his will nor his integrity!'

GOD SUPPLIES ARMOUR SUFFICIENT FOR THE BATTLE

To allow a well-armed fortress to fall into enemy hands would be a disgrace to the defending soldiers. Spiritually speaking, such a defeat is even more dishonorable, because God in Christ gives His soldiers all the power they need to resist the devil at every turn.

We should not be surprised when an unregenerate soul yields easily to a temptation that promises carnal pleasure or profit. Those without Christ have no armour with which to repel the enemy's attack; they know nothing of

His sweetness. So it is natural that they – for want of better food – would sit at the devil's table. The goat, we say, must graze where it is tied; the sinner, likewise, must feed on earthly things because he is staked to the earth by his carnal heart.

But the Christian has a hope for higher things than this world can offer. His present faith is a promissory note written in the Holy Spirit's own hand, to assure him of ultimate victory. The helmet of salvation (if put on) and the shield of faith (if lifted up) will ward off a whole shower of the devil's arrows.

God has good reason to be displeased when His child, who could have resisted by using his graces and calling to heaven for help, instead yields to the enemy. In the garden God said to Adam, 'Hast thou eaten of the tree whereof I commanded thee, that thou shouldest not eat?' (*Gen. 3:11*). The emphasis here is on *thou* – as if God were saying, 'I know you did not eat because you were hungry; you had a whole paradise to choose from! How could *you* fall when you were so well-equipped to withstand!' In the same vein, God may say to you, 'Have you been eating the devil's treats when you carry a key to My bountiful cupboard? Are your Father's provisions so meager that the devil's scraps sit well with you?'

THE CHRISTIAN'S SAFETY LIES IN RESISTING

God provides armour to defend the Christian while fighting, not to protect him while retreating. Stand, and the day is yours; flee or yield, and all is lost. I have read of great captains who purposely cut off all avenues of retreat so their soldiers would fight to the death. William the Conqueror, as soon as his army set foot on English soil, sent away his ships in full sight of his men. Similarly, God makes no provisions for cowardice. In His armoury there is not a piece to be found for the back. Here is an awesome truth: 'The just shall live by faith, *but if any man draw back, my soul shall have no pleasure in him*' (*Heb. 10:38*). He who faces the battle with confidence comes off with his life, but he who defects wins only God's displeasure.

What a poor exchange – to turn from fighting against Satan and engage God as your enemy. There is comfort in fighting sin and Satan, even when it draws blood. But there is no comfort at all in enduring the fiery indignation of an avenging God. What Satan lays on, God can take off. But who can give relief from what God lays on? Would you not rather die in the heat of battle fighting for your country, than be executed for cowardice or treason?

THE ENEMY IS OVERCOME ONLY BY FORCE

There are three reasons why this is so.

I. SATAN IS A COWARDLY ENEMY

Though he wears a brave countenance when he tempts you, he actually harbors a fearful heart in his breast. As a thief trembles when he sees a light or hears a noise in his victim's house, so Satan is startled to find a soul awake and ready to oppose him. 'Jesus I know, and Paul I know,' the devil said (*Acts 19:14*). That is, 'I know them to my shame; they have both put me to flight.' And if you are like them, Satan will fear you as well. Believe me when I say he trembles at your faith. Use it to call for help against him, and exert it vigorously to repel his advances; then you will see him run.

Suppose the soldiers defending a castle learned that the invading army was weak and disorganized and would quickly scatter at any show of strength from within the castle. Would this not greatly increase the courage of the defenders? The Spirit of God, who knows everything about the enemy, sends the Christian an intelligence report with these instructions: 'Resist the devil and he will flee from you' (*James 4:8*). The enemy cannot hurt you unless you let him. Your steadfast resistance strikes a heavy blow to his confidence.

At the time of Christ's temptation and unswerving resistance, Satan is said to have 'departed from him for a season' (*Luke 4:13*). When the devil persists in tempting you, it may be that, though you have not yet yielded, neither have you openly repulsed his advances. Like a determined suitor, Satan looks for the slightest encouragement and, upon seeing it, continues to advance. The only way to be rid of him is to shut and bolt the door, and refuse to entertain the matter further.

II. SATAN IS AN ENCROACHING ENEMY

Therefore, you must resist him constantly. 'Let not the sun go down upon your wrath,' warns the apostle; 'neither give place to the devil' (*Eph. 4:26, 27*). A soldier assigned to guard duty on the outskirts of a city must keep watch as faithfully as the king's personal bodyguard, or the enemy will break through the outer limits and thereby gain access to the heart of the town.

If you yield to temptation along the perimeter of your heart, you give the devil a foothold from which to create havoc in your inner spirit. For example, you may become angry and thoughtlessly spew out some bitter words. At the very moment this unholy language spills from your mouth, the devil finds the floodgates open and enters. Then come gushing forth such things as you never dreamed of saying! He is a cunning opponent and will not easily relinquish any ground he gains. The safest strategy, then, is to give him no ground at all from which to work. If you so much as hesitate as you walk by the door where sin dwells, you give Satan more time to entice you to enter. Then you are on his territory.

Who will stop by a tavern to enjoy the company of drunkards, or frequent places of sin, and yet pretend he does not intend to partake? Who will prostitute his eyes to unchaste objects, and yet remain chaste? Who will lend his ears to any corrupt doctrine of the times, and yet be sound in the faith? Such a person is under a strong delusion. If a man is not strong enough to resist Satan in the lesser thing, how can he believe he will be able to repel a greater temptation? You say you cannot avoid being surrounded by deep waters of temptation, yet you think you have the strength to hold your head above water? Then give careful thought to some practical advice: It is far easier, when in the ship, to keep from falling overboard than, when in the sea, to get safely into the ship again.

III. SATAN IS AN ACCUSING ENEMY

He is a foolish man indeed who, knowing what an accuser the devil is, will provide him with ammunition for his charge. Some say a witch cannot hurt you unless she has received the gift of money from you. Similarly, the devil cannot harm you unless you let him get hold of some weakness in you that he can use to his advantage. I advise you to take up Job's resolution: 'My righteousness I hold fast . . . my heart shall not reproach me so long as I live' (*Job 27:6*). If your own heart or conscience does not accuse you, then the enemy's accusation cannot stand.

2. Stand in Your Own Place – Do Not Usurp Another's

To stand implies proper rank, order, and station for each soldier, as opposed to disorder. When soldiers unaccountably break rank, their captain shouts, 'Stand!' Military discipline allows no one to stir from his proper place without special reason. It should be the concern of every Christian to stand in order in his assigned place. The devil's method is first to rout, and then to ruin.

Order presupposes company – one who walks alone cannot break rank. Therefore, the Christian's place and rank correspond to the company in which he walks. As a Christian, you must relate to a threefold society: community, church, and family. Each has ranks and places. In the community, there are public servants and private citizens; in the church, pastor and laymen, officers and members of the congregation; in the family, parents and children, husband and wife. The welfare of these societies depends upon every wheel turning smoothly in its place and everyone performing his duty for the benefit of the whole.

Three things are necessary for a person to 'stand in order.' First, he must understand the particular duty of his place. 'The wisdom of the prudent is to understand his way' (*Prov. 14:8*). What good will it do to ask the way to York if you are headed toward London? Yet how prone we are to inquire into another's way and work while neglecting our own. Some Christians, for instance, spend more time fretting about what the minister should do than praying for God's direction in their own lives. It is not in knowing another's duty nor in judging his neglect of it, but in fulfilling our own duty that we will come safely through the conflict. And how can we do our duty unless we know it? Solomon showed the greatest proof of his wisdom when he asked God for wisdom to fulfill his duty.

Second, once we know the duty of our place, we must conscientiously attend to it. Paul's charge to Timothy applies to every Christian: 'Meditate upon these things, and give thyself wholly to them' (*1 Tim. 4:15*). That is, devote yourself to performing your duty in the place and calling God has given you. The very power of godliness lies in such consecration. Religion which has no practical impact on our daily lives quickly becomes a vague, abstract notion that amounts to nothing. Yet many have nothing more than an empty profession to prove they are Christians. They are like the cinnamon tree whose outer bark is more valuable than all else that remains. The apostle speaks of such people in his letter to Titus: 'They profess that they know God, but in works they deny him, being abominable and disobedient, and unto every good work reprobate' (*Tit. 1:16*).

What is meant by 'good works' becomes clear in the following chapter (*Tit. 2:2–8*), where the apostle presents the duties which Christians ought to perform. A good Christian but a nagging wife, a godly man but a negligent father – these are contradictions that cannot be reconciled. The man who does not walk uprightly in his own house is nothing more than a hypocrite at church. If you are not a Christian in your shop, you are not a Christian in your closet – even though you may pray there. If your faith founders in one way, it cannot flourish in any other. Some professing Christians fail in their duties toward their fellow men, while maintaining an outward show of worship to God. Others falter in acts of worship while seeming to be steadfast in their duties to their fellowmen. Both inconsistencies are destructive to the soul. The soldier who stands *in order* is conscientious toward the whole duty that lies on him in regard to both God and man.

Third, to stand in order means we must stay within the bounds of our place and calling. The Israelites were commanded every man 'to pitch by his own standard' (*Num. 2:2*). This meant they were to be 'arranged in order,' as in a military formation. God allows no stragglers in His army of saints. 'As the Lord has called every one, so let him walk' (*1 Cor. 7:17*). You must walk in the path which your call prescribes for you. The apostle commands you to 'do your own business' (*1 Thess. 4:11*). Just as the general's business is not the private's, so the minister's is not the congregation's. Do not forget – that which is justice in a judge's action is murder in another's. Paul says we are to tend with all diligence everything that comes within the scope of our particular calling; beyond this, we are tilling someone else's field.

What a quiet world we would have if every thing and every person knew his own place! If the sea kept its place, we would have no inundations; if men had kept theirs, we would not have seen such floods of sin and misery as have almost drowned this present age. It must be a strong river bank indeed that can contain our fluid spirits within their proper boundaries. Peter himself was scolded sharply for prying into that which was not his affair. 'What is that to thee?' Christ said to him (*John 21:22*). In other words, 'Peter, tend to your own business; this does not concern you.' Someone has surmised that this sharp rebuke caused Peter later to denounce this sin in the strongest terms – ranking the 'busybody' among murderers and thieves (*1 Pet. 4:15*).

FIVE CONSIDERATIONS TO PERSUADE ALL TO STAND

To fix every Christian in his place and persuade him to stand without breaking rank, I offer the following considerations. They must carry weight with us if we say that we accept the authority of Scripture in directing our thoughts and actions.

1. YOU LOSE GOD'S APPROVAL WHEN YOU LEAVE YOUR APPOINTED PLACE TO WORK OUTSIDE YOUR CALLING
Why? Because you cannot do it in faith, and 'without faith it is impossible to please him' (*Heb. 11:6*). It cannot be done in faith because you have no call. God will not thank

you for doing that which He did not commission you to do. Perhaps you had good intentions. So had Uzzah when he steadied the ark. Yet we see that 'God smote him there for his error' (*2 Sam. 6:7*). Saul himself gave an impressive excuse for offering a sacrifice, but he was out of his appointed place, and God rejected him for it (*1 Sam. 13:8–14*).

It is not enough to ask, 'What shall I do?' You must also ask, 'Who is telling me to do it?' To be sure, God will at last put that question to you, and it will be in your own best interests to show that your commission was from Him.

To be occupied with anything which is not your duty means you are neglecting that which is your task. The spouse in the Song of Solomon confesses, 'They made me the keeper of the vineyards, but mine own vineyard have I not kept' (*1:6*). She could not mind others' vineyards and her own, too. You cannot expect to honor God by leaving the work He assigns you and doing something of your own choosing instead, no matter how worthwhile it may seem. Suppose a teacher asked a returning truant why he had been absent from school, and the wayward pupil replied that he had been in the blacksmith's shop, lending a hand there. Would this be a satisfactory excuse? Of course not! His business was to be in school, not in that shop.

II. YOU LOSE GOD'S PROTECTION WHEN YOU IGNORE HIS RESTRICTIONS AS TO PLACE AND CALLING

The promise is to 'keep thee in all thy ways' (*Ps. 91:11*) When you go out of your way, you go from under His wing. The Apostle Paul says it like this: 'Brethren, let every man, wherein he is called, therein abide with God' (*1 Cor. 7:24*). Mark that phrase, 'abide with God.' If you love to walk in God's company, you must abide in your place and calling. Every step in a different direction is a departure from Him. How much more blessed to stay at home in a humble place and low calling and there enjoy God's sweet presence, than to go to a sumptuous palace and live without Him. Truly, when you are in any place or about any work to which you are not called, you may be sure God is not in that place or enterprise. And what a bold adventure it is to stay where you cannot expect His presence to assist or protect!

In doing the duty of our place we have heaven's word for our security; but if we wander, we have heaven's word for our peril. It is just as dangerous to do what we are not called to do as to neglect or leave undone the duty of our place. As the earth could not bear the act of Korah and his company in usurping another's authority (*Num. 16:30–33*), so the sea could not harbor Jonah, the runaway prophet. Refusing to be his escape route from God's command, the raging sea caused Jonah to be cast overboard (*Jon. 1:4, 15*). Nor would heaven harbor the angels once they had left their God-appointed place and office (*Jude 6*).

The ruin of many souls rushes in upon them at this door. First they break rank, then they are led further into temptation. Absalom first looked over the hedge in his ambitious thoughts: He would be a king! This wandering desire to go beyond his place let in the bloody sins of rebellion, incest, and murder, and these at last delivered him into the hands of divine vengeance. The apostle joins order to steadfastness: 'I am with you in the spirit, joying and beholding your order, and the steadfastness of your faith' (*Col. 2:5*). That army alone is invincible in which every soldier stands in close order, attending to his duty and content with his work.

III. GOD DOES NOT HOLD YOU ACCOUNTABLE FOR
ANOTHER MAN'S WORK

'Give an account of thy stewardship,' the rich man said to his steward (*Luke 16:2*). The man was asked to justify his own affairs, not to give an account for what had been entrusted to someone else. Certainly we are to help one another, and it is a serious sin not to assist a brother whom God has placed within the scope of your duty. But if, in reaching out to compensate for someone else's sin you step beyond the boundaries of your own duty, there is a real danger of becoming an accessory to the very sin you are trying to prevent.

God does not expect you to compensate for another man's negligence when it does not belong to your place and calling. We are to pray for judges to rule in the fear of God. But if they do not, we are not to don their robes, take the bench, and do their work for them. God requires no more than faithfulness in our place. Surely you would not find fault with an apple tree laden with apples because it did not produce figs or grapes. We expect these only from their proper root and stock. Spiritually speaking, that man is a fruitful tree in God's orchard who 'bringeth forth his fruit in his season' (*Ps. 1:3*).

IV. YOU SUFFER NEEDLESSLY WHEN YOU BEAR BUR-
DENS GOD NEVER INTENDED YOU TO CARRY

Before launching out into any undertaking, we should seriously ask ourselves how well-equipped we are to complete the task if a storm should overtake us. What folly to engage in an enterprise which will in all likelihood leave us shipwrecked, yet pay the charge of all the loss and trouble it puts us to. Do not expect comfort from God unless you can give Him title to the business you suffer for. The psalmist said, 'For thy sake we are killed all the day long' (*Ps.44:22*). But if suffering finds us out of our calling and place, we cannot say 'for thy sake' we are thus and thus afflicted; rather, we must admit, 'for our own sakes.'

The apostle Peter differentiates unmistakably between suffering 'as a busybody' and suffering 'as a Christian' (*1 Pet. 4:15, 16*). To the latter he says, 'Let him not be ashamed, but let him glorify God on this behalf.' The carpenter who cuts himself while working at his own trade accepts the mishap more graciously than one who injures himself through careless meddling with the saw. The needless sufferer has this to add to his pain: he can expect nothing from anyone but a sound rebuke. The same is true of the Christian who comes to harm by interfering in someone else's affair. A child who gets hurt while gadding about away from home without permission, suffers the added pain of a spanking from his father for his disobedience. So it is with the Christian.

V. A FLIGHTY SPIRIT USUALLY CARRIES MEN OUT OF THEIR PLACE AND CALLING

No doubt some servants of God receive a special calling from heaven to do extraordinary things – as in the case of Moses, Gideon, Phinehas, and others. They are, however, rare exceptions, and it is dangerous to assume we have been given such an exceptional divine call when God most often issues His commissions in a more ordinary way, such as through His Word. We may as well expect to be taught in an extraordinary way without the Bible, as to expect to be called in an extraordinary way without the corroboration of God's Word. When I see any who are miraculously gifted – as the prophets and the apostles were – then I shall believe the authenticity of the extraordinary calling they claim.

Let us consider for a few moments why so many are carried out of their place and calling. The reason is not always the same.

Sometimes it is a spirit of *idleness*. Men neglect what they should do, then are easily persuaded to meddle with what they have no business doing. The Christian who will not serve God in his own place will soon be found doing the devil's errand and putting his sickle into another's corn. The apostle states this quite plainly: 'They learn to be idle, wandering about from house to house; and not only idle, but tattlers also and busybodies' (*1 Tim. 4:13*).

Others abandon their assigned place because of a spirit of *pride and discontent*. Their calling may be low and humble, but their spirits are high and prideful. They make the mistake of trying to raise their calling to the proud level of their spirits, rather than humbling their spirits to the level of their calling. In the case of Korah, it was not the work of the priest that he wanted so much as the honor which went with the position (*Num. 16*). As for Absalom, it was not a zeal for justice that made his spirit strive for his father's crown, but rather greedy ambition that hid itself behind a zealous facade (*2 Sam. 15*). Positions of prominence in the church and community are such fair flowers that proud spirits of every age have sought them for their own gardens. However, such flowers do not thrive well except in their proper soil.

Another unsettled spirit that carries some out of their place is *unbelief*. This made Uzzah stretch forth his hand to steady the teetering ark (*2 Sam. 6:6*). Since he was only a Levite, he had God's command not to touch the ark (*Num. 4:15*). But when the ark began to shake, the poor man's faith shook more. By fearing the fall of the ark, he fell to the ground himself. He had not learned a vital truth: God does not need our sin to shore up His glory, His truth, or His church.

In some, the flighty spirit is *misinformed zeal*. Many think because they *can* do a thing (preach, for example), that they *may* do it. Certainly the gifts of such saints need not be lost. The layman has a large field in which he may minister to his fellowman, even if he is not called to full-time ministry. But he is not to trample down the hedge which God has placed about the ministry and thus cause disorder in the church. According to Jewish law, one who set a hedge on fire and accidentally burned the corn growing in an adjacent field was required to make restitution (*Ex. 22:6*). Though he did not mean to hurt the corn, his action was the reason the corn burned, so he was responsible. We have all seen private Christians who have taken upon themselves the work of a minister. I daresay most of them never intended to cause such a combustion in the church as generally results from this kind of insubordination. But because they have set fire to the hedge which God has put between the minister's calling and the people's, they are responsible for the damage.

If we acknowledge the ministry to be a particular office in the church – which I think the Word compels us to do – then we must agree the work of that office should be done only by one who is called to it. There are many in a country who could be statesmen, but only those who can show a letter of appointment are recognized as official ambassadors. Those who are not commissioned by God's call for ministerial work may speak truths as well as any, yet we observe that only the one who acts by virtue of his calling preaches with true authority.

If you insist on preaching but do not have God's commission to the ministry, you are like one who joins his country's army on the battlefield and announces he has come to fight against the common enemy. Yet he stands by himself at the head of a troop he has gathered, and refuses to take orders from any of the officers or to let his troops join ranks with theirs. I question whether that man's service will do as much good against the enemy as his action does harm by distracting the entire army.

3. Stand – Do Not Sleep

Standing is a waking, watching posture. In the military, 'Stand to your arms!' means 'Stay alert and watch!' In some cases it is death to a soldier to be found asleep – when he is assigned to guard duty, for instance. He is to watch so that the rest can sleep. Shirking his duty endangers the lives of the entire army, so he deserves his sentence of death.

Watchfulness is more important for the Christian soldier than any other. In temporal battles soldiers fight against men who need sleep the same as themselves, but the saint's enemy, Satan, is always awake and walking his rounds. Since the devil never sleeps, the Christian puts himself in grave danger by falling asleep spiritually – that is, by becoming secure and careless. Either the unregenerate part of his nature will betray him, or grace will not be alert to discover the enemy and prepare for the assault. Satan will be upon him before he is awake enough to draw his sword. You should be aware that the saint's sleeping time is Satan's prime tempting time.

Even a fly dares to creep on a sleeping lion; unless he wakes up, there is nothing to fear. The weakest temptation is strong enough to foil a Christian who is napping in security. While Samson slept, Delilah cut his locks. While Saul slept, his spear was taken from his side and he was none the wiser. A drunken Noah slept and his graceless son took pleasure in seeing his father's nakedness. Eutychus slept, nodded, and fell from the third loft, and was taken up for dead. Thus the Christian sleeping in false security may be taken by surprise. He may lose much of his spiritual strength – be robbed of his spear or armour (graces, I mean) – or have his nakedness uncovered by graceless men, and bring shame to his profession.

Sleep steals upon the soul as quietly as it does on the body. The wise virgins fell asleep along with the foolish ones, though not so soundly. Take heed that you do not indulge yourself in laziness; stir yourself to action, as we tell someone who is drowsy to stand up and walk around. Yield to idleness and sloth and they will grow upon you; busy yourself in your Christian duties and spiritual drowsiness will flee. David first awakened his tongue to sing and his hand to play on the harp; then his heart awakened also (*Ps. 57:8*). I have heard that when the lion first wakes, he lashes himself with his tail to stir and rouse his courage. Then away he goes after his prey. We have reason enough to excite and provoke us to all the care and diligence possible.

WHY THE CHRISTIAN MUST REMAIN WAKEFUL

I. THE CHRISTIAN'S WORK IS TOO IMPORTANT AND DEMANDING TO BE DONE WHILE HALF ASLEEP, OR IN A HALF-HEARTED FASHION

If you have ever walked along the edge of a raging river or hiked to the crest of a steep hill, I doubt that you grew sleepy. As a Christian, your path is so narrow and the danger so great, it calls for both a nimble eye to discern and a steady eye to direct. A sleepy eye can do neither.

Examine any duty and you will find it lies between two dangerous extremes. Faith, the great work of God, cuts its way between the mountain of presumption and the gulf of despair. Patience is the grace necessary to keep us from suffering a stroke of sleepy stupidity which would deprive us of our senses, or from flying into a rage of discontent that would deprive us of our reason. Keeping a proper balance is essential. Any duty we perform for the cause of Christ takes us very near the enemy's quarters. Do not think you will pass by undetected. Your approach sounds an alarm, and Satan comes out immediately to oppose you. Thus it is necessary that you remain constantly watchful.

II. WATCHFULNESS REAPS ADVANTAGES FOR THE
CHRISTIAN IN THREE IMPORTANT WAYS

First, by watching, you frustrate Satan's intentions. Is it not worth watching to keep your house from being robbed? How much more worthwhile to prevent your heart from being invaded by the devil! 'Watch . . . that ye enter not into temptation,' Jesus said (*Matt. 26:41*). Getting your throat cut is a high price to pay for sleep, even if the wound should finally heal. It is better to be watchful now and keep yourself from mischief than to sleep and be kept awake later because of the wound you suffered for your negligence. David was in a state of spiritual slumber when he rose from his bed, walked upon the roof of his house, and cast his eye upon Bathsheba (*2 Sam. 11:2*). He fell headlong into Satan's trap, bruising his spirit badly. And how many restless nights this wound brought to David you may perceive by his own complaints of this sin, which is the theme of several mournful psalms.

Second, it is by faithful watching that you best learn the dangers of sleeping. A sleeping man is not aware of his own snoring, nor of how he annoys and troubles others. But anyone who is awake is conscious of it. If you stay awake spiritually, you will surely see the improprieties of those professing Christians who do not watch their hearts. Let them serve as a warning to you not to fall prey to the same temptations. Sleep levels all men. The strongest is no safer than the weakest while they both slumber. A napping wise man and a sleeping fool are equally vulnerable. Likewise, spiritual sleep makes even the best of saints as vulnerable as any other man as long as the sleep prevails.

Third, your watchfulness is an open invitation to the Lord Himself to keep you company. And when He comes to you, the time will fly by in sweet communion. His revelations about the things of the Father's kingdom will keep you from envying sleepy Christians their seeming ease, knowing they are missing the blessed fellowship you enjoy. Would you not, if you love your soul more than your body, rather have David's songs than his sleep in the night? And is it not better to keep your soul awake and know Christ's comforting presence, than to let it sleep and miss the Savior's visit? It is the watchful soul that Christ delights to be with, and to it He opens His heart.

We do not choose to visit our friends while they are asleep. In fact, if we are with them and sense they are getting sleepy, we excuse ourselves and leave them free to retire. Christ does the same with His spouse; He withdraws from her until she is better awake and more fit to receive His love. Put a purse of gold into the hand of a sleepy man, and the next morning he will hardly remember what you gave him. A groggy Christian will not recognize the true value of Christ's gifts nor remember to thank Him properly for them. Therefore, God gives His special blessings to the wide-awake soul, not only to bless His child, but also that the child may bless Him by speaking well of Christ for them.

HOW TO STAND AND WATCH

I. YOU MUST WATCH CONSTANTLY

The lamp of God in the tabernacle was to 'burn always' (*Ex. 27:20; 30:8*); that is, always in the night. And what is our life in this world from beginning to end but a dark night of temptation? Christian, it is so very important to make sure your sentry lamp does not go out in this darkness, and your enemy catch you unawares. If you drift off into spiritual slumber, you are an easy mark for his wrath. And you may be sure if you do let sleep overtake you, the devil will hear of it. He knew the apostles' sleeping time and desired to sift them like wheat (*Luke 22:31*). A thief is just getting up when honest men are going to bed. The devil, I am sure, begins to tempt when saints cease to watch. So be consistent in your watchfulness; otherwise you stand to lose everything.

Some Christians, having been injured by a serious fall into sin, will be very careful for a while as to where they walk and the kind of company they keep. But as the soreness of their consciences wears off, they forget to keep watch and become as careless as ever. A shopkeeper who has just been robbed is very careful to lock up his store thoroughly. He may even stay up late to watch it for several nights, but as time passes he relaxes his guard and at last gives it no further attention.

Josephus, in his *Antiquities*, tells us that the sons of Noah lived only on the tops of high mountains for some years after the flood, not daring to build houses on lower ground for fear of being drowned by another deluge. But as time passed and no flood came, they ventured down into the plain of Shinar where their former fear gave way to one of the boldest, most arrogant attempts against God that man ever pursued. They tried to build a tower high enough to reach heaven (*Gen. 11:2-4*). The very men who at first were so fearful of drowning that they would not venture down the hill, at last ventured on a plan to protect themselves against all future attempts from the God of heaven to judge them.

[305]

God's judgments often leave so strong an impression on a man's spirit that for a while he stays away from his sins. But when fair weather continues and he sees no storm clouds gathering, he descends to his old wicked practices and grows bolder than ever. If you want to be a true soldier for Christ, always remain watchful without slacking. Do not lie down by the wayside like a lazy traveler; reserve your resting time until you reach home and are out of all danger. God did not rest until the last day's work in the creation was finished; neither should you cease to wake or work until you can say your salvation is complete.

II. YOU MUST WATCH UNIVERSALLY

The honest watchman makes his rounds faithfully and compasses the whole town. He does not limit his care to only one or two houses. You also must watch over your entire being. A pore in your body is a door wide enough to let in a disease. Likewise, any one faculty of your soul or member of your body can let in an enemy that may endanger your spiritual welfare. It is sad that so few are watchful in every area. You may set a watch at the door of your lips so that no impure communication comes out; but do you also keep watch at the door of your heart to see it is not defiled with lust (*2 Chron. 23:6*)? Perhaps you keep your hand out of your neighbor's purse, but does your envious heart begrudge him the blessings God has given him? The Christian who is truly scrupulous in one duty may be falsely secure in others.

If the apostle bids, 'In every thing give thanks' (*1 Thess. 5:18*), then it behooves us in everything to watch, so that God may not lose His praise. No action is so small but that in it we may do God or the devil some service. There is nothing in all God's creation that is so insignificant His providence does not watch over it – even to a sparrow or a hair. By the same token, no word or work of yours should be thought too inconsequential to be watched over. Jesus said we would be judged by every idle word that we speak (*Matt. 12:36*).

III. YOU MUST WATCH WISELY

Tithing of 'mint, anise, and cummin' must not be neglected. But do not let a preoccupation with the small things make you blind to your wickedness in the larger things. 'These ought ye to have done, and not to leave the other undone' (*Matt. 23:23*).

Begin at the right end of your work by giving careful attention to your primary Christian duties. Suppose a man about to leave on a trip asks his servant to look after his child and to put his house in order while he is away. When he returns, will he reward the hireling for tidying the house if he finds that the servant became so preoccupied with the task that he let the child fall into the fire and seriously injure himself? Of course not! The child was the more important charge and should have been given top priority, then the other duty tended to. But when you have attended to your primary duties, do not neglect the smaller ones.

Lately there has been much attention given to the small details of worship, but who is looking after the little child – that is, the main duties of Christianity? Was there ever less love, compassion, self-denial, or power of holiness than today? Unfortunately these cardinal duties, like the child, are in great danger of perishing in the fire of contention and division which a perverse zeal for lesser things has kindled among us.

Be especially careful to watch yourself in those areas where you know you are weak. The weakest part of the city needs the strongest guard; in our bodies, the most vulnerable parts are covered and kept the warmest. I

[307]

would think it most unusual if the fabric of your grace was so consistently strong that you could find no weakness at any point.

Take my advice in the matter, and watch most carefully the area you find weakest. Is your head weak – your judgment I mean? See to it that you do not keep company with those who drink only the strong wine of 'seraphic notions' and high-flown opinions. Is your weakness in your passions? Watch over them as one who dwells in a thatched-roof house is careful of every spark that flies out his chimney, for fear one should land on the thatch and set the whole house on fire. When our neighbor's house is ablaze, we throw water on our own roof, or cover it with a wet sheet. When flame breaks out at another's mouth, throw water on your own hot spirit to prevent a fire breaking out in you. You should always have available some cooling, wrath-quenching scriptures for just such a situation.

These preventive measures will enable you to secure your house against any attack by the devil. And when the enemy has been put down, you will still be 'standing'.